D0469657

LISTENING TO MIDLIFE

LISTENING TO MIDLIFE

Turning Your Crisis into a Quest

Mark Gerzon

SHAMBHALA
Boston & London
1996

SHAMBHALA PUBLICATIONS, INC.
Horticultural Hall
300 Massachusetts Avenue
Boston, Massachusetts 02115
www.shambhala.com

© 1992 by Mark Gerzon

All rights reserved. No part of this book may be
reproduced in any form or by any means, electronic or
mechanical, including photocopying, recording, or by
any information storage and retrieval system, without
permission in writing from the publisher.

9   8   7   6   5   4

Printed in the United States of America

∞ This edition is printed on acid-free paper that meets
the American National Standards Institute Z39.48 Standard.

Distributed in the United States by Random House, Inc.,
and in Canada by Random House of Canada Ltd

Library of Congress Cataloging-in-Publication Data

Gerzon, Mark.
[Coming into our own]
Listening to midlife: turning your crisis into a quest
by Mark Gerzon.
p.   cm.
Previously published as: Coming into our own. 1992.
ISBN 1-57062-168-3 (alk. paper)
1. Midlife crisis.   2. Self-actualization (Psychology)   I. Title.
BF724.65.M53G47   1996   95-30767
155.6′6—dc20   CIP

For my parents, who gave me life.
And for all my elders, living and dead,
who have showed me its infinite possibilities.

Contents

Acknowledgments

There are those who are interviewed in these pages; those whose work is cited in the text and in the footnotes; those who have discussed the themes of each chapter and added their expertise; those who have read the manuscript, often many times; and, finally, those who have never seen these pages but who have nurtured, challenged, and guided me during the years I have worked on this book. Since I cannot even try to thank these scores of men and women here, I will simply say that you have given me gifts for which I am truly grateful.

Specifically, I want to thank my colleagues at Shambhala, whose enthusiasm and commitment to the publication of this edition have given this book new life. I also wish to thank my agent, Jill Kneerim, at the Palmer & Dodge Agency, for bringing this book from conception to creation. And my deepest gratitude goes to my wife, Shelley Kessler, who has been my guide, follower, and companion on the journey which I share in this book. She and our three sons appear frequently in the pages of this book because each of them, in their own way, has helped me to listen to midlife.

Preface

I have written this book because I needed to. Midway through my life, I was living as if most of my deep, fundamental growth was behind me. Without knowing it, I had accepted our culture's stale and simplistic view of adulthood —that the person you are at midlife is the person you will always be.

But I was wrong.

We have many words to describe less than twenty years of the life cycle: newborn, infant, toddler, preschooler, child, teenager, adolescent, and so forth. We need all of these words because children grow so fast. But to describe *the next half-century*—the period of fifty years or more after we reach the age of twenty-one—we have only one generally accepted word: *adulthood.* The poverty of our language reveals that we still do not understand that "grown-ups" grow too. We act as if adulthood is one long, stable, predictable period. We act as if we have signed a protracted, long-term contract, like paying off a mortgage.

I was jolted from this narrow view not long ago after certain events in my life, which I describe in this book, threw me into a state of confusion and uncertainty. At precisely the time when I thought my development was coming to an end, I found myself embarking on a totally unexpected journey of growth and change. I entered what the great Swiss psychoanalyst Carl Jung called the "second half of life."

> Wholly unprepared, we embark upon the second half of life . . . we take the step into the afternoon of life;

worse still we take this step with the false assumption that our truths and ideals will serve as before. But we cannot live the afternoon of life according to the program of life's morning—for what was great in the morning will be little at evening, and what in the morning was true will at evening have become a lie.[1]

We cannot tell if we have entered the afternoon of our lives by counting the number of candles on our birthday cake. We do not enter the second half just because we reach a certain age that ends in a zero. To know where we are in our process of transformation, we must learn to look inside.

Once we look within, we discover that adulthood can be a time of transformation. It can be a time of spiritual unfolding. Dramatic as it may sound, adulthood can be metamorphosis. If you find this hard to believe, remember that a creature as simple and primitive as a caterpillar enters a cocoon; its body partly dissolves and "dies"; it is reconstituted in another shape; and finally it emerges as a butterfly. *Is it therefore not at least possible that a creature as complex and evolved as a human being might also have an equally profound metamorphosis?*

Based on interviews I have conducted with a wide variety of men and women, and based on my research of the literature on adult development, I am convinced that the answer to this question is yes. There *is* an adult metamorphosis. However, unlike the caterpillar's metamorphosis, our transformation is invisible. It happens in a part of us that does not show up on X rays, cannot be measured by medical equipment, and cannot be tested in a laboratory. It happens inside us. And it happens over a lifetime.

Our metamorphosis is, in fact, a quest. The signposts on our quest are *quest*-ions (from *quaerere:* to search). They may not automatically point us in the "right" direction. But if we ask these questions and seek answers with an open heart, they will move us forward on our journey. Some of them include:

- You no longer look young. You cannot hide the signs of aging anymore. Why does it bother you so much?
- Your sense of purpose is draining away. Everything seems to be losing its meaning. What has happened to the spark?
- Another side of your personality is suddenly asserting itself. This "shadow side" bubbles up unexpectedly. You find yourself doing things that are out of character. Who is this "other person" inside you?
- You are searching now for a different kind of relationship—something deeper, more authentic. But where, and with whom, can you find it?
- Without warning, you get a "crush" on someone. You're shocked. That person is not even "your type." Why are you thinking about them so much?
- When you made your career choice years ago, you brushed aside certain talents that you had. Why are they coming back, demanding to be expressed?
- Your kids are growing up, and fast. They have consumed so much of your energy and focus. You wonder: what would life have been like without them?
- Or, you are childless. It seemed fine before. But now the question gnaws at you: Should you have a child? Or is it already too late?
- You have always known that you would die. But now you feel it in your gut. Why does time seem shorter now . . . sometimes too short?
- It's been years since questions about God or faith were on your mind. You thought they were settled long ago. So why are they coming up again?

This is book for people who are facing these questions. It is a book for those who dare to confront the unexpected challenges of the second half. It is a book for those who are ready to come into their own.

Already on the shelves of bookstores and libraries are scores of books, both academic and popular, telling us about the crises or stages of our lives. You will pass through certain "psychosocial stages," says the renowned psychoanalyst Erik Erikson, who was my teacher and adviser at Harvard University. You will progress through a sequence of "transitions," reports psychiatrist Daniel Levinson, whom I interviewed for this book. You will undergo a set of interrelated "transformations," advises another expert on adult development, Roger Gould. You will experience predictable "passages," counsels journalist Gail Sheehy, whose book popularized these experts' theories. Because their collective advice is often wise, and based on considerable research and investigation, their counsel will appear often throughout the pages of this book.[2]

But what they cannot do, I believe, is predict the path your life will take, or mine. To paraphrase Abraham Lincoln, some of their generalizations apply to some of us some of the time—but the times when they *don't* apply to us are usually the most crucial. They don't apply to us when our lives are "interrupted" by major historical shifts that are unique to our generation. They don't apply to us when we are challenged by either unexpected illness or unusual longevity. They don't apply when we are expressing the talents or gifts that are uniquely ours. And, perhaps most important, they apply less and less to us as we move into and through the second half of life.

You may recall that the best seller *Passages,* which effectively brought the issue of adult development into public consciousness in the mid-seventies, bore the subtitle *"predictable* crises of adult life." Just as children go through specific phases of child development, Sheehy marshaled life stories and anecdotes which suggested that adults similarly pass through a specific sequence of developmental stages. While Sheehy demonstrated beyond a shadow of a doubt that grown-ups do grow, I do not believe our growth is predictable. If it was, why would any of us get lost? Indeed, why would the experts *themselves* get lost? If you read between the lines in these experts' books, or interview them (as I have done), you soon learn that they are just as confused about their journey through adulthood as any of us.

The truth is: The experts could not predict their own growth, much less ours. The more we truly grow for our whole lives, the harder it is to reduce to a statistic. Try as the experts may to make us fit their theories, we won't. Try as they may to make our life histories follow their stages, they can't, because *as we mature, we are less predictable.*

Perhaps child development researchers can predict when, and in what order, children will learn to crawl, walk, speak, and so on. After all, a child's development is visible. It has clearly identifiable, observable, sequential stages. But this is only the beginning of the human journey. When we reach our full height physically, we are still in the caterpillar stage of our journey. What happens next is not clear, not observable, and not sequential. What happens over the next five, six, or seven decades is a mystery. We can study it, probe it, interview it, map it—but in the end, the mystery remains.

When the experts try to describe what happens in various stages of adulthood, they run into trouble. Can they generalize that in the early twenties young adults marry and have children? No. Can they assume that men and women in their twenties will select a career ladder? Hardly. Can they predict that forty-year-olds will be less fit than when they were thirty? Not anymore. We know precisely what "grade" in elementary school to find a child who is ten years old. But can we predict what grade in life we will find forty-year-olds? They may be grandparents—or they may have just had their first child! They may be experiencing the first signs of energy loss and decreased vitality—or they may be more fit than they were a decade earlier! They may have stopped being so ambitious and become concerned about spiritual matters—or they may have finally decided to express the secret ambitions they never before dared to show! There is simply no way that the modern lives of men and women can be categorized in neat, standardized chronological stages.

Instead of answers, we are left with questions. How do adults grow? What exactly is our metamorphosis? Does it happen to everyone? How do we enter the cocoon—and how do we get out? And finally, how do we come into our own and learn to fly? Although these questions are metaphorical, they are real. I know they are because I have listened to scores of men and women tell their own true stories of transformation. I have been so inspired by their stories that I want to share them—and my own—with you.

As you learn about the transformations of adulthood, both the breakdowns and breakthroughs, you will see for yourself that no one's process of growth or change is like your own. As Walt Whitman wrote, "Not I, not anyone else, can travel that road for you. You must travel it for yourself." Nevertheless, the stories of those who have gone before you can serve as a guide. When you get lost on your journey, turn to their wisdom. But they can show you the way inside yourself, where the voice most important to you lies.

When you find that voice, listen to it. It will help you along the journey through adulthood. It will help you come into your own.

LISTENING TO MIDLIFE

1

ENVISIONING A QUEST, NOT A CRISIS
The Quest for Wholeness

Buddha left a road map, Jesus left a road map, Krishna left a road map, Rand McNally left a road map. But you still have to travel the road yourself.

STEPHEN LEVINE, *Who Dies?*

When American astronaut Buzz Aldrin set foot on the moon, he achieved his life's ambition. A former combat pilot and holder of a doctorate from MIT, he was as tough and as smart as they came. ("All meat and stone," wrote Norman Mailer at the time.) But after he returned to earth, he became depressed, confused, and tearful. After achieving what he called "the most important goal of all," he finally confronted himself: "I had gone to the moon. What to do next? What possible goal could I add now? There simply wasn't one. I was suffering from what poets have described as the melancholy of all things done." In his depression, his marriage unraveled and he began to drink. He took antidepressant medications and sought help from psychotherapy. "My depression forced me, at the age of forty-one, to stop and for the first time examine my life," Aldrin later concluded. "The circumstances . . . were extreme, but I now look upon this experience as one of the most valuable things I have ever done. It taught me to live again, at an age when it is very possible to begin anew."[1] Having entered the second half of his life, he began a journey that would test him in ways that flying to the moon had never done.

Not only stolid military men like Aldrin seek transformation in the second half of life. This very same urge also emerges in lives that have been as far-flung as his was focused. Timothy Leary, a reflective, well-traveled psychologist, spent the first half of his life studying the nature of human relationships and consciousness. He was not a military technocrat in a sterile NASA space suit, but a dazzlingly intellectual author dressed fashionably in the tweedy clothes of academia. Yet when he sat down in his sixties to write his autobiography, his opening line was: "Exactly in the middle of the allotted term of this life's journey, my thirty-fifth birthday, I entered a dark place." Years of philosophical and psychological training had not prepared him for the challenges of the second half, which began to expand his mind long before he ingested his first hallucinogen at the ripe old age of forty.[2]

Many writers have implied, and some have actually argued, that the "midlife crisis" of Aldrin and Leary is primarily a problem for men. But women, too, are finding the second half to be a time of profound transformation. Like Aldrin and Leary, they suffer at midlife from what they have *not* done, and they embark on a quest for greater wholeness.

After marriage and early childbearing, Betty Friedan felt a growing emptiness. She had spent her life directed toward a goal—marriage, children, suburban house, happiness. But just when she "had it all," she felt empty. Like many other women in their middle and late thirties, she lay in bed at night afraid to ask, "Is this all?" Years later, when I asked her if she considered *The Feminine Mystique* to have been a midlife book, she replied without hesitation. "Absolutely! I began it when I was thirty-six and finished when I was forty-one." For her and her generation, she later wrote, "the feminist movement meant the marvelous midlife discovery of a whole new identity, a new sense of self."[3]

Natalie Rogers is almost a generation younger than Friedan. The daughter of the renowned psychologist Carl Rogers, she grew up in a cultural milieu apparently dedicated to psychological thinking and personal self-expression. She married and raised a family. Yet at precisely the same age as Friedan, she became profoundly dissatisfied. "Why?" she asked herself in her diary. "When I love my kids, I have a nice home, I have a husband who loves me (we never argue), I have security. Why am I in this awful funk?" Realizing that she had created for herself during the first half of her life an existence that she now found unbearable, she eventually left her husband—and temporarily even her children—to discover the parts of herself that she did not know. After forty-six years of "living a life *with* and *for* people," she decided it was time to live with and for herself. Few women can hear her story without recognizing aspects of their own struggle for selfhood.[4]

All four of these stories record one common experience: the shock of beginning life's second half. And stories of men and women like Aldrin, Leary, Friedan, and Rogers are only the tip of the iceberg. I interviewed men living apparently ordinary lives without death-defying trips to outer—or inner —space, who are also transforming their lives in their thirties, forties, fifties, and beyond. Similarly, I have interviewed career women as well as homemakers, women without children as well as mothers—all are encountering this crisis of the second half.

Some almost died from heart attacks and then began their process of renewal. Others plunged into divorce, or despair, and emerged to find new dimensions of love and hope. Some resigned from their jobs and discovered new callings that enabled them to express their deepest selves. Still others, imprisoned in lives of meaninglessness and passivity, liberated themselves and found spiritual meaning and social involvement that profoundly enriched their lives and their world. And some, of course, passed through their crisis without outward signs of tumult. To move beyond the crisis, however, all of them needed to consult their inner compass.

Consulting Your Compass: Before the Quest Begins

In the second half of life, our old compasses no longer work. The magnetic fields alter. The new compass that we need cannot be held in our hand, only in our heart. We read it not with our mind alone, but with our soul.

Now we yearn for *wholeness*. We yearn to remember the parts of ourselves that we have forgotten, to nourish those we have starved, to express those we have silenced, and to bring into the light those we have cast into the shadows. On this quest for wholeness, we must let go of clichés of adult life, both positive and negative. The standard maps of "growing up" and "growing old" will not serve us well. Using the best information available, each of us must find his own way.

To varying degrees, all of us are trying to break out of what Yale psychiatrist Daniel Levinson, in *The Seasons of a Man's Life,* called the "life structure" that we have built during the first part of our lives. "Every life structure necessarily gives priority to certain aspects of the self," wrote Levinson, "and neglects or minimizes other aspects."[5] No wonder, then, that the second half is the time when these parts of ourselves that have been neglected, ignored, or otherwise suppressed begin to emerge. It is now—or never.

"In this phase of life—between thirty-five and fifty—a significant change in the human psyche is in preparation," concluded Carl Jung, based on years of clinical research and reflection. "At first it is not a conscious and striking change. . . . Often it is something like a slow change in a person's character; in another case certain traits may come to light which had disappeared in childhood; or again, inclinations and interests begin to weaken and others arise to take their places."[6]

But what the measured prose of psychiatrists and the carefully calculated statistics of social scientists rarely capture is the experience of inner struggle. These "significant changes" do not occur automatically. In fact, they must often fight against our resistance. In this sense, midlife is a drama more worthy of a playwright than a scholar. We are characters in the play, caught at the opening of the second act, and we do not know what will happen next.

Jung wrote more than fifty years ago that, when we begin the second half, "the elements of the psyche undergo in the course of life a very marked change—so much so, that *we may distinguish between a psychology of the morning of life and a psychology of its afternoon.*"[7] Although my friend Peter Goldmark had never read Jung's words, he wrote these lines of poetry at the age of forty-five:

> If life is a day, in mine it is after one
> And only until dusk will daylight last.
> If life is a year, for me August is come.
> The young green afternoons of June have passed.[8]

Just as Jung predicted, Peter had noticed a shift within himself. Noon had passed. He had entered a different part of the day, about which he knew very little. But he was aware of crossing the threshold. He was aware of the quest.

Our quest is waiting for us—but only if we listen to these quest-ions. If we ignore our questions and act as if we are still in life's first half, we do so at our own peril. Whoever pretends that the second half of life is no different from the first, wrote Jung, "must pay with damage to his soul." If you don't find the time, the time will find you. Whether you begin your midlife quest on purpose with your eyes open, or against your will with your eyes shut tight, it will one day begin.

Indeed, without your knowing it, it may already have.

"Entering a Forest Dark": Why the Quest Is Not a Crisis

If you were to meet Dave and Donna Stapleton in their living room, they would seem at first glance to be just an ordinary American couple in their sixties. You would see his musical instruments in one corner and her stained-glass handiwork in the other. They would proudly show you pictures of their grandson. But if you listened to them describe the course of their rich and varied adult lives, you would notice: *They do not fit a pattern.*

At what was supposed to be the height of their productive years in their early forties, they were running a dry cleaning business in Chicago and were broke. In their late forties, they were operating a successful rug cleaning business in Florida. In what was supposed to be their stable fifties, they rode motorcycles around the country. When they reached retirement age, they were working seven days a week as hosts of a bed and breakfast. When these gray-haired grandparents take out their family scrapbooks, with recent photos showing them posing in front of their gleaming black Harley-Davidson, you confront the reality of the second half of life that so many of the well-packaged theories obscure. It is impossible to squeeze the lives of this couple into neat and orderly "stages" or "passages."

"By the time we were in our forties, we weren't afraid anymore," says Donna. "Even if people called us crazy, we did what we wanted to."[9]

I invite scholars and authors who think they can predict the stages of "adult development" to spend a day with the Stapletons, for they will discover an exception to their rules about the life cycle. I wager that most of us are exceptions too.[10]

Consider another exception, sixty-year-old Michael Murphy. I spoke with him one morning while he was making breakfast for his six-year-old—not his grandson, but his first and only *son*. At the age when the Stapletons were sending their grown-up children off into the world, Michael had not yet even become a father. He was too busy with the life of the spirit in his twenties to be involved with marriage, parenthood, and householding. Unlike what so many theorists predict, spiritual concerns gripped him in early adulthood, not at midlife. He founded the Esalen Institute, a center dedicated to exploring the frontiers of human consciousness that has over the last three decades enriched the lives of thousands who have visited its majestic acreage in the mountains of Big Sur. For him, seeking wholeness in the second half involved marrying and raising a family. He married at forty and had his first child at fifty-four.

"I am a householder," he now says, intentionally using the phrase from the Hindu tradition to make his point. According to the Hindu view of the life cycle, the householder stage characterizes early adulthood; after the age of forty or fifty, one is supposed to distance oneself from material concerns and become more involved with the spiritual. But Michael's experience was, of course, just the opposite.

"There is something a little bit old-fashioned about these stage theories," he says. "Our world is so pluralistic. We have so many new choices today. There are more options than ever before, more patterns and life sequences, more possibilities than these intellectual grids can take into account. Of course there is a role for classification. But I have a real problem with trying to make our lives fit the theories. I am driven by my own experience, and by the data I have been collecting over the past fifteen years, to a simple conclusion: *many people's lives today cannot be so easily categorized.*"[11]

I learned this firsthand in 1989 when an article I had written about the second half was published in a magazine. In the article, I requested that readers write letters describing their experience in their thirties, forties, fifties, and beyond. As a result of that article, which was subsequently reprinted in several different publications, I received scores of letters from men and women telling me their stories of second-half transformation. This one, for example, came from a man in a small town in Washington.

> I am a 48-year-old who has had a wonderful/painful midlife experience. At 41, I was a branch manager of a local insurance company, a practicing alcoholic and drug abuser. I had a family with three sons, mortgage, cars, bills, and no college degree.
>
> Seven years later, I am in graduate school majoring in psychology, remarried, out of debt, a practicing thera-

pist, skier, mountain climber, backpacker, and two years
ago ran in and finished in the Emerald City Marathon.
In 1982, if you had told me that this is where I would
be today, I would have thought you were crazy. Today, I
have no idea where my limits are.

This man now envisions the rest of his life as a quest, not a
crisis. His quest does not follow any experts' one-two-three
"stages of midlife growth." The experts' maps are theirs, not
yours. You will want to find your own map.

Influenced by the great theorists such as Jung and Erikson, I at first tried to make my life and the lives of those I
interviewed fit into some orderly pattern. It was tempting to
take refuge in abstract, generalized theories in order to escape the uniqueness and complexity of the actual life stories
I was hearing. After sifting through countless first-person
accounts and conducting scores of personal interviews, however, only one generalization stood the test of time: As we
age, we human beings yearn for wholeness. We yearn for the
parts of ourselves that have been in the dark to find sunlight,
and those that were sunburned to find shade. We yearn for
the parts that have been underdeveloped to grow, and those
that were overdeveloped to be pruned. We yearn for the
parts that have been silent to speak, and those that were
noisy to be still. We yearn for the parts that have been alone
to find companionship, and those that have been over-
crowded to find solitude. *We yearn to live our unlived lives.*

No one has witnessed this more intimately than Anthea
Francine, who has spent over a decade leading "questing
circles" for women in the San Francisco area. Each of the
over one thousand women with whom she has worked is
seeking something different as she enters her second half.
Some want to enter a marriage, some to leave; some want to
find a more committed vocation, some want leisure; and so
on. But behind these vast differences is an underlying common thread. "They are questing for authenticity," says

Anthea. "They want to be who they are, and not be tied down to someone else's demands or stereotypes."

To explain what she means by authenticity, Anthea draws a circle. "People come onto the wheel of life at different points," she says, "just as people are born at different times of the year. To complete the circle, each needs something else. For each, the journey is unique. I have found that people may be highly developed in one part of the circle and completely underdeveloped in other parts. For most of the people I work with, their challenge is to reclaim what they have forfeited and become whole."[12]

To be true to Anthea, and to so many others who have recently shared their lives with me, I cannot construct a series of stages for the second half of life against which you can chart your own path. Yes, I can pass on other people's maps that describe the terrain from their perspective, indicate some of the landmarks that you may pass, and suggest ways of creating your own compass that may keep you on your chosen course. But ultimately, your path toward wholeness is unique. It depends on where you have been and where you are going. Your quest is just that—*yours.*

What we share, I believe, is this quest for wholeness. Have you ever heard of anyone upon their deathbed who said: "If only I had specialized more narrowly in my field"? Have you ever heard of a last will and testament in which the deceased said they wished they had not made love such a high priority; that they had not spent so much time with their children; or that they had not taken such good care of their health? Have you ever heard reports of wise elders who, looking back upon their lives, said they wished they had spent more time in the office; paid more attention to other people's expectations of them; or been more cautious in exploring new parts of themselves?

We never hear such regrets because the second half of life is a quest for wholeness. It turns the tables on the first half. It weights the balances in favor of integrity. It asks us not to

defend who we are but to be open to the mystery of what we
have not yet become, the mystery of coming into our own,
whoever we may be. It connects us to a quest that goes far
back beyond our time, long before the phrase *adult development* was ever coined. Dante opened *The Divine Comedy*
with the famous lines:

> Midway upon the journey of our life
> I found myself within a forest dark,
> For the straightforward pathway had been lost . . .

Although longer lifespans have heightened our awareness of
the second half, its mysteries have been explored as far back
as the *Odyssey.* The quest runs through literature from
Dante to Sartre; is present in all the great religions; continues into the birth of modern psychology with Freud and
Jung; and moved into popular culture through books like
Passages and *Necessary Losses,* as well as through movies,
television, novels, board games, advertising, and pop music
lyrics.

The quest for wholeness in the second half is ancient and
universal. Joseph Campbell defined it well in his classic
study of world mythology, *Hero with a Thousand Faces.* He
showed that in virtually all the world's myths could be found
a shared quest for meaning and transcendence, a "heroic"
quest that took place during the years we call adulthood.
According to Campbell, the drama of the quest itself was far
more than a mere extension of our personal or family
psychohistories. It was a joining with the cosmic and timeless
tales—what Jean Houston calls "the Larger Story"—that is
crystallized in dreams and codified in myth.

"So these old stories live in us?" Bill Moyers asked Campbell during one of their interviews held at George Lucas's
Skywalker Ranch.

"They do indeed," Campbell replied, and he went on to
outline the challenge of the second half.

As a child, you are brought up in a world of discipline, obedience, and you are dependent on others. *All this has to be transcended when you come to maturity,* so that you can live not in dependency, but in self-responsible authority. If you can't cross that threshold, you have the basis for neuroses.

MOYERS: But I can hear someone saying, "Well, that's all well and good for the imagination of a George Lucas or for the scholarship of a Joseph Campbell, but that isn't what happens in my life."

CAMPBELL: You bet it is—and if he doesn't recognize it, it may turn him into Darth Vader. If the person insists on a certain program, and doesn't listen to the demands of his own heart, he's going to risk a . . . crackup.[13]

Unfortunately, too many of us are locked into the "certain program" of life's first half. Physically, socially, economically, psychologically, and spiritually, the agenda of the second half of life varies greatly from the agenda of the first. And yet, lost under the bland generality of "adulthood," we continue to treat each other and ourselves as if nothing has changed. We turn the second half into a "midlife crisis" by pretending that everything is supposed to stay the same— only to discover, to our surprise, that nothing does stay the same. Possibilities for growth and change in the second half that we never knew existed now emerge.

"Who knows?" said Paul McCartney, in the sixties. "At forty we might not be able to write songs anymore!" Yet the former Beatle is now writing original songs that top the charts even as he enters his fifties. Mick Jagger, meanwhile, entered the 1990s still wearing his tights and strutting across the stage before sell-out crowds. Bonnie Raitt, in her forties, won a Grammy Award for her hit album *Nick of Time,* filled with lyrics resonant with the second half. The list goes on of minstrels who did not fade away or recycle their old music, but who continue to produce spellbinding new music to this day. Although some were casualties of drugs and other inner demons, many musical leaders of the rock-and-roll generation have given us inspiring examples of how to grow and heal deep into the second half.

Similarly on the sports field, where only the young and hardy can survive, many athletes now entering the second half are not hanging up their cleats or retiring to the "senior circuit," but are pushing themselves well past the stereotypes of aging with which they grew up. In addition to the superstars who are pushing the limits, the generation as a whole is more active than ever. Membership in the United States Masters Swimmers (average age: forty-six) has more than doubled in the last eight years. The U.S. Tennis Association, the New York Road Runners Club, and scores of other sports organizations all report sharp increases in membership among men and women in their thirties, forties, and fifties.[14]

Beyond the high-profile world of entertainment and sports, many others are proving that growth is a built-in part of the half century we lump together as "adulthood." Stories abound of dramatic achievements and profound life-changes. The people who accomplish these midlife break-throughs are not heralded on television or given awards, but they are pathfinders that others will certainly follow. Twenty years ago, Lourdes Baird was a mother of three making Toll House cookies, taking night classes, and worrying that her discount coupons would fall out of her purse and she would be discovered as "nothing but a housewife." In her forties, she graduated from law school. Now in her fifties, she is a U.S. attorney in California, one of the most powerful federal prosecutors in the country.[15]

How many inspiring, startling, trend-setting stories of second half reawakening are out there? No one knows—*but there are more than we can imagine.* Not only on the concert stage and sports field, but in homes and workplaces throughout America, the generation now in the second half is dispelling once and for all the self-destructive equation, "Growing Older = Stopping Growing." Men and women in their thirties, forties, fifties, and older are proving with their lives that growth in the second half of life can be as breathtaking—and as confusing—as in youth.

Denial and Confusion: The Fine Art of Getting Lost

The journey of adulthood, however, involves a different dimension of growth from the first half. It is not incvitable, biologically determined growth, as it was in childhood. Nor is it the built-in, socially recognized "growing up" of adolescence. It is much more mysterious, unpredictable, and often invisible. An adolescent boy who suddenly sprouts up two inches in half a year, begins shaving, and falls in love is obviously growing. So is a teenage girl who menstruates for the first time, develops breasts, and refuses to wear her old "kid's stuff." But the growth of grownups cannot be as readily "proved" or "disproved." It is more elusive.[16]

If I were to pick a single moment when I recognized that I had entered this new dimension—begun my metamorphosis, so to speak—it would be the day several years ago at my son's baseball game. A few months prior to that day, my wife Shelley had suggested I read a book entitled *In Midlife*.[17] I flipped through several pages and put it down. I told her that I found it tedious, academic and uninteresting. Then about half a year later, she mentioned that she had given the same book to a friend who had collected the most powerful passages in the book and edited them down to a few pages. Along with some other paperwork, I took the photocopied pages with me to the Little League diamond, where our son Ari was about to have a game. While he shagged flies in the outfield, I glanced down at the pages in my lap.

Crash! The next thing I knew, a foul ball slammed into the

fence directly in front of where I was sitting. I looked toward
the outfield; Ari was gone. I checked the scoreboard; the
game was already in the second inning. I had been lost for
almost half an hour in excerpts from a book that less than a
year ago had bored me. Now I was staring at these pages
mesmerized, like a primitive tribesman first encountering a
mirror. Almost every passage I read felt as if someone had
taken a photograph of my inner life. The passage on which
my attention had been riveted when the foul ball struck was
an uncanny single paragraph describing what happens when
we enter the second half:

> Midlife is a crisis of the spirit. In this crisis, old selves
> are lost and new ones come into being. . . . Typically,
> the midlife transition lasts several years and occurs
> somewhere between the ages of thirty-five and forty,
> usually falling around the age of forty. . . . Most stu-
> dents of it agree on certain characteristic features: there
> are often persistent moods of lassitude and depression,
> or feelings of disillusionment and disappointment. . . .
> death anxiety steals in, and a sense that time will run
> out before one can get down to "really living" is fre-
> quently reported; physically a person is beginning to
> show signs of aging, and so an earlier self-image starts
> cracking and altering.

Every one of the features mentioned in the paragraph had
been hovering around the edges of my consciousness. When
I read them one by one, loaded together in a single paragraph, I felt as if I had just seen a CAT scan of my unconscious.

Obviously, I did not enter the second half of my life consciously or deliberately. On the contrary, the discovery was
so startling that I proceeded over the ensuing months to
deny it ever happened. When I began writing this book, in
fact, I totally blocked out the experience of what happened

at the baseball diamond. I actually wrote in one draft that I had "just happened" to see the book on a shelf in our bedroom. But Shelley reminded me of what occurred at the baseball game.

It was only then that I remembered how the book had gripped me; how I had proceeded to take it with me on a business trip a few days later; how on planes and trains I had read it a second time, and then a third; and how, finally, I had located the publisher in Dallas and ordered ten copies to share with others. Why, if I had been so enthusiastic about the book at the time, did I later totally block out the moment of its first impact? Why had I tried so hard to resist something so valuable?

The answer to these questions is clear: denial and confusion. Both are a vital part of the quest. Since none of us unconsciously wants to be lost, we begin the quest by denying it. The journey therefore takes us by surprise. "Midlife befalls us," writes Murray Stein, the author of the book. "We don't ask for it." This is why, in so many cases, we try to stop it from beginning. We pretend it hasn't started, even when it clearly has. We deny that the metamorphosis of adulthood has begun. And we become confused about where, and who, we are.

Unlike the conventional view of the "midlife crisis," the quest does not necessarily begin with a tumultuous upheaval in one's life—an affair, or a red sports car, or a move to a new job. Whether we know it or not (and usually we don't), it often begins with resistance to change. It begins with our pulling against the future and clinging to the past. It begins with our unconsciously saying "No, not yet!" to what is happening inside us.

Denial is a kind of quest in reverse. We are actually trying *not* to journey. We think our challenge is to stay young, and so we pretend that we are still in life's first half, that the transformation isn't taking place. We cling to our youthful selves with all the determination of a shipwrecked sailor gripping a piece of driftwood. Sometimes it requires suffering the loneliness of watching others leave us behind as they set off on new paths. It involves blocking out the sights and sounds and smells that suggest new lands and new possibilities. It demands that we silence our questions, doubts, wonderings, and inner yearnings.

The word *midlife* itself, for example, often produces an adverse reaction. Most people in their thirties and forties (and even many in their fifties) assume that it refers to someone older than themselves. Thirty-five-year-olds think it begins at forty; forty-year-olds think it begins at forty-five; forty-five-year-olds push the entry point back to fifty; and so on throughout our final years. When Katharine Hepburn tells Henry Fonda in the film *On Golden Pond* that they should get together with another "middle-aged" couple like themselves, her cantankerous husband replies: "We're *not* middle-aged. People don't live to be a hundred and fifty!" We resist applying the word *midlife* to ourselves because it acknowledges two interconnected truths: that we may no longer be "young" (whatever that means to us), and that, since life has a *mid*point, it must also have an *end*point—and it is not one hundred and fifty!

While in this period of denial, we tend to dismiss these internal signals and wait for them to go away. This is another form of denial: postponement. Postponers accept that they are beginning a journey into a new phase of life, but they arm themselves with the illusion of control. They "decide" that their entry into life's second half will begin at a later date. It will happen when they reach a certain age (usually five to ten years ahead). It will happen when they reach a certain income (usually significantly more than they currently earn). It will happen when their children leave home, or when they reach some other landmark that, like a mirage, always recedes into the distance. They dismiss what is happening inside them as premature, as if such feelings were permissible only in "old people." (The title of one comedic book expresses this feeling well: *Who Needs Midlife at Your Age?)*

For my friend Anna, then in her late thirties, the phase of denial was extremely painful. Married to a successful physician, the mother of three children, and a homemaker in a charming suburban home, everything was "picture perfect" for Anna except for one strange detail. Beginning at the age of thirty-seven, whenever she was alone in her house, she would begin to cry. Her husband would leave for the office; she would take the children to school; she would come home and shut the door behind her—and cry. It went on for weeks, then months. *It will pass,* she would think to herself. *It's just a phase. It will go away. No point in telling other people; it would be so embarrassing.* So she tried to ignore her tears. To follow them to their source, she later discovered, would threaten everything she had and everything she was. And she was not ready—not yet.

For Dr. William Nolen, a fifty-year-old surgeon at the peak of his professional life, the second half messenger was not tears but sleeplessness. His medical career was flourishing. He had even written a highly acclaimed book. His marriage was strong, and his children all successful. But he found himself waking at three in the morning, unable to get back to sleep. It happened not once, not twice, but again and again. Like Anna, he thought the solution was to ignore the message—ignore it, and it would go away. But it persisted, and his fatigue deepened. He began drinking, then taking sleeping medications. He would not listen to his insomnia; instead, he tried to overpower it. Only after several months of deepening pain and confusion did Dr. Nolen realize that he could not fight insomnia that way. The harder he fought it, the stronger it became. He was not ready yet either.[18]

Although experiences like Dr. Nolen's, Anna's, and mine are common nowadays, we experience them alone, in isolation, with little or no support for the quest on which we are about to embark. If only we knew that this process of transformation is part of our human heritage. So mysterious is this process that we refer to it only through metaphor— caterpillars entering their cocoons, embryos preparing to be born—because we feel we are entering a zone that is beyond our knowledge, literally off the map. We use metaphors because, as Dr. Ralph Metzner has observed, they are tools for carrying ourselves beyond the known *(meta,* "beyond"; *pherein,* "to carry"). They are trying to carry us beyond the first half of our lives and into the mysteries of the second.

For Anna it was tears, and for Dr. Nolen, insomnia. For others it may be illness or impotence, depression or divorce, weight gain or job loss, fatigue or hyperenergy, or scores of other symptoms. *What matters is not the symptom itself but the message it carries.*

The message is: It is time to prepare. Something is happening to us. We are undergoing a change. We may choose to deny it, but ultimately we must recognize that our passage into the second half of our lives is beginning. This is the positive purpose of denial: It permits continuity. It avoids premature encounter with chaos. It maintains a facade behind which the forces of change can gather themselves. It allows us to maintain necessary control. It gives us more time.

Imagine that someone suddenly offered you a dream vacation, with one condition: You must leave in two hours. Your excitement would be mixed with panic, for even the journey of your dreams requires some advance warning. You must get time off from work and find someone to watch the kids and water the plants. You must pack. You must make several large adjustments in your life in order to get away for that length of time. You need time to get ready.

So if you feel you are in this stage of denial, do not immediately assume it is inappropriate. It does not necessarily mean you are being lazy, or obstinate, or otherwise stuck. In fact, you may be working very hard just trying to resist the change you sense is coming. Resistance may be your way of allowing yourself time to prepare for what lies ahead.

Sadly, though, denial is not just the first stage of the quest for some people; it is also the last. They sense the possibility of a journey, usually unconsciously, and postpone it indefinitely. They do not feel prepared for such a quest—and who can blame them? None of us is prepared for the unknown. It is frightening, unpredictable, the first step toward losing control. That it is also the first step toward finding our deeper selves, we do not know. Since it preserves the status quo, the incentives for denying, for waiting, appear great. Since it involves upheaval and uncertainty, the incentives for moving forward on our quest appear small. Until this changes, we stand still. Sometimes we even regress. We make one last stand, trying to avoid leaving the familiar land of the young and journeying toward the unknown country ahead.

But the time comes when denial no longer works. Looking back on what she called "the most painful year of my life," Jane Fonda reflected shortly after her divorce on the choice she had made between denial and moving forward. "You can either pretend," she said, ". . . avoid [the pain], stay real busy, numb yourself through drink or drugs or promiscuity, use your kids as a battlefield, stay angry. . . . Or you can say, if God is having me feel this much pain and suffering, *there's got to be a reason.*"[19]

Indeed there *is* a reason. But we cannot find it yet. Only one foot has crossed the threshold. We are not in our old world, but we are not in the new world either. We are in a gray area, neither here nor there, living in two worlds at once. In this twilight zone, we experience confusion *(fundere,* "to pour"; *com,* "together"). We are con-fused because two worlds are indeed becoming fused: the personality that in the first half of life we grew accustomed to calling "I," and the self that is trying to break through into consciousness in the second half. Finally, when the change becomes so massive that we simply can no longer deny it, we awaken as if from a dream. We accept the truth that we are, in fact, lost. We don't know what is happening to us. Inexplicable exhaustion, mysterious pain, insomnia, uncontrollable crying, profound dissatisfaction at work—whatever our personal symptom may be, we begin to question ourselves, to seek the wound that is not healed, to identify the source of our pain.

Recalling his own quest, Jung called this his "confrontation with the unconscious." Today, many contemporary psychologists are shedding new light on the process and naming its various dimensions. Jungian analyst Murray Stein calls it "the return of the repressed." John Bradshaw calls it the "wounded inner child," who is finally demanding to be heard—and healed. Maureen Murdock, speaking of women, calls it "the descent to the goddess," when a woman "meets the dark mother within and reclaims the discarded parts of herself." Robert Bly, speaking of men, calls it "taking the road of ashes," when we feel that our dreams have turned to dust and we are forced to confront "the long bag we drag behind us." Perhaps Connie Zweig, in her prologue to *Meeting the Shadow,* puts it most directly: "At midlife," she wrote, "I met my devils."[20]

But whatever we name the shadow, the fact is that we can't just talk about our anger, pain, or hurt anymore. We are now compelled to live it. We can't observe it; we *are* it. What in the first half of life we decided was *not* us now comes back to *become* us. Two selves, the I and the not-I, are now pouring together inside us. The question is: What is this new compound, this new self, that will emerge? And at this point, there is no answer—only confusion. The form that it takes usually depends on what parts of yourself you have neglected or minimized—that is, whatever you are least ready for.

In the movie version of Anne Tyler's novel *The Accidental Tourist,* Macon is a writer (played by William Hurt) who is totally dependent on order, predictability, and rationality.

He falls in love with wacky, spontaneous, emotional Muriel Pritchett (played by Geena Davis). He discovers this dormant side of himself through this radically different human being. Speaking of his new love at midlife, Macon says: "She gave me another chance to decide who I am." In fact, Muriel was only his muse. It was Macon who gave *himself* another chance to discover his "other side."

For each of us, the parts of ourselves that we have hidden are unique. But they can be summarized by Jung's deceptively simple concept of the *shadow*. We forge our identities in adolescence by highlighting parts of ourselves that Jung called the *persona*. This is what we show the world, what we claim as "me." We define ourselves by keeping the shadow in the dark. As men define their masculinity, they tend to place their feminine side (or anima) in this shadowy underworld, just as women submerge their masculine side (or animus). What may superficially appear to be a "midlife crisis" is the much deeper, long-term psychological process of our shadow seeking the light.

This process is confusing because at least two voices inside us are now claiming to be the I: the old persona, the identity formed in the first half of our lives that is determined to disown these new elements in our psyches; and the awakening shadow, asking—sometimes demanding—to be let in. As the crack widens between who we are and who we are perceived to be, it can be more than confusing. It can be totally disorienting. If we have had the courage to embrace these new parts of ourselves, the alchemy of the second half can combine these two into a new I that is more whole, more wise, and more compassionate. But at this point, all we feel is confused.

Recall Anna, for instance: Is she the wife of a successful physician, who is lovingly raising her gifted children? Or is she a depressed woman who is out of control and on the verge of a nervous breakdown? And Dr. Nolen: Is he the brilliant surgeon and author whose body and mind perform

with skill and precision? Or is he the insomniac who is taking more and more drugs in order to sleep, the drunkard
who is embarrassing himself and his wife at parties? They—
and we—are both, of course, which is logically true, but *psy-
cho*logically misleading. If we are both, then what is the con-
tainer that holds these warring elements in our psyche? The
old self, formed in the crucible of adolescence, was based on
banishing the shadow. Our new self is being called upon to
embrace it. Following Jung, let us call this all-embracing self
that emerges in the second half just that: *the Self.*

In this confused and questioning stage of our journey, the
Self is barely glimpsed. At this point, we are divided against
ourselves. As Ralph Metzner points out, the metaphors
abound: "We may be 'shattered' by an experience; we may
think we are 'falling apart'; 'coming apart at the seams,' or
'falling to pieces' . . . feel 'torn' between conflicting demands, be 'crushed' by a rejection, 'crumble' under stress,
until [the] mind 'snaps'." It is a time when we speak for-
lornly about wishing we were "more together," but it is, in
reality, when we feel—and couples do—"split up."[21]

We are likely at this stage of the quest to describe ourselves as torn between alternatives. We may feel torn *between lovers,* unable to decide which to choose, or even
wanting both. We may feel torn *between jobs,* one that offers
security and prestige and another that offers challenge and
uncertainty. We may feel torn *between life-styles:* for example, an urban existence with all its rewards and stresses, and
a new life in a rural area with lower income, fewer options,
but more beauty and peace. Ultimately, we are feeling torn
between selves: who we have been versus who we are becoming on the quest.

Now suddenly the structure of our lives does not fit us, but
we don't know why. Bargains we made, both professional
and personal, may suddenly seem unfair. Relationships we
chose may suddenly seem unfulfilling. Signs of aging in our
faces suddenly seem prominent. A car, home, or community

that once brought pleasure may now seem utterly inadequate. A life-style that seemed satisfying, or at least bearable, now grates on our nerves and becomes increasingly intolerable. Goals that seemed so clear may now become complex or blurred. Rewards that before seemed destined to bring pleasure now seem empty, not even worth the effort. A life-span that only yesterday seemed long now seems inexplicably abbreviated.

Like a swimmer flipped head over heels and submerged by a turbulent wave, we do not even know which way to go for air. We are confused, scared, and out of breath. As the contemporary poet Jan Struther observes,

> It took me forty years on earth
> To reach this sure conclusion:
> There is no Heaven but clarity,
> No Hell except confusion.[22]

We yearn for clear direction, but find only fog.

For a surgeon like Dr. Nolen, as for many professionals, his identity was built around being *under control.* To be sloppy or messy, much less publicly drunk, would be anathema to a surgeon's identity—which is why this is exactly how he behaved during his period of confusion. He was *out of control.* For Anna, as for many loving parents and spouses, her identity was built around happily *serving the needs of others.* Even when her persona began to break down, she did not cry when she woke up in the morning; she began sobbing only after the needs of her husband and children had been fully met. At this stage of her journey, Anna could let her tears fall only when no one else was there to see them. For her, the challenge of the second half was to begin *attending to her own deeper needs.*

When we are suspended in this state of confusion, we do not know whether to go forward or turn back. But we know now that we have never been in this place before. We are approaching the heart of our quest, the pivotal crossroads. Do we pretend that we do not hear the messenger? Do we ignore the call? Do we bury our heads in what Murray Stein calls "the illusion that nothing is actually different"? Do we try to hold on to our old persona at all costs, "even after it has long since outlived its usefulness"?

When we are confused, many of us act out in ways that reveal the undeveloped (or what Jung called the inferior) sides of ourselves. These emerging parts of ourselves simply do not fit within the confines of the self we constructed in the first half of our lives. Just as teenagers burst the seams of their old clothes, we are bursting at the seams of our old identities. Who we were and how we lived may now feel like prisons to us. We feel (usually unconsciously) a desperate need to escape. At this critical stage, we may speak of being "trapped" in a marriage, "tied down" to a family or job, "stuck" in a rut, "roped in" by certain constraints, or otherwise held captive.

For some, the jail cell is marriage. They feel they must escape from the deadly limitations of their domestic life. For others, it is their job. They feel suffocated, almost incarcerated, by their employment and harbor desperate fantasies of freeing themselves from the Alcatraz of their office. For still others, it may be a physical addiction or psychological obsession, an invisible set of steel bars that prevents them from becoming a free man or woman. In some cases, the prison may be the body itself and the experience of being overweight, ill, in pain, or simply unattractive. Given these various forms of imprisonment (which we explore more deeply in later chapters), our behavior at this stage not surprisingly resembles those of actual inmates: We are angry and depressed.

At this point, we feel trapped by everything we have done in the first half of our lives. As one executive at a Chicago advertising agency put it, "My past life had such a grip on me that I felt helpless to change things. I felt trapped in my marriage. I felt trapped in my life-style. Trapped in my career. Trapped in the high-rise I lived in. Trapped in the high-rise I worked in. Trapped in my skin." For him, these feelings of imprisonment led quickly (as we will explore in Chapter 5) to a total life change.[23]

When trapped in confusion, we may actually feel as if we are dying, trying to prop up a corpse—an enterprise obviously destined to failure. We may buy our dying youthful persona a new Porsche. We may give it a young lover. We may change the old persona's mask cosmetically, buy new clothes, or change hairstyles. But nothing can hide the stench of a dying body or a dying self. If we do not dare to let go and bury the dead, we will be stuck in confusion and mourning. The ghost of the first half of our life will haunt us.

By no means does everyone who begins the quest continue on it. We may be so terrified by the confusion that we try to turn back. We abort our journey. We may revert to the stage of denial, postponing the quest as long as we can. Or we may attempt to make superficial, cosmetic changes on our old persona while avoiding any profound change. We do not want to face the truth that something is rotten in our own home. So we call in the building contractor and interior decorator to do some remodeling. Ignoring the deep structural flaws, we add on a bedroom or a lovely deck or some modern skylights in the hope that, once the remodeling is over, life will feel better. Perhaps for a while it does . . . but not for long. We cannot half-bury a corpse. We cannot partially emerge from our cocoon. Similarly, we cannot *sort of* begin a quest. Either we do, or we don't—and the time to decide has arrived.

There is only one way out, and that is *through.*

Turning Points:
Breakdowns, Breakups, and Breakthroughs

"The death of my husband triggered my quest," Leni told me matter-of-factly. "Although we had been separated, we were still very close. After his death, all my attention was focused for a few years on my teenage daughter. But when she left for college, I was left alone . . . with an aching emptiness. When I entered that new zone, nothing felt the same. All the ways I had related to people didn't work anymore. Everything felt intolerable; everything was painful; everything was confusing. I knew I had to do something.

"So I took a year leave of absence from my job and moved to the mountains of Idaho. I lived inexpensively. I didn't have much to do. I didn't know many people. I had no diversions. I let go . . . let go of control—of the *illusion* of control. It was so obvious I could not control the pain. So I just let go.

"A year later I came back. I came back to the *same* parents, *same* house, *same* job . . . yet it all feels wonderful. I realized that midlife is a very inward journey. It is a process with its own timetable, its own rhythm. It's like grief . . . like mourning."

There, once again, was the same metaphor I had heard so many times. Something inside was passing away and being buried. But what, I asked her, is dying?

"An old self," she replied. "A self that no longer fits."

As Leni's answer illustrates, words betray us if we take them too literally as we describe this next stage of the quest. Obviously, no doctor would confirm that something inside Leni had died. No electrocardiogram would provide evidence that some part of her had passed away. Yet to describe the emotions of the next part of the quest, we are compelled to use words such as *dying* and *being born*. We are compelled to use this metaphor because these are the words that spring to the lips of virtually every person who describes this stage of their quest.

Why do we encounter this death/rebirth metaphor from so many people as they pass through this phase of their quest? I think it is because this is what, in fact, happens in the second half—not physically but spiritually.

For some, this process of death/rebirth is a time of miraculous transformation. Lifelong alcoholics suddenly go sober (and uptight teetotalers allow themselves a brandy); isolated singles suddenly find love (and long-married couples rediscover loneliness); bitter atheists suddenly discover a spiritual home (and devout fundamentalists break free of their dogma). But the process does not automatically lead to a breakthrough. It may also lead to a breakdown and breakup that can be disorienting and painful. It can be a time of casualties—of marriages that disintegrate; of midlife drug overdoses and suicides; of unexpected first-time violence between couples, and between parents and children; of illness and premature death.

The quest into the second half doesn't just *feel* frightening. It *is* frightening. The risks are real. If we leave our old home, we risk becoming homeless. If we want to expand or otherwise transform our marriages, it can lead to dissatisfaction, distrust, and divorce. If the demons hiding in our shadow selves are powerful, they can push us to within an inch of our lives. We may experience profound depression or paralyzing fatigue during this period. Our bodies may generate illnesses that are life-threatening. Our "spiritual emergencies" can wreak medical, sexual, marital, and often financial havoc in our lives. Midlife can raise the ante of living so high that we no longer dare to play.

My dear friend Craig, who grew up with me in Indiana, struggled with suicidal feelings for most of his life. After playing varsity quarterback at his Ivy League college, he became a Rhodes scholar at Oxford. I eagerly visited him there one summer, only to discover that he had not been in his dormitory for days, but rather in a small hospital room. Had his roommate not discovered him soon enough to get his stomach pumped, Craig would certainly have died. He had taken enough cyanide, as his doctor put it, "to kill a horse."

Craig survived and became a surgeon—that profession of consummate control. He had a gift for healing others in a way that he could never heal himself. He held his dark side in check enough to have a successful practice and start a family. But in his mid-forties, the shadow overwhelmed him again. After writing his wife a note apologizing for having been such a burden for so long, he climbed to the roof of the hospital in Houston where he had prolonged so many lives and leaped to end his own.

Craig was suicidal—we can say to comfort ourselves—and we are not. And indeed, many of us will traverse this part of the quest without personally encountering suicide, cata-strophic illness, or severe depression. But the demons that claimed him may approach us in other, less fatal guises. This is the time when the corporate executive suddenly resigns, or when the gifted speaker gets cancer of the throat and for a time cannot speak. This is the time when the famous actor takes LSD and shocks the studio executives, and the press, by proclaiming: "I have been born again." This is the time when the athlete becomes ill, the voiceless begin to speak, and the articulate fall silent. This is the time when "happily married" couples suddenly discover that they are caught in a romantic triangle (or even two); when we do not get the promotion we expected; when otherwise healthy men have unexplained "epileptic seizures" and otherwise healthy women have unaccustomed shifts in their weight. And it is the time when journeys, long postponed, are suddenly un-dertaken, often resulting in unforeseen transformations. It is the "rite, or moment, of spiritual passage" that Joseph Campbell explored so powerfully in *The Hero with a Thou-*

sand Faces—a rite "which, when complete, amounts to a dying and a birth."

For Anna, whose inexplicable tears began her journey into the second half, the death/rebirth process involved a painful breaking up during what was supposed to be an idyllic weekend with her husband celebrating their fifteenth wedding anniversary. As they rode up into the mountains, Anna was excited about their romantic getaway, far away from their three children and the house in which she had shed so many tears. Glancing at her husband, who sat silently and stiffly behind the wheel staring at the road ahead, Anna asked him what he thought had been the most wonderful moments of their married years.

"I don't know," he said, in the distant tone of voice she knew so well. "I can't think of any right now."

Although I was interviewing her five years afterward, the pain of the memory still brought tears to her eyes. "At that moment," Anna recalled, "I knew I wouldn't be asking him that question at our twentieth anniversary—or even at our sixteenth." Indeed, soon afterward they divorced, and Anna's quest began.

> I looked at my alternatives. It was scary! I looked around at what the culture was saying about aging women. The message I got was that we were worthless, useless, invisible. Some part of me decided that I just could not stay connected to those stereotypes. I wanted to age with grace, dignity . . . substance.
>
> As I considered divorce, I realized that I had to take complete responsibility for my own growth. I had to take care of *me,* provide for *me,* protect *me.* I couldn't use anybody as a buffer against life anymore. I had to trust myself, embrace myself, face myself.
>
> There was nothing to protect me against the whiplash of the forces I had repressed. I didn't know the pain would be that bad. It was like an earthquake. I was so

shaken that I could not operate on automatic pilot anymore. I didn't have anything to say. I didn't know who I
was . . . only that I could never again be who I *used* to
be.

Later, we will visit Anna again to see where her quest led
her. But even this brief episode illustrates how powerful and
scary breaking into the second half can be. The parts of
ourselves that we have disowned—the shadow—demand to
be reclaimed, implore us to become whole, and beckon us
onward.

Throughout antiquity, throughout the world's indigenous
cultures, throughout the world's religions, we find recognition of the process of renewal in human life. Human cultures
recognized that the Self must undergo renewal or rebirth.
Before modernity and what William Blake called our tech-
nocratic "single vision," sacred rites and rituals enabled human beings to move from one stage of life to the next. Life
was seen as a wheel, a perpetual cycle—not a chronological
ladder beginning at birth and ending in death. And at every
stage of the journey—birth, puberty, marriage, childbirth,
old age, and death—there were rites of passage that acknowledged change and renewal.

If such rites were needed in cultures where the average
life-span was perhaps forty, they are even more vital today,
when our life-spans have almost doubled. Dr. Nolen needed
insomnia and burnout at the age of fifty to reawaken and
reinvigorate his inner growth. Anna needed a divorce and
loneliness to revive the parts of herself that had become
deadened in a marriage that did not work and a self-limiting
life-style. Similarly, Shelley and I (and scores of other men
and women in the second half) have had to create rites of
passage to renew our growth. These crises of the spirit, or
what Stan and Christina Grof have appropriately called
"spiritual emergencies," lead us to encounter forces more
powerful and more mysterious than we have ever known.

We know we have reached this stage of the quest because of the rising level of our fear and anticipation. On the one hand, we have lost our way. But on the other hand, we have found it.

More than twenty years ago at the age of thirty-six, Scotty was sent by the U.S. Army Medical Corps to the headquarters of the National Training Laboratories (NTL), the organization that developed "sensitivity training" (or T-groups). His job was to explore a potential contract between NTL and the U.S. Army. On the one hand, he was a tough, pragmatic army officer; on the other hand, he was a wise, experienced psychiatrist. He was the perfect man for the job. But Scotty arrived for the twelve-day training session under considerable stress. He was exhausted from years of struggling against army bureaucracy, including his own stressful yet ineffectual lobbying against the Vietnam War.

On the tenth day, he received a message to call his office, and he learned to his dismay that his mentor in the Medical Corps had not gotten the promotion to brigadier general that he so richly deserved. Instead, the position was given to a far less visionary man, whom Scotty deeply distrusted. That night, he was terribly depressed about the call because it symbolized all that was wrong with bureaucracy. But when he informed his T-group, he spoke in a dull, expressionless monotone. When they asked him if he was angry, he denied it.

"Your hands are shaking, Scotty," one of the members of his group said matter-of-factly.

Still, Scotty denied his rage. He denied it until he began sobbing uncontrollably, overwhelmed at his feelings of exhaustion and despair.

> Waves of fatigue began to sweep over me. . . . I wanted to stop. I didn't want to make a fool of myself. But the fatigue was too much. I didn't have the energy to stop. . . . The first waves were of Washington, of

the "in" box three feet high, the talking papers written late at night, the lies I had seen perpetrated, the mixture of apathy, self-interest and conniving callousness against which I struggled. But as I let them come in, there were far older waves of fatigue, of struggling to make a marriage work, of almost endless nights in emergency rooms, thirty-two-hour tours of duty throughout medical school and internship, pacing the floor with colicky babies—wave after wave.[24]

After weeping for half an hour, he finally fell silent. He was more amazed than his colleagues were. "Please bear in mind," he told his colleagues, who had gathered around him in support, "that I've been saving it up for thirty years."

During the next months after his breakthrough, Scotty and his wife Lily moved to another community. He resigned his army job, opened a private practice, and began the second half of his life. He found his voice and gained a deeper wisdom, a wisdom that many others need as well. For Scotty is M. Scott Peck, whose wisdom in such books as *The Road Less Traveled* has guided millions of people toward their own true path. Without those tears at the age of thirty-six and his subsequent quest, his wisdom would have remained buried behind his dry eyes, and his healing touch locked inside his shaking hands.

This is the kind of breakthrough that is possible when the quest begins. For some, the breakthrough may be physical, a deep healing within the body. For others, it may be in a relationship, a deepening of intimacy with their mate or lover. For still others, the breakthrough may be professional, leading to the discovery of a true calling that draws forth their hidden gifts and talents. But as Scotty's story underscores, the breakthrough is not selfish or narcissistic. On the contrary, such personal renewal and growth is the building block of social transformation. By accepting the gift that is our quest, we pass it on.

The Quest Begins

You may be only thirty and already deeply engaged in the quest; or you may be fifty and still resisting it. This is because your chronological age is based on clock time; the quest moves through soul time. In this "time zone," which many of us encounter for the first time only in the second half, getting old turns out to have less to do with calendars than with fear; less to do with wrinkles than with truth; and less to do with death itself than with the deepest dimensions of life.

For some, the quest begins gently, like a sea breeze through the palms. But for others, it hits like a hurricane. If this happens to you, you will not know what hit you until you have been swept away. If you have experienced your life primarily through words, then on your quest words will fail you. If your life seemed under your control, it will now seem uncontrollable. If you have been passionate, you will now lose your passion; if passionless, you will find it. If you have been strong, your weaknesses will overwhelm you; if weak, your strengths will grip you. If you have been inactive, you will become energetic; if energetic, you will be tired. If you have been deeply intimate, you will encounter loneliness; if lonely, you will discover intimacy. If you have loved your parents, you will encounter your anger; if you have hated them, you will seek their forgiveness and love.

However the quest begins, you will be surprised, for you are entering the land of the second half. When Dr. Raymond Moody began his research into near-death experiences, he interviewed more than a hundred people who had clinically died and then recovered about what they experienced on the "other side." He was so startled by what he learned that he sympathized with the many people who would dismiss his book and its findings as inaccurate or irrelevant. "I have no room whatsoever to blame anyone who finds himself in this category," wrote Dr. Moody. "I would have had precisely the same reaction only a few years ago."[25]

So if you still find the idea of a quest alien and uncomfortable, honor your resistance. In retrospect, I realize that that is what I did, and I don't regret it. My denial gave me time to prepare. I needed to wait until I was ready, and perhaps, so do you. But if you feel ready now to venture further into this book—and perhaps into your quest as well—then allow me to offer you some preliminary markers for the journey ahead.

Follow the signs leading to intensity. Your ally is pain and bliss; your enemy is shallowness. If it feels safe, it's probably not the right path. If it scares you, it probably is.

Listen to the wind of your dreams. Unless your sails catch it, you will sit dead in the water. Your dreams are trying to remind you of what you have forgotten. They are your inner psychedelic, your own personal guide. Learn their language.

Denial is healthy—but only up to a point. Denying change allows you to get ready. But deny your body's message too long, and you may get sick. Deny your mind's warnings, and you may go crazy. Deny your soul for too long, and you may lose it.

Without confusion, no clarity will emerge. Keep pretending you are not confused, and you will remain stuck in your obsolete "understanding." Confusion is the mother of change. If you don't quest-ion, you will have no quest.

Better retreat than advance in the wrong direction. Your crisis is a warning that your old compass no longer works. Perseverance brings progress only if you are headed to your desired destination. If not, standing still—or even retreating—is true progress.

Discover new landmarks. The magnetic fields have changed. Your old compass does not point north anymore. It points toward wholeness. Better watch the stars.

Hasten slowly. You are in a new time zone. Stillness may be faster than speed. Progress has taken on new dimensions.

It's time now not just to break down, or up, or out—but to break *through*.

Follow your nose. As Jung once wrote in the final paragraph of a letter to one of his colleagues: "You get nowhere with theories. Try to be simple and always take the next step. . . . So climb down from the mountain . . . and follow your nose. That is your way and the straightest."[26]

2

COMING TO YOUR SENSES
The Quest for Deep Healing

And if the body does not do fully as much as the soul?
And if the body were not the soul, what is the soul?

WALT WHITMAN
"I Sing the Body Electric"
Leaves of Grass

Shelley and I are on a three-day vacation. We stay in a small wooden cabin by a mountain stream. After a long drive from the city, I expect to find myself enraptured by alpine splendor. But I pass the first day disappointed.

The stream is quite small, filled with rocks and unsuitable for swimming. Tall pines crowd the stream bed, keeping it in the shadows much of the day. After a quick look around, I am ready to get back in the car and do some sightseeing. I feel separate and distant from the landscape. Since the view by our cabin does not meet my expectations, I want to move on.

But the next day when I awaken, the area is for some reason more intriguing. The trees are varied and imposing. The shapes and colors of the rocks in the stream bed seem more exciting. Depending on the time of day, the sun plays different patterns across the water. I spend at least half an hour sitting still, watching and listening, feeling more and more connected to the scenery. I begin to relax. My body arrives.

On the third day, the stream is a glistening, mysterious thread, flowing through the fabric of stones and branches, embroidered with the lace of white rapids. The trees point like arrows to the heavens, their tips bending against a background of racing clouds. Through the branches sunlight filters across the landscape and across me, making everything appear to move, as if it were actually alive. I walk through the cold water barefoot and splash it on my face. I hold pine cones in my hands and smell their pungent resin sticking to my skin. I close my eyes, listening to the lullaby of water. I open my eyes again, and the view takes me by surprise, leaving me awestruck by its ever-changing beauty. I feel as if I am more alive. My sight has improved. My sense of hearing is keener, and my sense of touch and taste more vivid. I am coming to my senses.[1]

During those three days, the landscape did not change. But I did. By the third day, I was able to see what had been present all the time.

Throughout my life, I assumed that I was present, but God was not. But the river turns the question around. Can it be that God was present all along—but *I* was not?

Listening to Our Bodies: A Matter of Life or Death

On July 9, 1984, Assemblyman John Vasconcellos was fifty-two years old, weighed 232 pounds, smoked a pack of cigarettes a day, ate whatever was put in front of him, and worked as if he had the world on his shoulders. It was his eighteenth year in the legislature of California and the first day of summer vacation. "What better day for a workaholic to have a heart attack!" John chuckles now. But he was not laughing then, and he spent the summer recuperating.

Four weeks later, on the very first day of the next legislative session, he was ready to get back to business. He was on the phone with Nathan Pritikin, who was encouraging John to enter his exercise and diet program. Standing there talking about changing his life-style with the guru of preventive health care, he felt a twinge in his chest. Then the twinge became a spasm. It felt, John recalls, as if someone were gripping his chest. (He gripped my hand in his fist to show me exactly how it felt.) Arriving at the hospital in late afternoon, he was told that the same artery was clogged, only this time it was worse. It was a second, far more severe heart attack. Immediate surgery was essential. By the time the eleven o'clock news came on that night, the anchorman announced that John had survived his seven-bypass operation.

I interviewed John six years after his heart surgery. His physician, Dr. Dean Ornish, had just called him the day before with startling news. Not one, not two, but *all seven* of his arteries were now open.

"What does that mean?" John asked, unable to grasp the good news.

"They're all open, man," Dr. Ornish told him. "Your heart's healing."

John looked straight at me as he recounted their conversation. His eyes were ablaze, his face alive, his 190-pound body lean and athletic. The story of how John made the transformation is not unique. Throughout America, thousands of men and women in the second half are coming back to their senses.

How did John do it?

"Nothing special," he says modestly. "I stopped smoking the day of my heart attack and have never had another cigarette since. I exercise seven days a week, playing racquetball with somebody half my age. I watch my diet, keeping it low-cholesterol by going light on dairy and red meat. And I use several stress-reduction techniques and take more time away from the state capitol. That's about it."

Did it take discipline?

"Not really. Being at the verge of death really opens you up, makes you vulnerable. You learn fast. I immediately incorporated the lessons I had to learn. I'd always hated the taste of low-fat milk, for example . . . couldn't stand the stuff. Used to say: If God had wanted us to drink this stuff, he would have created cows that made it that way. But all of a sudden, after my heart attack, it tasted just fine!

"Given how I was living, my heart's probably in better shape now than it was thirty years ago. I am living with more verve, healthfulness, and clarity than ever. It's hard to believe, but it's true."

It *is* hard to believe—but why? Why is it hard for us to accept the rejuvenating powers of life's second half? Why did John need the terrifying experience of a heart attack to transform his life-style—and his life?

"A heart attack has a way of getting a person's attention," Dr. Ornish told me when I asked him to put John's experience in perspective. "When we are younger, we feel as if we'll live forever. But as we grow older, we start getting information that this is not true. We may have aches and pains; we may have friends who are dying; or, in some cases, we may have life-threatening illnesses. This awareness of mortality can hurt. But this kind of pain and suffering can be a catalyst for transforming our lives—not just behaviors such as how we eat, but the deepest motivations behind those behaviors."[2]

In other words, John Vasconcellos was not just healing his arteries. He was healing the self of which those arteries were only a small and vulnerable part. In coming to his senses, he was beginning the deep healing of the second half.

Like John Vasconcellos, Mary Kay Blakely is a kind person. She was always taking care of other people—*always*! There was no room for hostility and mistrust in this world of caring and nurturing for her family. She was trying her best to put everyone else's needs before her own. Mary Kay was always being just what a woman is expected to be—as Lillian Rubin aptly puts it in her essay on women's midlife search for self, "be good, be pretty, be patient, be kind, be loving."[3]

As Mary Kay tells the story of her own physical breakdown and psychological transformation, it begins as her husband, from whom she is separating, is driving her to the airport so that she can catch a plane to New York to be with her lover. Underneath her blouse, a six-inch rubber tube is sticking out of her rib cage, a remnant of an open-lung biopsy she had undergone a few months earlier. She is exhausted, tired, on antibiotics, stressed out—and late for her plane.

This slightly built, ailing woman arrives at the airport with only minutes to spare before her plane departs. When she does not see a porter or a luggage cart, she quickly hoists her heavy baggage and begins racing for her plane. She reaches the plane and collapses in the aisle on top of her luggage, still managing to disguise her emergency condition. A flight attendant notices her and asks if she is all right.

"Don't worry about me," she replies, adding the final haunting line: "I'm fine."

When the plane lands at La Guardia Airport, she is picked up by her lover at the airport, and they return to his apartment. He wants to make love, and they do. But the next day, Mary Kay Blakely never gets up. She drifts into a coma that lasts nine days. During her time in the intensive care ward at St. Vincent's Hospital, she almost dies. Almost everyone, including the doctors, fears they have lost her. In an endless series of hallucinatory dreams, her entire life plays back before her closed, comatose eyes. In this "near-death experience," she relives the years that brought her to this state of virtual self-destruction.

> I had been scheduled for death but—like other appointments I'd missed—I didn't make it. . . . I felt radically altered by my nine-day sleep, a passionate psychological journey that uncovered old, unextinguished yearnings. After wakening on March 31, I gradually discovered that *the life planned by the woman I had been no longer fit the woman I'd become.*[4]

The habit of ignoring her own pain, she observes in her memoir, *Wake Me When It's Over,* began in her Catholic girlhood when she received "thorough training as a young martyr. Suffering silence was thought to benefit the souls in purgatory." Whether Catholic or Protestant or atheist, the Type M (for martyr) personalities always put others before themselves. It is the archetype of devoted wife and nurturing mother taken to its most self-abusive extreme. She will meet everyone's needs, attend to everyone's feelings, and please everyone at any cost—even unto death!

Obviously, there are many levels to both John's and Mary

Kay's journeys from near-death to robust health. But both stories suggest to me a vital lesson: *The price we pay for being out of touch with our senses is enormous, and it is a price we cannot afford to pay in the second half of our lives.* Although our lives may not be threatened as a result of being out of touch with our senses, our lives will most certainly be diminished, and many no doubt shortened. The key to the second half is renewing ourselves, reawakening to our senses and to our lives.

"We need to return to feeling the textures of life," writes Diane Ackerman in *A Natural History of the Senses.* "Much of our experience in twentieth-century America is an effort to get away from those textures, to fade into a stark, simple, solemn, puritanical, all-business routine that doesn't have anything so unseemly as sensuous zest." And when she illustrates what she means by sensual, Ackerman does not mean Cleopatra, or Marilyn Monroe. She means Helen Keller, whose "senses were so finely attuned that when she put her hands on the radio to enjoy music, she could tell the difference between the cornets and the strings."[5]

In the early eighties, Jane Brody, the highly respected journalist who covered health issues for *The New York Times,* tried to address this issue objectively in a column that explored whether the "crisis" was inevitable—or imaginary. She concluded that there is indeed "an unsettled and life-disrupting period" that usually occurs between the ages of thirty-five and fifty and that usually involves "self-doubt, marital discord and divorce, extramarital affairs, abrupt career shifts, personality changes, sexual problems, depression and newly awakened anxieties about health and mortality." Those afflicted by this middle-age malaise are likely to be haunted by questions such as, "What have I accomplished? Is this all there is to life? What do I really want? Am I heading anywhere but the cemetery?"

Eager to help readers weather the crisis, Brody offered the usual commonsense advice (eat sensibly, exercise regularly, utilize marriage or family therapy, start new hobbies), and then concluded: "[T]urn your midlife crisis to your own advantage by making it *a time for renewal of your body and mind,* rather than stand by helplessly and watch them decline." She clearly stated her view that the spectacular body/ mind vehicle that takes us on our journey through life is indeed capable of renewal as well as decline in the second half. But she did not address why some of us *re*generate, and others *de*generate.

Put so starkly, the choice sounds harsh and unforgiving. Yes, genes matter. So does luck. And so does the economic system, which makes life easier and healthier for some, and harder and more injurious for others. But stories from the second half underscore that the most important determinant of whether we regenerate or degenerate is not our DNA, not our good fortune, and not our bank account, but ourselves. Neither genes nor luck simply explain the tales of transformation in the second half told to me by men and women whom I have interviewed. Nor does economic advantage or disadvantage explain why people with similar resources handle their second halves so differently.

Something else is at work here. It is, I believe, the mysterious quest for *deep healing.*

Renewal: The Machine Has a Soul

Fortunately, deep healing can occur without the inspiration of a heart attack or a nine-day coma. It often happens much more mysteriously, as it did with Jonathan, one of the people I knew when I worked in the labyrinth of the entertainment industry. He was not seriously overweight, but he carried his body as if it were a heavy, unwelcome load. His head usually rested on his hands, and he sprawled out in a chair as if he wished it were a bed. When he spoke, he always made sense and was sometimes brilliant. But his voice was heavy and slow, as if he were struggling to push each sentence uphill word by word from his lungs to his lips. But most striking, in retrospect, was Jonathan's face. Slightly balding, his long forehead sloped down to eyes that were strangely opaque. They never held mine—even for a second. His cheeks, forehead, nose—every feature seemed slightly swollen, like an overinflated balloon.

Jonathan and I had had many meetings together, but we had never become friends. Although I admired him and his work, I didn't know how to relate to him as a person. I felt an invisible wall. Because we never connected, we soon lost touch. I did not see him for over two years until we both happened to attend a meeting together. I was startled to notice that he looked, not two years older, but five or ten years *younger.* He sat like an athlete, his body erect. His eyes, alertly surveying the room, caught mine. He looked at me, actually *saw* me, then smiled. I had never seen him smile this way before. His entire face came alive. His face, no longer puffy, revealed cheekbones and penetrating eyes. It had, in a word, character. The change was so dramatic that, during a break, I asked him about it.

"I spent my entire adult life addicted to alcohol and drugs," he told me matter-of-factly. "I had thought about stopping, but the time was never right. Almost two years ago, I just stopped. I couldn't do it before. Nobody could get me to do it. The time just wasn't right.

"But then, *I just stopped,*" he repeated proudly.

To congratulate him, I reflexively offered him a glass of wine. He accepted the congratulations but not the drink. As it turned out, not only had he forsworn alcohol, he was also in the midst of a ten-day fast. Not satisfied with merely ending his addiction, he wanted to cleanse the organs and tissues of his body, which he knew still bore a toxic scar. His goal was to undo, as much as he could, the physiological patterns of the first half of his life. To whatever degree possible, he intended to revitalize every cell in his body. Within the limits of his physiology, he wanted to heal.

Springing from the lips of men and women in their second halves, I have heard more times than I can remember deceptively simple comments about ending bad habits ("Oh, I just stopped") and beginning healthier ones ("Well, I just started"). Inexplicably, a self-destructive body/mind habit—whether it's smoking a pack a day, or eating too much, or never exercising, or some other form of self-abuse—is let go. Such simple sentences are signals that change is under way and that an inner revolution has finally begun against whatever has limited the full unfolding of our being. Sometime early in the second half, many men and women break free of patterns of physical stress, pain, neglect, or abuse. Deep healing occurs—so deep that, usually, it seems a mystery.

"I just decided that the day I graduated would be the day I started taking better care of myself," recalls Sigrid McAllister, who was overweight, smoking a pack of cigarettes a day, and depressed. But the day she got her master's degree, at the ripe young age of forty, she started running. She improved her diet. She stopped smoking. She lost fifty pounds in seven months. The following year she won the over-forty division of the Rose Bowl Marathon. Now over fifty, she is a champion triathlete, combining long-distance running, swimming, and biking.

For McAllister, like most second half fitness converts, the goal is not winning or even looking good. "Feeling good is the important thing to me—feeling good *inside*. If I had known how good I would feel, I'd have started sooner."[6]

Although coming to our senses may seem like a sudden event, it isn't. It is a process that has been brewing in the unconscious for months, even years. John Vasconcellos's heart did not just happen to transform itself. Mary Kay Blakely did not just happen to transform her life following her coma. Jonathan did not just happen to end a twenty-year addiction. And Sigrid McAllister did not just happen to decide to transform her life. Each did it for a reason. We may not see the reason or understand it, but it is important to know that the reason exists. If we continue to consider such transformations as just coincidence or good luck, we are missing a golden opportunity. We are ignoring clues that can guide us on our quest.

People who make these breakthroughs often describe them with bodily metaphors, saying that they had to "get it off my back" or "off my chest," or that it was a "gut feeling" or a "change of heart." They do so because they know the transformation is coming from somewhere deeper than the clock-watching, money-counting, strategy-building part of us we usually call the mind. Whether we call these deeper regions soul or spirit or Self is a matter of personal faith. But all such terms have one thing in common: They acknowledge the *depth* of the healing process.

But why do some people make startling and profound changes in the way they take care of their body/mind, and others don't? Admonitions to eat sensibly and exercise regularly are not enough. If a negative pattern has taken shape over three, four, or five decades, it will not be banished by a journalist's exhortations or even a doctor's prescription. Changing how we care for ourselves is not only a question of mechanics, of pumping better fuel into our bodies and lubricating the moving parts. It is a question of spirit.

In Jonathan's case, for example, he did not just decide to stop abusing alcohol and drugs. He had the support of a woman who loved him deeply and who was allied with his healing. He had also learned that his father was dying of cancer, and for the first time in his adult life, he began going back to his hometown on weekends and rebuilding a relationship with his parents that had all but disappeared. During this same period, he also moved out of Los Angeles to a small rural town where he could see and smell and feel the earth. Within a year of stopping his alcohol and drug abuse, almost all the major facets of his life had changed.

Behind these apparently random stories of renewal—ending addiction, losing weight, building stamina, surviving heart attack or coma—is a common pattern. We are tired of the way we lived the first half of our lives. We are seeking a deeper grounding in ourselves—a deeper level of healing, nourishment, energy, and awareness. It is in the dark, moist earth of our inner selves that the seeds of renewal must take root. *Deep* self-renewal, concludes Dr. Roger Gould in *Transformations,* is not just a mental resolution. It is so deep that we cannot grasp its origins with the mind alone. "It is this fundamental task of *deep self-renewal,*" writes Dr. Gould, "that is the force that drives all mid-life experiences."[7]

The ceasing of old self-limiting patterns and the starting of new healing ones is tangible physical evidence of the spiritually transformative power of the quest. These endings are a form of death, and the beginnings are a form of rebirth. No matter how minor they may seem at first, these changes from negative habits to more positive ones almost never occur in isolation. One is followed, or accompanied, by another, which in turn triggers two more in another part of our lives. At first we rarely can see the pattern, but it is present nonetheless—perhaps invisible to us, but visible to others who have heard more stories of healing. When we marshal all our energies—body, mind, *and* soul—we can change deeply ingrained patterns of behavior in the second half. Indeed, true renewal is possible only when it involves these deeper "spiritual" dimensions as well.

Now our bodies can teach and enlighten us in ways that a robust twenty-year-old body simply cannot. By engaging in a heartfelt inquiry into the part of ourselves we call the body, we can know our own wounds. If we have the courage to recognize them before they in some way incapacitate us, we can prevent unnecessary aging. Dr. Alex Comfort once provocatively speculated that only 25 percent of what we call aging is rooted in the actual physical consequences of becoming older. The other 75 percent of aging he referred to as "sociogenic"—that is, caused by the social "role which our folklore, prejudices and misconceptions about aging impose on 'the old.' " It is in the second half that we face a crucial choice about what we intend to do with that crucial three-quarters.[8]

What do we mean when we make the vow that we are going to "take better care of ourselves"? If we determine that we are going to get or stay "in shape"—in shape for *what?* If we decide to "work out" several times each week, what are we working *toward?* Even if we decide that we want to take better care of this body/mind vehicle, we still have to decide where we are going to drive it—and why.

There are now several dozen books, ranging from mediocre to excellent, that outline in detail specific fitness programs for various target audiences. Most of these books tell you what fitness means. But your body is not a standard, replaceable machine part. Not everyone needs the same kind of body or the same kind of fitness, any more than everyone needs the same kind of car. *It all depends on the journey you intend to take.*

Whether it's ten sit-ups or ten vitamin tablets or another act of self-care, does it truly nourish or energize us? Do our well-planned diet and our personalized exercise plans truly take care of our vehicle? Or are there deeper wounds that these modern rituals never even touch? Are our efforts to stay fit truly bringing us back to our senses? Or are they just another set of rules that we impose on them? Do we want physical fitness to compete in professional sports? Do we simply want to prove our prowess to our peers? Do we want to look good in order to appear more sexually appealing to a particular person? Are we investing in our long-term health to prolong life as long as possible? Are we trying to reduce pain from certain afflictions? Are we using exercise as a stimulant to fight depression?

We cannot answer these questions unless we know our bodies—and our minds.

Wholeness: How Sincerity Can Keep Us Healthy

By the time we reach the second half, "health" means something more to us than it did when we took a high school class with that name. It means more than how fast we can run a mile or how many push-ups we can do. It depends on much more than our weight and blood pressure. It involves healing our deepest wounds. For no one I have ever met, and no one I have ever interviewed for this book, has reached the second half without having been wounded. Each of us has lost and sacrificed parts of ourselves. None of us reaches the second half whole. We have been injured—if not physically, then psychologically or spiritually. These wounds may be buried quite deep, but they are there.

Our *health* depends on beginning to *heal* these wounds and finding greater *wholeness*—and *holiness*—in the second half of our lives. *Health, heal, whole, holy:* all derive from the same linguistic root. This clearly implies that to be truly healthy is not just a physical and emotional challenge, but a spiritual one as well. Our bodies are messengers inviting us, with both pain and pleasure, to become more whole.

No doubt this is why the connection between mind and body, which is a vital key to deep healing, has attracted so much interest from those in the second half. Contemporary physiology has taught us that what we call the mind "doesn't really dwell in the brain but travels the whole body on caravans of hormone and enzyme, busily making sense of the compound wonders we catalogue as touch, taste, smell, hearing and vision."[9] But in the second half, we do not need to read textbooks to learn this. If our bodies could talk, they would be telling us loud and clear: "Express yourself. Let your energy flow. If you don't, watch out!"

Our bodies are calling on us to develop true sincerity. I do not mean the perfunctory "sincerely yours" with which we are trained to end our correspondence. I mean *sincerity* as it was intended in the original Latin: "clean, pure, genuine, honest." Unscrupulous marble dealers in ancient Rome would cover up unsightly cracks by rubbing in wax to make them less visible. But honest dealers would sell their marble without wax *(sin,* "without"; *ceres,* "wax"). We have the chance to learn how to express our *whole* selves, cracks and all. This is true sincerity. In the second half, our health depends on it.

Unfortunately, when our bodies fail to work, we do not treat them like honored messengers bringing important news. Instead, we often look like motorists stranded on the freeway beside our cars. We are annoyed and frustrated, even angry, that our vehicle has malfunctioned. Only moments ago we were zooming by the world; now the world is zooming by us. We suddenly go from being in control of our destiny and making rapid progress to being a helpless victim and getting nowhere. Particularly if we think we are taking good care of ourselves, we feel as if our bodies have betrayed us. But the truth may be just the opposite.

As we do aerobics at the health club or jog around the local track; as we do our yoga stretches in the morning or lift weights at the gym; how are we exercising? With enthusiasm and joy? Or with fear and self-criticism? As we eat fiber-rich foods or take megavitamins; as we count calories and monitor cholesterol; how are we eating? With pleasure and satisfaction? Or with anxiety and self-doubt? How we answer these questions is not merely of psychological concern, but of physiological concern. Our heart and our body are one.

Although eating right and exercising regularly can help us on our quest for wholeness, coming to our senses means more than diet and exercise. Scientists are reminding us that our "vehicles" are not mechanical, but human. Thanks to several decades of persistent pioneering work, the impact of diet and exercise on fitness is now well recognized. Researchers studying the impact of attitude on fitness and longevity have concluded that how we express—or fail to express—ourselves in our daily lives, through our words and actions and feelings, has a significant impact on our health. The public is most familiar with research in this area that concerns the so-called Type A personality, which becomes even more crucial as we grow older.

Type A behavior has been called "hurry sickness" by some physicians because its victims seem to be in a chronic state of unrest and agitation. They speak far more than they listen. They always feel other people are working, thinking, talking, or moving too slowly. They curse red lights, slow elevators, and backed-up traffic. Their friends or mates are constantly trying to calm them down. They never feel as if they are getting enough done. They are usually doing more than one thing at a time. They act as if they were trying to squeeze as much into each minute as it can possibly hold.[10]

Long-range studies of Type A personalities have established that careful diet and exercise are not enough. Our inner emotional life and how we express it also matters enormously. At a recent American Heart Association meeting, for example, data were presented demonstrating that law students who were the most hostile and mistrustful were *more than four times as likely to die* during the next twenty-five years than other law students. Exactly why the over one hundred law school students who had high "hostility scores" on psychological tests were more likely to die young is a psychological and physiological puzzle that will take many more years to fully put together. But enough pieces are already in place for us to see that, to a greater degree than we imagined, our emotions affect our health. Our attitude toward life can protect us—or endanger us.[11]

Quite conveniently, I have been referring to Type A personalities with the comfortably distancing pronoun *they,* which automatically implies that neither you nor I should be counted among them. This is the seductive danger of these medical categories: We are either A or B, in or out. But life, particularly midlife, is not so black and white. To refer to these Type A sufferers as "they" has made me feel uncomfortable because, unfortunately, I identify with them.

Consider, for example, my Red Light Syndrome. Unwilling to "waste time" in Los Angeles traffic, I have learned shortcuts and developed a driving style that cuts driving time down to a bare minimum, without breaking any laws. A few years ago, my mania for time-saving was so extreme that, when I encountered red lights and certain busy intersections, I would get visibly irritated.

Then, for the first time in almost twenty years, I started seeing a therapist. After one eye-opening appointment with this wise Jungian analyst, I got into the car, put my notebook open on the seat beside me, and headed into traffic to go back to my office. As I drove, insights would come to me that I did not want to forget. I wanted to write them down. When I came to the first red light, I reached for my notebook and began writing. But the light changed to green, and I had to stop writing in midsentence. For the first time in my life, I had looked forward to encountering a red light and was disappointed when it turned green.

In that instant, I saw my craziness in all its splendor. The entire ride home was a revelation. Every red light was a relief, a moment to relax, to breathe, to reflect, and occasionally to jot down a thought. I had been in a hurry all those years because I was not in contact with my inner life. I was impatient, bored, and irritated at red lights because all I could think about was where I was going, not where I actually was. In a chronic hurry to get *there,* I was afraid of actually being *here.*

If, by any chance, you are reading this and feeling complacent because you are *not* a chronic hurrier and *not* a hostile and mistrustful personality, let me add a word of caution. Your attitudes may also be undermining your health. In fact, if you are the opposite of Type A, as Mary Kay Blakely was, it is almost certain that your character is also taking its toll on your physical well-being. Even if you are the wife or husband of a Type A spouse, you have probably developed another compensating personality style, which may hurt you just as much as theirs afflicts them.

All too often these polarized types marry and find an eerie and unstable kind of balance. As we shall explore in the next chapter, for such marriages to flourish into the second half, both men and women must reclaim their lost selves. He must learn to become more vulnerable, to need, to cry. She must learn to be strong to take back the power she has given away. As Anne Morrow Lindbergh wrote long ago in her poignant memoir *Gift from the Sea,* both husband and wife must each become "free to fulfill the neglected side of one's self" and to discover "this greater wholeness in each person."[12]

To her credit, and to the benefit of her health, this is precisely what Mary Kay Blakely did. As harrowing as her ordeal was, she concluded that "it did not turn out to be a tragedy for me." Instead, it was the beginning of deep healing. She left her husband, married the man she deeply loved, enabled her children to join her, started listening to her body, and deepened all of her intimate relationships. She came to her senses and discovered, she says, *"another I."* Her new Self had the capacity for a deeper sincerity: the capacity to express herself more authentically. This will, of course, not always ward off illness or disease, but it definitely sustains our health. As we take care of our body, it in turn takes care of us, guiding us on our quest.

By the time we reach the second half, we know more about ourselves than we did when we were younger. We may even think that we have finished becoming who we are. After all, we have become someone. We have a social security number and credit cards. We have a job, family, and friends. We have an address, possessions, a resume. We have a reputation, an attitude, an identity. Given a checklist of adjectives, we could mark which describe who we are and which do not. By the second half, each of us discovers that certain patterns of stress, strain, and often pain have taken hold in our bodies.

Although we may think we know our bodies better than before, the opposite is often true. By the time we reach the second half, our bodies have changed. Much of what was true is no longer so. To come fully to our senses requires that we face the shadow side of our body knowledge, the parts of our physical selves that are hidden from view. After all, much happens to us physically before we are consciously aware of it. Much more is forgotten or repressed. By the time we reach adulthood, our bodies are like the earth. Only archaeological digs can uncover its history, because the clues are buried in strata of rock and soil deep beneath the surface. Precisely because we live in our own body and have never lived in anyone else's, there are aspects of it we take for granted. This is why we can walk into the office of skilled healers who are able to tell us in minutes something about our bodies that we, even after decades of inhabiting it, do not know.

At the end of a day in my office, often my neck hurts. I have not done that intentionally. In fact, I have tried to keep it relaxed. But I have inflicted pain on myself nonetheless. Despite my most determined efforts, I have not been able to stop myself from using my body in ways that produce this chronic, low-level pain. This is because habits are partly unconscious. If they were fully conscious, they would not be habits. We usually discover them only when their adverse impact on our health becomes noticeable. I have been misusing my neck and shoulders for decades; I am only becoming aware of it now because the pain is forcing me to do so.

To interview our bodies we must take into account that they do not speak in words. We must *give* voice to our bodies in order that they can be heard. Like an empathic actor who must work hard to get inside his character, we must work hard to get inside our bodies. This is not easy and can only be accomplished under the right circumstances. If we are preoccupied with other matters, under time pressure, blocked by fear, or otherwise not fully present, we will not be able to speak for our bodies. And unless we do, who will?

By taking a biography of our body, we can learn to know it better than we did when we were younger. So take a moment and interview your own body. Don't just look at how shiny your vehicle looks. Open the hood. Get your hands dirty. If you are visually rather than verbally oriented, draw a portrait of your body. Encounter not only the front, which you see in a mirror, but your sides and back. Probe its depths; discover its strengths; acknowledge its weaknesses; locate its wounds. Converse with the parts of your body of which you are proud, and those of which you are ashamed. Do not only speak the lines of an interviewer asking questions. Also play the part of your body giving its replies. Do not do this silently, but out loud. Be honest with your body, and ask it to be honest with you. It will help you decide what kind of nourishment, energy, and purpose you are seeking in the second half of your life.

Our bodies can be our wisest teachers, our most enlightened gurus. Perhaps it is a headache or backache, slumping shoulders or chest pain, failing eyes or constipated bowels. Almost always, hidden in our wound, is something that will enrich and deepen our lives. Your body ultimately knows itself far better than any other person can. In its cells have been stored every experience that has ever happened to you since before you were born. It knows more about you than your own mother, more about you even than your mind. Our bodies will teach us more than we can imagine, if only we will listen.

"I thought I was doing all the right things," says Art Lipski, forty-five, one of AT&T's district managers. "I'd given up red meat, ate lots of chicken and fish. It was a real startler when I discovered my cholesterol was 279." He was shaken after he received the results of a detailed "health risk appraisal" questionnaire and medical test. Dr. Dorothea Johnson, vice-president of medical affairs at this mammoth communications corporation, organized a program to require its employees to do a nuts-and-bolts body biography. Each employee then received an in-depth report—a kind of "state of the body" printout. The results shocked many of AT&T's personnel like Lipski, who responded by changing his diet and bringing his cholesterol down to 216.

The good news is that the entire procedure *saved* AT&T money. According to Dr. Johnson, for every dollar the corporation spent on wellness, it got back two in reduced medical costs and lowered absenteeism. But the bad news is that AT&T's program is the exception, not the rule. Most corporations are thinking short-term. Since it costs money now to save money later, it is easier to duck their heads in the sand rather to stick their necks out.[13]

Unfortunately, our consciousness reflects our culture. Most of us will spend money and time to fix bodies when they break down, but not to maintain them. We will celebrate cure, but not prevention. We can blame the health-care system hospitals, insurance companies, government bureaucrats, and profit-hungry corporations, if we want to. But ultimately, our health is our responsibility. If we want to stay healthy as we grow older, there are lessons we can only teach ourselves, and they lead us inexorably to that invisible frontier where mind and body meet.

To truly nourish ourselves, to find our deepest sources of energy, to express sincerely our whole selves: These are not overnight accomplishments. They are not the result of six-week "crash" diets or miracle fitness programs. On the contrary, they require a deeper self-knowledge—and a greater wholeness—than we have ever had before.

Deep Nourishment: Replenishing the Well

Thousands of mice in the National Toxicology Laboratories in Little Rock, Arkansas, were given a diet of 40 percent fewer calories than they would have eaten if given an unlimited food supply. The result? Compared with those who ate all they wanted, *they lived twice as long* (sixty months rather than thirty). They got sick less often, and they had quicker immune response. "You can't help but be impressed," says the director of the laboratories, Ronald Hart.[14]

Although Hart and his colleagues know that the scientific evidence is still preliminary, they aren't waiting to draw their own personal conclusions. They have already started eating less, and so have other researchers, from the UCLA Medical School to the National Institutes of Health in Washington. They are discovering what the long-living traditional tribes of the world knew long ago: Fewer calories (combined of course with adequate nutrients) mean longer lives.

What these indigenous tribes knew, and what even those mice learned, I did not realize until one festive New Year's Eve a few years ago. After eating an early dinner with our kids, Shelley and I left them with a baby-sitter and went out to a small party. We proceeded to consume the equivalent of a second dinner. And that night, as we began the new year, we felt sick.

Eating too much is not unprecedented in our lives or, I presume, yours. But doing so on this particular evening triggered a strong reaction. We realized that we had eaten the second meal not because we were hungry, not because the food was exceptional, and not because we sensually enjoyed it. On a superficial level, of course, our taste buds were stimulated by that second dinner. But on a deeper level of sensory awareness, it was a violation. We ate to please and to appease; we ate to fill an emptiness. Realizing we were eating for the wrong reasons, we decided to stop for a while and to wait until we were *truly* hungry before we had another meal. In other words, we began to fast.

If you consider three meals a day as natural as dawn, midday, and dusk, you will presumably be skeptical. But since you have spent long hours watching commercials exhorting you to eat whether you are hungry or not, it seems only fair that you give thirty seconds to the following message: *The post–World War II generations now entering the second half are the first to have been bombarded since early childhood with billions of dollars worth of powerful messages showing us that happiness and pleasure and joy can be found through purchasing and ingesting food. One of the reasons those of us now in the second half find ourselves concerned with diet is that we have listened since childhood to high-powered, high-priced electronic hucksters telling us what to swallow. Now it is time to stop listening to them and come to our senses. Our lives depend on it.*

Being out of touch with our senses disorients us in many different ways. Particularly for women, it breeds a fear of food and a terror of becoming fat. Burdened with anxiety and obsessive control, these women may become anorexic or bulimic, like the woman a friend of mine met in his Over-eaters Anonymous (OA) group. Her bulimia became so severe that her throat and mouth were bleeding from the years of daily vomiting. In desperation, she sought out yet another psychiatrist, who also felt overwhelmed by the hopelessness of her case. He suggested that she try attending some sessions of OA, one of the organizations where people with such problems congregate and share their experience and seek support. For two months this tormented woman attended meetings where she sat silently in a circle with my friend and others. But her condition only worsened. As she sank deeper into depression, the others in the group feared that she would die.

But then one day she arrived at a meeting looking very peaceful despite her frailness. As the meeting started, she was the first to speak. She told the group that the previous morning she awoke unusually early and went to the market where she usually shopped. For some reason, she began with the lemons.

"Please forgive me," she said to the lemons.

Then she moved on to the oranges.

"Please forgive me," she said to the oranges.

Methodically, reverently, as if in a sanctuary, she made her rounds, asking forgiveness from the fruits to the vegetables, from the breads and the milk, from the cheeses and the meats. She realized that she had abused them. She had taken their life-giving energies and their sensual delights and desecrated them. After seeking absolution, she left the market and spent the first day of her adult life without vomiting. In the following weeks and months, she was finally free of her addiction. In the face of death, she found the strength to forgive herself. And with that forgiveness she came to her senses.

For most of us, the struggle to regain our bodily wisdom is neither so dramatic nor so life-threatening. We do not suffer from extreme conditions like anorexia, bulimia, or obesity. We deny our senses much more subtly.

Unlike those whose bathroom scales gave incontrovertible proof that something was amiss, the evidence that I was overeating was not in my waistline but, more subtly, in my energy level and state of mind. I had eaten to fill an emptiness, a void inside me. I had overeaten as a child to make myself feel taken care of. I had overeaten in college to compensate for feelings of loneliness and confusion. I had eaten to chase away feelings I did not want to face. It was as if every mouthful were ingested to disprove the notion that I did not deserve to be loved or to be alive. But each mouthful only filled my stomach; it did not nourish my soul. I was taking in huge quantities of food, but very little deep nourishment.

In my thirties, a strange lethargy began to set in. I found myself needing to nap quite often and was often tired after meals, particularly large ones. Instead of feeling eager to jog or swim in the morning, as I had in my twenties, I usually couldn't get myself to exercise until midday. There were other signals, too, such as the fact that I was particularly hard hit by jet lag. With my worst fears about "middle age" coming true, I began to adjust to what appeared to be the realities of aging. I foresaw in the near future that I would lose my physical energy, stop having the desire to exercise, become more sedentary, and begin the slow but ultimately debilitating slide into "old age." We decided to fast.

Though I still struggle with overeating, our New Year's fast marked a turning point. Although it was not the first time I had stopped eating, it was the first time I had truly listened to what my senses had to say, which was: "Enough!" At the end of day one, Shelley and I decided to continue our fast. We both felt a process had begun that was important and that it needed more time.

To my amazement, on the second day I felt stronger and more energetic than the first. I felt so good that I decided to go for a swim at our neighborhood pool. As I drove there, I listened to my fears: that I would get quickly chilled because my body had no calories to burn; that I would run out of energy before I completed my usual forty laps; and that I would return home weak and depleted. But our senses can surprise us, if we let them. After two laps, my body was comfortably warm, and after forty, I had energy enough to spare that I swam an extra twenty. My nutritional paradigm exploded. After almost forty-eight hours of not pumping my body with food and vitamins, I had more energy swimming than I had had the last time when I had been eating regularly. By day three it was time to go back to work and get the kids back to school. We began eating again—but more simply, *and less.* The deeper energy and resilience continued.

As I finally broke through my youth-fixated eating patterns, my energy increased. I needed less sleep. I was quicker to arise in the morning and more alert. I no longer felt lethargic after meals. Occasional fasting and eating less became part of our quest.

The dramatic experience awakened me to the fact that, even into my forties, I had been eating as if I were a teenager at the peak of my physical growth. As I soon learned from my research, our midlife metabolism is slower. We use calories more effectively. As Dr. Gershon Lesser argues in his book explaining "nutritional rejuvenation for people over forty," those of us in the second half of life get "more miles per calorie—so that it requires less fuel and . . . fewer calories in order to maintain a healthy body weight."[15] If we eat like a college athlete or a young nursing mother, we overburden our bodies. Of course we must provide our bodies with the necessary nutrients, but we do not need the volume of calories that a young, high-metabolism body needs.

In our consumer society, eating less sounds almost unpatriotic. As one reporter observed, to stop pumping our bodies with the "best" and the "most" sounds "highly un-American."[16] But this is part of the challenge of entering the second half of life. If we haven't started to think—and eat—for ourselves, the second half is the time to begin. If mice can do it, so can we. In the second half, it is time to reexamine our relationship with hunger. It is time to put aside our habits and get to know our appetite again.

Deep Energy:
Strengthening, Stretching, and Stillness

Except for those who feel hopeless and despondent about their physical condition and so do nothing, everyone seems to be searching for that rejuvenating, exhilarating physical activity that will keep us young and healthy forever. But as with diet, the question quickly confronts us: What kind of exercise for what kind of journey? Is our goal to run a marathon or to fit into a size eight dress? To climb Mount Everest or to climb the stairs to the office without panting? To pump iron or to plant a garden? To win Wimbledon or to practice yoga? The clearer we are about our journey, the more likely we are to find the kind of energy we truly need.

When I was in my early thirties, I worked out every day. Blessed with a vigorous metabolism, I looked at "older people" and could not possibly understand why they were so inactive. I promised myself that, as I aged, I would continue to work out every day. As I envisioned it in my age-bound naïveté, I would engage in daily strenuous activity throughout my life simply because it was so much fun. Always trying to find a new way to exercise, I finally bought a windsurfer.

Loaded down with my windsurfing paraphernalia—board and sail strapped to the roof rack, other equipment filling the trunk—I would head out to nearby lakes. As surfers look for the perfect wave, I would seek the perfect wind, often spending hours of driving and loading and unloading equipment in pursuit of the elusive "perfect ride." The thrill of speed, the drama of competition, the human body harnessing the power of nature—this was my narrow yet Olympian view of the ultimate form of exercise.

But then I encountered a charismatic Indonesian named Mochtar Lubis. Approaching sixty, Mochtar was one of several foreign journalists who worked on a global magazine that I helped start called *World Paper*. Mochtar was over six feet tall, his skin color a soft and lustrous bronze. His posture was erect, his body lean. He moved with quiet grace and power. Whenever we met at our editorial meetings, in cities scattered across many time zones, his face showed little evidence of jet lag. Although half his age, I (and most of the other journalists) would struggle to adjust to our new time zone while Mochtar, beaming with enthusiasm, would be setting off for a brisk walk. Finally, at one of our meetings in Geneva, I asked Mochtar what he did for exercise.

"Nothing in particular," he said modestly. "Yoga and walking, mostly."

Typical activities for an old man, I thought to myself. To confirm my prejudice, I asked him at what age he started doing yoga.

"In my twenties," he said, "during the years I was in jail."

Intrigued, I learned that Mochtar Lubis was not only a journalist but a hero in his country's independence movement. He had been put in jail by the Dutch colonial government for being a leader in the resistance. He had spent months of solitary confinement in a small jail cell on an inadequate diet. After independence, he was jailed again by the new government, which he had persistently criticized for suppressing basic freedoms. I was so impressed with Mochtar's courage and integrity that I asked him many questions about those turbulent years before I returned to the personal question that had been on my mind. "How could a man who had been trapped for years in a jail cell have such deep, resilient energy at your age?" I asked him.

"In my cell, I learned to stretch and tone every muscle in my body by doing yoga exercises," he told me. "I combined them with meditation. I would do exercises that simulated running in the hills, swimming in the ocean, everything! By the time I was finished with what you would call my 'workout,' I felt as if I had been freed from my cell. I felt as if I had smelled the trees, touched the water, seen the sky. That is how I survived."

Now, no matter how small his hotel room, Mochtar can exercise. In fact, he told me he could even exercise strapped into an airplane seat. He didn't need Nautilus equipment or free weights or Jacuzzis; he didn't need swimming pools or health clubs. (And he sure didn't need a windsurfer or the "perfect wind"!) He had discovered a far more rejuvenating workout: He had found his deep energy.

By deep energy, I do not mean the hyped-up zip that so many people exhibit in public before they go home and collapse. Like actors and actresses, many of us have learned by the time we reach the second half how to put on our psychological as well as facial "makeup" before we go out the door in the morning. We make our performance as vital and dynamic as possible and then return home to the reality of our actual feelings, which are usually considerably darker. (As

Wendy Wasserstein's protagonist asks in her play *The Heidi Chronicles:* "But what if I'm too sad to go to aerobics class?")

Shallow energy is far better than no energy, but the private toll can be immense. This double existence can make us feel like impostors. It can enrage those who are close to us, who justifiably wonder why so much of our precious energy is invested in performing for others, leaving so little for those we love.

Now that I am closer to Mochtar Lubis's age, I recognize in his "workout" the three ingredients that become more and more important as we search for deep energy at midlife: strengthening, stretching, and stillness.

Strengthening—getting stronger and sweating—is an important element in a fitness regime. Indeed, the cleansing and rejuvenating powers of sweating that "tune up" the endocrine system and stimulate positive hormonal changes are often overlooked as we age.[17] Only a small minority of Americans work up a sweat at least once a week, and the percentage declines as we age. Less than one out of five Americans exercise at least 150 days a year (or every other day). Three out of five exercise fewer than twenty-five days annually, less than once every two weeks. Since sports doctors recommend we have vigorous exercise three or four times a week, we are clearly in trouble.

No one is "too old" to benefit from strengthening exercises. Researchers have discovered that proper training exercises can build muscle in men and women at any age, even in their eighties and nineties. In one study, 299 women ranging in age from 19 to 91 were ranked in terms of their levels of physical activity. At every age level, those who were moderately or very active had stronger bones (greater bone mass) and leaner bodies than those who were less active. In other words, strengthening our entire bodies—muscles, organs, bones—can happen at *any* age.[18]

But as you begin exercising, keep in mind that what you

strengthen may already be strong, and what you neglect to strengthen may be weak. The simple truth is that every body is different. What works for one person may not work for another. Someone with a sound skeletal structure and posture but with a weak cardiovascular system should not do the same workout as someone else who has great stamina and energy but a weak back. You must recognize your unique pattern of strengths and weaknesses before you can develop a sound exercise program that will improve those areas that need strengthening.

I learned this lesson myself after spraining my back bodysurfing. I decided that I needed to strengthen my back and, for the first time since college, began weight training. Using Nautilus machines, I gravitated toward some machines, which I used regularly, but disliked others and so avoided them. Then one day my friend Chris, who is an expert in sports injuries, happened to be working out in the weight room at the same time. I told him why I had started training with weights and described what I did—and did not —include in my workout.

The one Nautilus machine I always skipped was precisely the one he recommended that I use. This particular machine used the muscles in my midback that were underdeveloped; my stronger muscles in my shoulders were useless on it. Since it pinpointed my "wound" with uncanny accuracy, I had avoided it. With Chris's advice, I changed my workout, focusing more on my weaknesses and less on my strengths. It not only helped heal my back injury but helped me find a balanced strength that I had never had before.

While useful at any age, this lesson about strengthening is particularly important in the second half of life. Physically as well as psychologically, each of us by this age has developed strengths and weaknesses. We hold ourselves together and function effectively by letting the former compensate for the latter. By the second half, this system of checks and balances often starts to malfunction and the weaknesses start to show.

They signal us with the body's SOS: illness, pain, and fatigue. We cannot ignore them any longer. We have to pay
attention.

Unless you are an exceptional athlete, it is doubtful that
you will be playing full-court basketball or running mara-
thons in your seventies and eighties. (If you can do so, more
power to you.) For most of us, it is far more likely that we
will be swimming, biking, or doing yoga. The time to start
finding sports that will last a lifetime is *before* you need to. It
will make the transition far easier.

So begin now to broaden your range of exercise. Vary
your exercise pattern, alternating workouts each day: for example, weights and aerobics one time, swimming or biking
the next. Particularly if you have had a relatively uniform
approach to exercise during the first half of your life, you
should strongly consider trying something quite different
now. If you have played competitive basketball ever since
high school, you don't necessarily have to stop—just blend
in something else that balances you. Start exploring new terrain.

Although we all like to do what we do well, try something
you do poorly, or at best moderately well. Perhaps you have
strength and endurance, but no balance—then try yoga or
dance. Perhaps your legs are strong but your arms are weak
—try rowing or weightlifting. As you become better ac-
quainted with your weaknesses, they often bring rewards
that strength itself cannot. So find out what your weaknesses
have to teach you. Remember: The goal is not to become as
good as or better than others. It is to heal—that is, to become whole.

Had I listened to Mochtar Lubis, I would have known
long ago that *stretching* is just as important as strengthening.
Unfortunately, I needed to be instructed by that most authoritative teacher, pain. After running a five-day around-
the-clock conference, I returned home exhausted. The next
day I went to the gym and began "stretching." Seated on the

floor, I reached my right hand and grabbed my left foot to stretch my hamstrings and my back muscles. Suddenly, I was contorted in pain. I couldn't move. I couldn't even breathe without feeling a searing pain in my side. I had to be carried out on a stretcher. The doctor's diagnosis: I had pulled a ligament. I had injured myself because the so-called "stretching" I had done was not a slow, relaxing, healing movement, but hurried, forced actions that were counterproductive.

Our bodies have a mobility and flexibility as infants that many of us begin to lose in adolescence, or even in childhood. Unless we have made a conscientious effort to activate the body's natural flexibility, we find ourselves in the second half with a seriously restricted range of motion. Out of ignorance the body's growing rigidity is often dismissed as "aging." The truth is far more encouraging, but also more demanding: Much of that rigidity can be prevented by precisely the yoga-style stretching that Mochtar Lubis did daily in his prison cell.

I had first encountered yoga long before I ever met Mochtar Lubis. In college, I had taken a course that involved some yoga, and I had found it both relaxing and invigorating. But as soon as the course was over, I stopped. When I had time for exercise, I would do something more vigorous running, rowing, basketball, swimming Despite my positive experience, I decided yoga was boring. For the next two decades, I neglected it almost entirely. Before working out I would take a minute or two to stretch my legs or back, but I was always in a hurry to get started.

By the time I reached my late thirties, however, my physician prescribed specific stretches and yoga postures as part of my physical therapy. I learned that stretching does *not* mean perfunctory toe-touching or rapid-fire backbends. A genuine stretch means holding a position of muscle extension *for at least thirty seconds*. And it does not mean simply, passively holding that position. As any yoga instructor will explain, it means breathing as well.

I had turned away from yoga because it involved *stillness,* the third component of deep healing. After years of defining exercise in terms of being out of breath, here was yoga with its emphasis on deep, slow breathing. If one is addicted to motion, not to mention commotion, yoga may seem boring. Yet without stillness, exercise loses its meaning. If we cannot tolerate a genuine and healing state of rest (except when sleeping), then physical activity is not self-expression. It is addiction. Just as speech becomes blabber if we are unable to remain silent, so exercise becomes hyperactivity if we are unable to be still. It is precisely in such a state of stillness that we come, at last, to our senses.

Indeed, stillness is as important as exercise because at rest we can hear our own rhythm. Exercising and dieting have become so chic that the keeping-up-with-the-Joneses syndrome has taken root. But asking too much of yourself is as bad as asking too little. The fact is, even moderate exercise, including walking or leaf-raking, has marked health benefits.[19] So listen to your own drummer. Ground yourself in your own senses. Be guided by your own vision. You do not need the latest diet book or work-out tape. In the second half, you now have a personal trainer you can trust: your own body.

3

SEARCHING FOR YOUR SOUL/MATE

The Quest for Love

I talk to lawyers in Houston and Chicago and New York and divorces are getting nastier all over. It's a spiritual crisis. The whole damn society is suffering from an excess of greed and a fixation on material things. That makes this a very tough era for relationships.

STUART WALZER, divorce lawyer[1]

Marriage is a psychological and spiritual journey. . . . Whether or not you realize the full potential of this vision depends . . . on your willingness to acquire knowledge about hidden parts of yourself.

HARVILLE HENDRIX, marriage counselor[2]

Love is not a feeling. . . . I define love thus: The will to extend one's self for the purpose of nurturing one's own or another's spiritual growth.

M. SCOTT PECK, psychiatrist[3]

In the following pages, you will read about falling in love and out again; about marriage and divorce; about monogamy and infidelity.[4] These subjects deal with some of the greatest pleasures in life, some of the deepest pain. Unlike these subjects, however, this book cannot stroke your cheek or make you dinner. It cannot argue with you or challenge you to be more honest with yourself. It cannot do all the things that a mate or lover can do that make you feel loved or abandoned. All it can do is rest passively in your hands and invite you in.

So it is entirely up to you whether to accept my invitation not just to read "about" these subjects but to enter fully into them. Your intimate relationship is, in fact, a doorway into another dimension of life, a dimension that often becomes available to us only in the second half of life. Seen in this light, "the difficult challenges that men and women encounter in joining their energies together are not just personal travails," as John Wellwood says so beautifully in *Journey of the Heart.* "They are also invitations to open ourselves to the sacred play of the known and the unknown, the seen and the unseen, and to the larger powers born out of intimate contact with the great mysteries of life."[5]

There is a reason, of course, why you may not accept this invitation. If it were easy to walk through this doorway into deeper, more authentic relationships, we would all do it early in life. We would spend our entire lives in this joyous place of everlasting love. All marriages would be blissful. No one would get divorced. All children would be raised by two loving parents. And we would all live happily ever after.

Unfortunately, there is an entry fee into the further reaches of love. Before we cross the threshold, we must feel pain. As C. G. Jung put it in one of his most frequently quoted lines: *"There is no birth of consciousness without pain."* What is less well-known, however, is the essay where this line can be found, "Marriage as a Psychological Relationship," and the fact that the line follows this sentence: *"Seldom or never does a marriage develop into an individual relationship smoothly and without crises."*[6] This is not only true in my life, it is true in every marriage or long-term relationship with which I am personally familiar or about which I have read during the years I have researched this book.[7]

Intimate relationships without pain are virtually impossible because of a simple yet mysterious emotional algebra:

> Love depends on intimacy.
> Intimacy requires vulnerability.
> Vulnerability involves getting hurt.
> And getting hurt causes pain.

In *The Art of Loving,* a book that I first read a quarter of a century ago, Erich Fromm explained why the conscious, spiritual consummation of marriage involves pain. Contrasting "the initial experience of falling in love with the ongoing experience of being in love," Fromm explained how easily lovers mistake "the intensity of the infatuation, this being 'crazy' about each other, for proof of the intensity of their love, while it may only prove the degree of their preceding loneliness."[8]

At the age of fifteen, how could I have understood these words? I had barely begun to date, much less to love. By the time I reached twenty-one, I had met three women to whom I had said "I love you." Each time, of course, I had meant it. But I could only mean it to the extent that I knew who "I" was. And at that age and level of inexperience, there was only so much I could know about the strange, mysterious, archetypal frontier where self and lover meet.

When I "fell in love" with Shelley in my early twenties, I once again assumed that this was truly what love was all about. We felt that, now that we had found each other and our "true love," we would live happily ever after. We both had enough education and enough common sense to know that marriage takes work. But we were so enraptured by each other, so convinced that we had finally found our one true love, that we believed that the pain of loneliness and misunderstanding, disappointment and betrayal, was behind us. Out of the depth of our love, we married and had children.

Just as the experts predict, "falling in love" was an engrossing, ecstatic period. Love gripped us in its awesome power. We were inseparable. Like flowers to sunlight, our bodies gravitated toward each other. For weeks we hardly slept because we were so busy making love, yet somehow we were not tired. I am sure that it was true, as psychopharmacologists have since proven, that in this intoxicating state natural hormones and chemicals were actually flooding our bodies with a sense of well-being. We were literally "high" on love, transfixed in an altered state of sexual awareness and desire.[9]

Literature and film, not to mention soap operas and pulp paperbacks, thrive on depicting this state of mind in all its infinite variations. As a culture, we absolutely adore this stage of love. Unlike traditional societies, with strictly limited courtship rituals and arranged marriages, we are in love with "falling in love." No wonder *Romeo and Juliet* is Shakespeare's most famous play; we love youthful romances, and in this drama, conveniently enough, death spares us having to watch the lovers grow into adults. We are so mesmerized by the light of romantic love that we do not even notice its shadow.

Falling Out of Love: Encountering Our Shadow

Writing about the sacred marriage requires language—and our language about mature love is in shambles. Most forty-year-olds, not to mention seventy-year-olds, do not have the same experience as do teenagers when they "date," "fall in love," and "marry."

Consider, for example, what would happen if Shelley and I, graying and in our mid-forties, got divorced. When we began dating again, we would be caught in a bizarre linguistic time-warp. The woman I dated would call me her "boyfriend," and Shelley would be someone's "girlfriend." We might "fall in love" again—the same phrase that we used decades earlier, when we were in our early twenties. Although our experience would be fundamentally different, the same anachronistic, adolescent vocabulary would be applied to us again. This is a warning sign that something is missing in our view of love in the second half.

What is missing is an understanding of the natural process of falling *out* of love. In the second half, if not before, the curtain falls on this act in the drama of romance. Disillusionment sets in. Pain rears its ugly head. As one Jungian analyst observes, marriage becomes for countless people "the greatest disappointment."

> It is well-known that most people get on each other's nerves even when they undertake only a fourteen day trip together. The two marriage partners, however, promise to live their whole lives (thirty, forty, fifty, sixty years) together in the greatest physical, spiritual, and psychological intimacy. And this lifelong commitment they make to each other in their youth! Perhaps in ten years they are both completely different people. They make this promise at an age when they neither know who they are themselves or who the other is. . . . That a decent, responsible society not only allows, but actually encourages, young people in their complete ignorance to bind themselves together permanently . . . seems incomprehensible.[10]

And, of course, it doesn't work. According to sex therapists Phillip and Lorna Sarrell, whose book *Sexual Turning Points* explores these themes in detail, "sexual disenchantment" often begins within two years of marriage.[11]

One four-letter word—*love*—now becomes coupled with another: *pain.* The person with whom we unpack groceries and coordinate work and child-care schedules no longer seems to be the person with whom we once frolicked in the grass or kissed in the moonlight. To cope with this unexpected problem, we want them to change (or change *back),* or they want us to change. We feel our mate has let us down or broken their promise (or they feel we have). The joy and ecstasy have diminished, if not disappeared. Sometimes we actually feel betrayed.

As the malaise deepens, the urge to blame our mate is strong, and it receives considerable support in popular culture.[12] Whether we blame our mate or ourselves, the glow is gone. In mild cases, we resign ourselves to lowered expectations. In severe cases, we feel that our dream has turned into a nightmare. We discover our mate's negative qualities, and, if we are honest, our own. At this point, observe the Sarrells, who have counseled hundreds of couples in distress, "many people panic. They think that they no longer have a happy marriage or any chance of one with this mate." Couples who fall out of love believe that they have "misread the stars." All too often, they decide that they have only two alternatives: live *un*happily ever after—or get divorced.

But there *is* another alternative. We can decide to make our marriage part of our quest. This does not mean that we know beyond a shadow of a doubt that we will remain together forever. What it does mean is that we will consider our wedding a beginning, not an end. As one longtime married couple put it: "A wedding is *not* a marriage. A wedding is only the beginning of an undertaking that may or may not, someday, develop into a marriage."

When we fall in love as teenagers or young adults, the

shadow of both mates is usually still in hiding.[13] Two people fall in love, but not two *whole* people. Their shadows, the parts of themselves that are "in the dark," will seek expression as the urge for wholeness intensifies, often in the second half. We become dissatisfied with our relationships based on fundamental and usually widening polarities (for example: he is the boss, she is not; he mistrusts, she trusts; she handles the kids, he doesn't; she values intimacy, he values power; and so on.)

In *We: Understanding the Psychology of Romantic Love,* Jungian analyst Robert Johnson writes that one of the critical challenges of mature love is "to live consciously with romantic love—that is, with the vast psychological forces that it represents." Speaking in the metaphor of myth, Johnson advises both men and women that they must move toward wholeness in the second half if their marriage is to remain alive. "Two things are required for a hero [or heroine]: a sword and a harp. . . . To be complete, the hero [or heroine] must have both. Without the sword, the harp becomes ineffectual. But without the harp, the sword is reduced to egotistical brute force."[14]

In family therapy, this is often called "splitting," which means that one person owns one set of qualities and their mate owns the other. When such "splitting" becomes ever more deeply entrenched in the relationship, it cripples either the husband and wife, or both, and often they literally "split." It is no coincidence that this is the slang expression for divorce because this is the ultimate way we act out what Jung called our shadow. By the second half of life, each of us must discover these hidden parts of ourselves, the parts of ourselves we failed to water and feed, the aspects of our characters that have remained undeveloped. It is the part of us that we have withheld from the world and denied to ourselves. It is the "lost self," which we repressed because of social pressure; the "false self," the image that we present to the world and behind which we hide; and the "disowned self," those qualities that were condemned in our childhoods and therefore buried. It is the self we have left behind. Until we "embrace the shadow side of our personality," we are split within ourselves—whether or not we legally "split" from our mate.[15]

As the experience of Jungian analyst Murray Stein illustrates, if our marriage does not force us to face our shadow, divorce will. Like most scholars and therapists who write about the second half, he did not share his personal experience in his book. But now, a decade later and in his late forties, he is able to share how much of his insight came from the confusion and pain of his own divorce.

Stein had chosen to become a Presbyterian minister and had adopted a self-image that was sturdily constructed out of only the most pious virtues. "I thought of myself as an honest, genuine, straightforward person," he told me, as I interviewed him in one of the small conference rooms at the C. G. Jung Institute of Los Angeles. "During the divorce, however, I did things I couldn't believe I ever would. I felt so hurt, so angry, that I lied, cheated, deceived. It was shadow . . . just running wild. The man who I had thought was 'me,' that goody-goody minister, was just a narrow part of me. It was something that I had constructed, *something that was not whole.*"

So Stein experienced what he would later write about so eloquently: the death of his old self-image, the emergence of his shadow, and the end of the first half of his life. Fortunately, his quest has led him through his pain and into a deep and rewarding authenticity. He left the ministry and trained as a Jungian analyst, and now he sees his patients facing the same challenge to give birth to unacknowledged parts of themselves. A few years after his divorce, he remarried and, with his new wife, began teaching a college course on the second half. As they outlined the material for the class, he realized that a book was inside him, just waiting to be born. "Although I have written many books and papers," he says, *"In Midlife* was the closest I have ever come to feeling truly inspired. I would go to sleep at night and wake up early in the morning with chapters simply waiting to be recorded."

No doubt your circumstances, like mine, are different from those of this minister-turned-therapist. But the shadow does not seek the light only if you are married, or only if you are male, or only if you are a therapist or writer. It also seeks the light if you are single, female, and in a mainstream occupation. One way or the other, the quest leads us to bring the shadow sides of ourselves into our search for deeper intimacy.

Delia is a strong and savvy woman who is respected both for her work in the media and for her leadership in politics. She is able to identify a cutting-edge story and is decisive about whether to assign a reporter to cover it. As a feminist, she helped organize many major political events, and everyone who knows her would consider her tough and clear-headed. Yet the story she told me over lunch recently showed a very different side of her—her shadow side.

Having reached her mid-thirties, Delia was eager for love, marriage, and family, and Norman seemed to offer all three. He said he loved her, was open to marriage, and definitely wanted children. Over the year they dated, their relationship deepened. She spent most days and nights in his new home and completely redecorated and landscaped it as if it were her own. They talked of marriage so frequently, she thought *his* home would soon be *theirs.*

Then Delia discovered she was pregnant. She was overjoyed, yet apprehensive. When she told Norman she wanted to have the baby, his face registered surprise but nothing else. They agreed they had some big decisions to make together, and quickly. But Norman decided to make those decisions by himself. He stopped returning her phone calls; he returned all her possessions to her apartment; and he changed the locks on *his* house. He refused to speak to Delia again either in person or by phone.

"I was ready to commit myself to love, more ready than ever in my life," she recalled, enraged. "But he betrayed me."

According to Delia's account, he had shown her one side of himself (which was honest, loving, caring, and devoted) but had masked his shadow (which was self-deceptive, self-ish, irresponsible, and cruel). As I watched this lovely, tear-ful woman tell her story of heartbreak, I felt sorry for her. But by sharing her story, Delia wanted something more from me than sympathy. She wanted to derive some mean-ing from the sense of loss following the abortion, the sting of his betrayal, and the anguish of her loneliness. As her friend, I felt compelled to ask her if she was not hiding part of herself too.

For a moment, Delia stared at me blankly. But then I saw her eyes widen. She knew I was referring to the tough, in-sightful, savvy editor who could smell a story—or a phony—quicker than anyone. Had that editor never once glimpsed the hidden side of her lover's character? Had there never been even a single clue?

Slowly, Delia laid out the *other* story—hers. It was the story of a woman so eager for love that she left her judgment at the office; so willing to please that she put aside her own needs for his; so ready to start a family that she ignored his self-centeredness; so deeply yearning to move ahead with her life that she refused to see that she was being taken for a ride. She became a passive victim to this unconscious con man and might never have woken up were it not for her accidental pregnancy, which forced Norman's shadow—and ultimately hers as well—into the open.

She did not collapse into being a self-pitying victim or a self-righteous man-hater. On the contrary, she recommitted herself to her quest for wholeness. For six months she stopped drinking any coffee or alcohol, she recalls, "because

I did not want to hide from the pain. I wanted to be conscious—psychologically, emotionally, spiritually." During this period, she also refused to date. "It felt like a lie to say, 'Yeah, I'll go out with you . . . but I don't know who *I* am.' It was a time of cleansing, of purifying, of letting go."

What followed then was a period of spiritual seeking. "I began trying to listen to the voices from within, voices that are ultimately wiser and more timeless than the one I was used to hearing come out of my mouth. These voices had always been there, but I had been moving too fast to hear them. I had focused too much on other voices, like Norman's, and not enough on my own."

When Delia started dating again, it was a completely different experience. Powerful, successful, attractive men were courting her, but she was not quickly swept off her feet. "The packages were phenomenal," she said, "but now I was looking beneath the packaging. It was as if I had X-ray glasses on. Because I was listening to myself deeply, I automatically listened to them deeply. I could spot a phony now a mile away."

Now in her early forties, she is looking for a relationship again, but looking for one quite differently from the way she did when she first married in her early twenties. "Then I didn't want to deal with all the *un*romantic stuff. Now I am ready for the *whole* experience. I am willing to work things through. I want to be in a relationship because you get lessons about life; if you're alone, you don't get those lessons. And I want them. I realize that I am the maker of my own happiness. Happiness, ultimately, is an 'inside job.' "

Whether you are still single (as Delia was), divorced (as Murray Stein was), or remain in your first marriage (as I do), the challenge of facing the shadow confronts us all in the second half. In the second half we finally reach a turning point, a time in life when we don't have the answers. It is a time of confusion and pain, when old ways of loving no longer work. We are striving toward wholeness now, for a balance of the masculine and feminine within us. Whatever patterns have trapped us for the first half our lives—a marriage that needs to be revitalized; a divorce that has left us bitter; a solitude that we are aching to break through—must change. To do so requires a new way of looking not only at love but at our entire inner lives.

More than Monogamy:
The Challenge of Being Free and Faithful

If you find it hard to recognize your shadow, much less accept it, be gentle with yourself. The shadow has its own rhythms, and healing has its own season. You can hurt yourself and others just as much by being in a rush to change as by being opposed to it. It takes wisdom tempered by humility to harvest wholeness in our lives. Even the most experienced, best-trained experts need to learn this painful lesson.

Dr. Harville Hendrix had been a therapist for many years with a highly respected practice. No one could accuse Hendrix and his wife of not working hard to save their marriage. For eight arduous and painful years prior to their divorce, they did everything possible to rescue their relationship, including intensive self-examination and numerous kinds of therapy. But their wounds were too deep and could not be healed within their marriage. As he sat in divorce court waiting to see the judge, Hendrix felt "like a double failure, a failure as a husband and a therapist." He knew that, after the proceedings were over, he was scheduled to teach a course on marriage that afternoon, and the next day had several couples coming to him for counseling. Despite all his training, all his expertise, he felt just as confused and demoralized as the other men and women seated beside him, waiting for the judge. Like Murray Stein, Hendrix's vast knowledge was of no use. He felt like a beginner again.

After his divorce, Dr. Hendrix did not return to his work as if nothing had changed. He began to plumb the depths of his own pain. He was determined to learn not only why his own marriage had failed but why so much therapy with couples also fails, and from his search came his book *Getting the Love You Want.* What's important to remember is this: Encountering your shadow and feeling pain do not necessarily mean your marriage has failed. Instead, it may mean that it is actually starting to work. "Marriage is not a static state between two unchanging people," Hendrix insists. He traces it as it begins "in the ecstasy of attraction, meanders through a rocky stretch of self-discovery, and culminates in the creation of an intimate, joyful, lifelong union."

Hendrix's story, and countless personal tales of many other couples' reawakenings, are all part of the great untold story of the quest for wholeness in the second half.[16] I have encountered again and again in the lives of those I have interviewed how hard it is to make ourselves vulnerable enough to acknowledge our shadow to ourselves, much less to others. Why else would we wait until the second half to do so? But as evidenced by Murray Stein, by Delia, and by Dr. Hendrix, embracing the shadow is what brings meaning and growth into relationships in the second half.

It would be convenient for me to end this section with these case studies of *other* people's shadows. But that would send the wrong message to you, and to me. My challenge is to face *my* shadow; your challenge is to face *yours.* And that is ultimately more painful—and more liberating—than telling other people's stories.

Shelley and I had been together for almost fifteen years in what we, and others, had often described as a good marriage. But ours, like most, had its own particular tensions. We were in the stage that marriage counselors know only too well: the power struggle. We knew that the person we *thought* we had married was different from the one to whom we actually *were* married. We alternated between denying this fact to ourselves and to each other, and bargaining with each other in a futile attempt to get the other to change. ("If only you'd stop doing this, I'd stop doing that, and then we'd be happy," and so on.) To minimize the tensions of our two warring egos, we tried to "please" each other by hiding feelings that we feared might be troublesome. Over the years, the amount of unshared feeling had accumulated to the point that both of us constantly edited out emotions. For example, I would be hurt by how she spoke to me, but I would hide it so that I would not have to explain it to her or own it within myself. Or, she would be angry because she felt I paid too much attention to my work and not enough to her, but she would hide her anger to avoid pushing me even farther away.

Over the years, these concealed selves grew to the point that vitally important parts of ourselves were in almost permanent hiding. *Of course* I sometimes felt enraged that my fair damsel was depressed or hostile and imagined having a shiny, brand-new lover who would see me through her innocent eyes as the man of her dreams. *Of course* Shelley sometimes felt betrayed when her knight in shining armor was grouchy, exhausted, or confused and fantasized that a young man would romantically see her as a worldly, passionate woman of his dreams. But for years we kept these feelings to ourselves.

We thought our silence was evidence of our loyalty to one another. In fact, it was evidence that we did not dare to face our shadows.

Part of not being aware of the shadow in the first half of life involves denying its existence. This was certainly my frame of mind when, in my early thirties, I wrote in a previous book about Clark and Rena. This is what they said to each other, only weeks before they divorced, as they sat on the couch in our living room with Shelley and me:

CLARK: But why didn't you say something? Why did you wait until it was too late?

RENA: I did say something. Many times. But you weren't listening.

CLARK: But if you were so unhappy all those years, why didn't you tell me? It's not fair to say suddenly: "It's all over."

RENA: I told you long ago. . . . You were always too busy. Five years ago, remember, I wrote you a letter. I thought that way you would have to hear. I wrote you a memo so you'd pay attention to it like you do at the office. I told you then that our marriage was not working for me. But you still didn't pay attention. You thought I was just going through a phase. . . .

CLARK: What do you mean? I loved you more than anyone then, and I still do.

RENA: On your trip to England: She was just for fun, right? And that woman at work: She was only a passing thing, right? And the last one. That's what hurts. I could forgive you for your failings, and they were many, as long as I trusted you. But when you destroyed that trust, you took away the only thing I had left.[17]

The old projections of "falling in love" had worn off; the couple felt like strangers. Rena was in despair; Clark in denial. When I learned of their decision to divorce, I thought they simply hadn't tried hard enough. To protect myself and Shelley, I saw them as having failed to work at their relationship—Clark as too insensitive, and Rena too timid. I saw their shadows ever so clearly—but I did not see my own. In my arrogance, I thought their marriage had a problem, but ours was fine. In fact, sooner or later, most couples face their own version of this dilemma: wanting to become whole in our marriages, but discovering that we are not.

After a dozen years of marriage, I was proud of my marital fidelity. Our code of monogamy was one of the ways

Shelley and I proved to ourselves that our marriage worked. To help me observe the code, I used a quick fix that is quite common among loyal married couples: I persuaded myself that I simply was not attracted to other women, and that they were not attracted to me. Occasionally Shelley would ask me if I found a certain woman attractive, or if I had noticed that a woman had been drawn to me. Invariably, I would say no—and mean it. If you had told me that I was repressing part of myself, I would have flatly disagreed.

The discovery that the person we married is not the one we imagined, but in fact *a real and separate human being whom we do not know,* is frightening. It forces us to realize that we do not know ourselves. At the time I recorded Clark and Rena's words, I had not reached this painful juncture in my marriage yet. I still thought Shelley's and my love was somehow immune from this midlife malaise. This attitude characterized my life until my mid-thirties, when, before I knew it, my quick fix lost its hold over my consciousness. Suddenly, all kinds of women attracted me and were attracted to me, and before long I found myself having my first and only affair. Although it was brief, the pain it caused to all concerned lingered. And with that pain, as Jung predicted, came a birth of consciousness.

Recognizing that we needed help as we grappled with our relationship, Shelley and I entered couples therapy. During our third session together, I indirectly expressed some anger —and then quickly denied it. When the therapist pressed me on the matter, I admitted that Shelley had made me angry. I hid my anger, I explained, because I was afraid she wouldn't love me if I told her what I was really feeling.

"Tell Shelley that," the therapist said softly.

So I turned to Shelley, who looked as nervous as I did. Looking directly into her eyes, I repeated myself: "I am afraid you won't love me if I show what I am really feeling." As the words came out of my mouth, I felt my eyes begin to burn, as if salt had just been dropped in them.

"Tell her what you want from her," the therapist instructed.

I hesitated. Shelley watched me, sensing my inner struggle. She did not know what I was to going to say, but I felt her support as I struggled to find the words. "Shelley, I want to know that you will love me even when I show you what I am really feeling."

It was something I had needed to say to her for years, but never had. (It was also something, as I would later learn, I had needed to say to my mother for a quarter of a century, but never had.) As my tears began to flow, for the first time in our entire marriage, I cried not alone, but in Shelley's arms. My shadow began to come out of hiding, out of the darkness and into the light.

For me, this was a pivotal turning point in our relationship, a moment of truth. It was a moment of healing because I stopped hiding my shadow from my wife, and from myself, and brought its energies and mysteries into our marriage. (Shelley, too, had similar moments, which are hers to tell.) As I did so, the parts of myself that I had held back from our marriage for a dozen years or more began to spring forth. As the new currents of passion and authenticity in Shelley's quest flowed together with mine, we found ourselves on a frightening yet exhilarating journey that has made our relationship more alive, vital, and mysterious than it has been in years.

This period between falling in love when we are young adults, and the hoped-for joy of our later years together, is difficult, painful, sometimes traumatic. It may last months or years. It may strike as an intense, one-time trauma, or intermittently over a long period. This pain means that the shadow is being awakened. Our childhood wounds are healing. It means we have allowed our mate to touch us, that we have opened our soul to love. We take this risk for the same reason a baby who can crawl tries to walk. We do it even if we fall down and get hurt. We do it because it is the next step on our quest.

Yes, it is possible that your marriage, or mine, will not survive. But do not run at the first sign of your shadow. Perhaps it is not your marriage but your old way of loving that is dying. If so, then bury it. Mourn. Take stock. With an open mind and, more important, an open heart, embrace the mystery of the sacred marriage.

Virgin Territory:
Lovemaking with Our Whole Selves

The day I cried for the first time in Shelley's arms, another dimension of my quest began. Now I had to find out more about this strange and vulnerable self that had dared to cry in a woman's arms. The experience was powerful because I experienced then an incredible release of tension that was not sexual, but spiritual. The part of myself I had always held back I finally dared to share. I was reminded of adolescence because the only way I can describe the feeling is to say: *I felt like a virgin once again.* When I cried in Shelley's arms, I felt a part of me open to her that had never been touched, a wounded place within me that I had hidden since earliest childhood. When I followed my tears and found that deepest dwelling place, which is often called the soul, I recognized that it was virgin territory.

Since those of us in the second half have been sexually active for many years, my use of the word *virgin* will seem odd. Sexually speaking, we have not been virgins for decades. But what if there is another dimension that is just as important (if not more so) than sexuality, a realm that has no name, a zone that cannot be explored until we are older? Just as sex represents the unknown and invisible frontier for adolescents, what if there exists a similar frontier in the second half of life? If so, then it is possible that we may be

virgins again—not sexually, but in some other, more mysterious way.

Only as a second-time virgin could I clearly see the split
personality in which I had been living my marriage. I was
faithful but unfree. Because I did not feel free to act on my
feelings of sexual attraction toward other women, I did not
feel free to have those feelings. And by cutting myself off
from those feelings, I cut myself off from my own manhood.
I realized that I had been sexually faithful, not as a free and
willing act of a mature man but as a resentfully obedient
boy. Whether or not I obeyed the rules was not the point.
The point was, *faithful or not,* I had not given my whole self
to my marriage.[18]

As we break into this tender new domain where we can be
free *and* faithful, the virginal feelings of our teenage years
may return—the excitement of self-discovery, the fear of ex-
posure, the lure of the mysterious, the trembling first steps
into the unknown. But do not be misled. Although the feelings are indeed reminiscent of adolescence, they are not
identical. If you do not recognize the crucial difference, you
will not find your soul/mate but simply have another affair.

That this should be so is understandable—time is running
out. By the time we reach our late thirties and forties, most
of us feel that we have loved and been loved, probably more
than once. We must either decide that the mate we have
chosen is the best person with whom to share our lives, or
we had better begin looking for someone else. As Judith
Viorst frames the dilemma in *Necessary Losses:* "Why not
seek a new relationship before we get too faded and juice-
less and scared? And our answer, as the spate of midlife
divorces seems to suggest, may be—why not?"[19]

Most couples, I believe, reach this *divortium* ("fork in the
road"), whether they divorce or recommit themselves to
their marriage. So did Shelley and I. When we recommitted
ourselves to the road called marriage, it was a commitment
more whole than we possibly could have had in our early

twenties. For the first time in my marriage, I felt I could be faithful *and* free. Instead of focusing on all the mystery and adventure that awaited me with other women, I became aware of the mystery and adventure *within* my own marriage that I had not yet dared to explore. By reconnecting with the part of me that was still a virgin (as Shelley, in her own way, did the same), we became aware that it would take years, indeed probably a lifetime, to finish having "an affair" with each other, and ourselves.

Looking back, both Shelley and I realized how much we and our generation had rushed to "lose" our virginity. In a culture where tradition had been turned upside-down, losing our virginity meant becoming grown-up. Traditional cultures offer their young people rites of passage that confirm them as adults. These rites are both psychological and spiritual, since both the secular and the sacred are interwoven in the ceremony. Only *after* these initiation rites do young men and women become sexually active. In our culture, however, with no recognized rites of passage, having sex (or, consequently, having a baby and getting married) often by default becomes our initiation into adulthood. So we lose our virginity in order to gain status as "grownups"—if not in our parents' eyes, then in our own.

This sexual shortcut is a burden too heavy for marriages to bear. Instead of being initiated into adulthood by adults of our own sex, we are initiated by the other sex. Our status as adults depends on our romantic relationship. If we lose that relationship, through breaking up or through divorce or through falling out of love, we have symbolically become children again. We can only regain our lost status by finding another mate or lover who will once again confer on us the mantle of maturity. For maturity is defined sexually and socially, not spiritually.

The next time of initiation in the life cycle is the second half, which inherits the unfinished business of adolescence. But this time we are called by the spirit, not the flesh. It is the time when we are called to identify ourselves, and to be identified, not as our parents' child or as our mate's lover, but as mature adults in our own right. Although this is true for both men and women, this challenge holds special meaning for each.

For women, rediscovering their inner virginity is a powerful rite of the second half passage. This is the missing ingredient in so many marriages, the wisest women psychologists agree: they did not develop their virginal selfhood enough before they lost it and became wives. As Jung's colleague M. Esther Harding stressed, women need to reclaim "this term *virgin* in its psychological connotation" to make clear that "it refers not to external circumstances *but to an inner attitude.*

> "A woman who has a psychological attitude to life which makes her dependent on what other people think, which makes her do and say things she really does not approve, *is no virgin in this meaning of the term.* She is not one-in-herself but acts always as female counterpart . . . to some male."

The virgin woman, Harding explains, "does what she does— not because of any desire to please, not to be liked, or to be approved . . . but because what she does is true. She may have to say no, when it would be easier . . . to say yes." Concurs Jean Shinoda Bolen, author of *Goddesses in Every Woman,* the virgin woman "will be motivated by a need to follow her own inner values, to do what has meaning or fulfills herself, apart from what other people think."[20] This is why, for example, after Delia broke up with Norman, she did not date for more than half a year. She needed to make herself a virgin again.

For men, rediscovering our virgin selves can be equally powerful, but it requires removing layers of armor unique to our gender. Our generation of men now entering the second half has begun to do so, in part because we now have mentors (or what later in the book we will call elders) to whom we can turn for guidance. Robert Bly *(Iron John)*, Sam Keen *(Fire in the Belly)*, Robert Moore, and Douglas Gillette *(King, Warrior, Magician, Lover)*—these gifted guides, each in his own way, are all encouraging men to reclaim the original innocence, vitality, and wildness that they have forfeited. A network of male initiation experiences has emerged around the country, calling upon men to reclaim their virginal manhood—defined not by their mothers or wives, but by themselves.[21]

Unlike the early 1980s, when I first wrote about the changing archetypes of masculinity in Western culture, the men's movement is no longer small and fragile. Just as women (like Delia) are moving beyond defining themselves in terms of their reflections in men's eyes, so the men's movement is moving beyond being pro- or antifeminist. Just as women stopped doing whatever they thought would please men, men have stopped doing whatever they thought would please women. Instead, they are finally trying to be themselves. It is as if both sexes were concluding that it is not worth having a mate if the price is losing one's own soul.

Of course this puts pressure on marriages in the second half. Both wives and husbands are asking more of their mates, and of themselves. They are seeking a marriage that, as Scott Peck puts it, "nurtures . . . spiritual growth." This is only possible when we free ourselves as men and women from sex role limitations and move toward the place where masculine and feminine merge into one. It is often not until the second half when wives and husbands break out of their predefined roles and begin their quest for a deeper, more authentic experience of love.

"Will you and Mommy ever get divorced?" my son Mikael, then seven, asked me a few years ago after I had picked him up from the birthday party of a friend whose parents lived apart. Tired after a long day in the office, I was in no mood to field tough questions from this pint-size investigator.

"No, pal," I replied. "Your mom and I will be together for the rest of our lives." I was confident that this fatherly reassurance would ease his mind.

"Are you sure?" he probed, throwing me off guard.

With no time to think, I shot back, "Pretty sure."

"Why just *pretty* sure?" he probed.

"Because life isn't always completely under our control."

He put his hand on my arm. (Was he just wanting to feel close? Or was he making sure I wouldn't leave?) "But Daddy," he asked me bluntly, "what would happen if you *did* get divorced?"

As I turned into our driveway, I reminded myself that what he wanted was reassurance. "That's *not* going to happen. Shelley and I love each other very much." But then I added: "Even if we did divorce, you'd do what many kids do: live part of the time with me and part of the time with Mommy."

"But I don't want to. I want to live *every* day with both you *and* Mommy."

Instinctively, we hugged. And then we went inside.

Many children, myself included, did not grow up living every day with both parents. On the contrary, we grew up in a brave new world of broken homes, blended families, "serial" marriages and single parents—and we survived. But all of us, just like my son, need the masculine and feminine to be connected in our everyday lives. We seek the sacred marriage, the union for which the child within each of us so deeply yearns.

In the second half, we begin to see that the sexual and spiritual are two branches on the same tree. In his brilliant study of romantic love, Robert Johnson lays bare the roots of this tree. According to Johnson, what we are ultimately seeking in our erotic connection with our mate or lover "is the inner truth of [our] own soul.

What we seek constantly in romantic love is not human love or human relationship alone; we also seek a religious experience, a *vision of wholeness*. . . . Unknown to our conscious Western minds, our souls and spirits are psychological realities, and they live on in our psyches without our knowledge. And it is there, in the unconscious, that God lives, whoever God may be for us as individuals.

"This," says Johnson, "is the secret key that unlocks the mystery of romantic love."[22]

One does not have to agree with Johnson's sweeping conclusion to recognize that, for modern Westerners, this profound split between sexuality and spirituality wreaks havoc in our personal (and, as we shall see later, public) lives. As the lawyer, marriage counselor, and psychiatrist who opened this chapter agreed, our search for love compels us to look beyond its visible, physical aspects and into the invisible and spiritual. "It's a *spiritual* crisis," says attorney Stuart Walzer, when asked about the divorce epidemic. It's a *"spiritual journey,"* writes Dr. Harville Hendrix, in describing the challenge of lifelong love. The goal of true marriage is *"spiritual* growth," concurs Dr. Peck.

Not only do I agree with them wholeheartedly, but I believe that, in the second half, our failure to embrace the spiritual dimension of marriage can stunt its growth. It can undermine every dimension of marriage, including sexuality. Despite all the talk about sex, it remains a mystery. What is actually occurring in the spiritual/sexual dimension of our private lives is so intensely personal that, even in this age of polls and computers, the truth remains elusive. One can read questionnaire responses about how satisfying sex is, or polling data about how many times per week couples in various age groups make love. But there are no statistical surveys that explain why, if "having good sex" helps make a good

marriage, spirit has something to do with whether sex remains good.

Faced with the mystery of long-term marital sexuality, we
readily resort to stereotypes. The most popular is the bitter,
often sarcastic stereotype that portrays long-term marital sex
as increasingly boring. According to this view, the longer
you are married, the more boring sex becomes. Since passion inevitably dries up within a long-term monogamous relationship, only extramarital affairs can be exciting.

After reviewing the literature about sex in the second half,
I have found nothing that persuades me that, as a rule, sex
gets better—*or* that it gets worse.[23] As a rule, *there are no
rules.* For some, sex gets so uninteresting that it virtually
ends; for others, it becomes such a profound, erotic way of
communicating, it feels like a sacrament; and for still others,
sexual ennui and sexual discovery flow together throughout
the course of their marriage, depending on the pressures of
their lives.

Analyze all the data, and in the end, certain questions
remain beyond the scope of statistics: *Why for some second
half couples is sex cold and brittle, and for others warm and
tender? And even more mystifying: Why for the same couple
can sex sometimes be so hollow and other times so ecstatic?*
The two questions are, I think, deeply connected to our
quest for wholeness. Both are directly related to what we
bring to bed and to what we leave packed away in the
"closet."

Some couples chronically leave many of their most vulnerable, tender feelings in the "closet." They never dare to
bring those feelings into lovemaking. They bring to sex only
part of who they are. If one is a beginner, such sex can
nevertheless be gratifying. But if one has been making love
for years or decades, such sex eventually becomes stale.
Imagine playing cards a few times a week for twenty years.
How interesting would the game be if every player always
held the same cards in his hand? Similarly, if we bring only a

part of ourselves, and bring that same part year after year, emptiness and boredom will certainly displace fulfillment and passion. To renew sex involves bringing the new and growing parts of ourselves with us to bed. In relationships that stay sexually alive well into the second half, both partners bring their emerging selves into their marriage. If we take these healing (and therefore more whole) selves into our marriage, we can find love that will last—and grow—for a lifetime.

Some years ago, on a two-week business trip to the Soviet Union and Europe, I had a stark, unexpected encounter with just the opposite fragmented kind of sex. I lay awake one night in Frankfurt, West Germany, caught in a nerve-jangling state of jet lag. Alone in a hotel with around-the-clock, sexually explicit erotic movies on the cable channel, I decided to watch whatever was playing. For the princely sum of fifteen deutsche marks, I was suddenly witnessing the "lovemaking" of several pairs or trios of men and women. Like most men, I found the sight of naked women's bodies sexually arousing. But soon, and quite inexplicably, I became bored. As I watched the energetic copulation, I tried to explain my lack of interest in terms of the uninspired dialogue, the flat acting, or the unattractive actors. But then I realized that I was bored with the sex itself. After twenty minutes, the total absence of relationship—spontaneity, enthusiasm, compassion—totally eroded eros. I was turned off, not turned on.

The experience made me realize that most of the "sexually liberated" generation now entering midlife has had the opportunity for multiple sexual relationships *before* marriage. Few of us are married to our first lover. For the baby-boom generation, moving beyond the rules that governed the first half of our lives may lead us, not to blondes and Porsches, but rather to a deeper kind of commitment—not only to our marriage partners, but to ourselves. As we become more whole, so can our relationships.

For couples seeking a sacred marriage, sex at forty-five can be very different—not necessarily "better" gymnastically, but certainly deeper spiritually—than at twenty-five. When lovemaking encompasses the more authentic parts of ourselves that we have discovered only later in life, the sexual experience can be more illuminating than ever before. The people between the sheets are two very different people from who they were when they met. They are not only older; they may also be more conscious, more vulnerable, and more open. Consequently, they do not measure their sexual life in terms of number of orgasms, frequency of intercourse, length of physical contact, or any of the other variables that sexologists can so readily tabulate. On the contrary, they ask whether it touches their souls.

But why, then, do even couples on the quest sometimes have days (or weeks, or months) when sex seems shallow or unappealing, followed again by periods when it is as, or more, fulfilling than before?

Growth through the life cycle is neither continuous nor smooth. It moves forward and back, zigs and zags, coalesces and disintegrates, then reintegrates in new and unexpected ways. Combine the lives of two people (mix in jobs, kids, in-laws, fatigue, and all the rest) and the number of variables dragging a couple down—or lifting them up—is astronomic. Under such circumstances, it is not puzzling that sex runs hot and cold and then hot again. It would be puzzling if it didn't.

Before Shelley and I entered the second half, it almost seemed as if an invisible script lay beneath our bed. It was not a bad script—it had many wonderful moments of passion, playfulness, and pleasure—but it was nevertheless a script. We knew how sex started and how it finished; what we liked and what we didn't; which lines belonged to her and to me—and which ones neither of us dared to read. Why did our lovemaking follow this script for so many years? Why were we unconscious of its power? And why, beginning in our late thirties (as Jung predicted), did its hold over us

loosen? What exactly happened that began to liberate us
from predictability? How did we discover new ways of communicating with each other that made our sexuality more
mysterious and enthusiastic than ever before?

Although I can articulate the questions, I cannot answer
them except in terms of my own experience. Speaking personally (for I am at liberty here to invade no one else's
privacy but my own), I know that bringing my shadow into
lovemaking was a vital change that, after moving through
the pain, brought a new joy, pleasure, and yes, spirit into
sexuality.

As a child, I was raised to see my body as sinful. The body
was not to be enjoyed, but rather controlled. It was a burden
to be carried—something that, finally, we would let go of as
we entered heaven. In the meantime, it was a temptation.
Yes, we should take care of it, but for God's sake, not enjoy
it. Eros was the enemy of the divine. God was reached
through prayer, not pleasure; devotion, not desire. Thus
the world I entered was divided into the lower realms
and the higher realms. The road to hell was through the
genitals; the road to heaven was through the head (and "the
pure heart," as instructed by the head). In the battle for my
soul, the higher realms held dominion during my childhood.

Only decades later, on a cassette tape given to me by a
friend, would I understand what had happened to me.
"Shame has to do with spiritual deprivation," explains Patrick Dougherty, who lectures widely to men's groups.
"Where shame is, God is not. Shame is godlessness. Shame
is darkness. Shame says, 'Something is so wrong with me
that God does not love me'. . . . Shame does not trust even
the Holy One. Shame is the darkness of the soul."[24]

But then came puberty. Into our bodies is set an unfolding
plan, which includes the awakening of eros. The lower
realms assert themselves and demand to be included in our
worldview—and self-view. It is no coincidence that this is
the time when, like so many others, I lost my religious faith,

for that faith was built on the denial of much of God's creation, on the denial of the body, of pleasure, of the earth, of love—not the abstract "love" of a heavenly father, but the embodied, mature, erotic love of each other and ourselves.

Forced to choose between heavenly and earthly love, my choice was preordained. Since sex was opposed to the spirit (or so I was taught), then I would oppose the spirit as well. From adolescence on, I greeted anyone who spoke of the "spiritual" dimensions of life with distrust. I assumed that they were simply trying to impose their worldview on my experience. By invoking higher (and always invisible) powers, they would try to divide me into right and wrong, good and bad, believer or heathen, saved or damned—higher or lower. My very being resisted being torn in half. Like any of God's creations, I wanted to be whole.

Then in high school—oh, sweet delight!—I entered into my first sexual relationship. In college, I was blessed with a relationship with a woman who was a warm and gentle companion in and out of bed. I was fortunate to be initiated into the sexual world with women who received what I then had to give, and who gave to me what I was then capable of receiving. For me, from the very beginning of my adult experience, sex fell securely and snugly into the category called "good."

But my deeper wound was not healed. Sex was separate from the rest of my life. When I engaged in sex, it had nothing to do with spirit, certainly not with "God." Good sex, in my divided mind, somehow disproved religion. The more pleasure and intimacy and love I experienced through sexuality, the more I distanced myself from the repressive religious notions of the body and sex as evil. I remember taking almost vengeful pride in discovering how good "loving a woman" could feel compared with how empty and bored I felt when told to "love God." The former was a rich and tender reality that energized and revitalized my life; the latter was a platitude I viewed as a hypocritical charade.

It was with this split that I entered my marriage at the age of twenty-five. From our very first encounter, Shelley and I felt drawn to each other in ways that were rationally inexplicable. We felt lucky enough to have "great sex," as if it were an experience like winning a lottery rather than a reflection of our inner beings. We referred to this mystery as "chemistry," as if by using this scientific term we made this spiritual mystery more fathomable.

Although I would not become conscious of the spiritual dimension of our marriage until years later, I caught glimpses of it repeatedly during the first decade of our marriage as a consequence of our passion. Shelley and I gave birth to three sons, and each time one of them was born, I cried in awe of what I was privileged to witness. (Even many of our mothers, who gave birth during an era tyrannized by drugs and forceps, have never been so blessed.) Each time I was so moved by the spirit in the room that I felt the presence of a force greater than Shelley and me, greater certainly than sex, greater than our bodies, greater than human consciousness—something as great as the very force of Life itself. The room was filled with the light of the Spirit, and I stood awestruck before it, like Moses before the burning bush. I would look at our baby and be overwhelmed with awe. Then I would look away, into Shelley's face, and be overwhelmed again. The Latin *spiritus,* from which the word *spirit* is derived, means "breath" (or "breath of God"), and I felt it clearly when I saw these three new souls first draw this *spiritus* into their lungs.

Yet my capacity to deny the spirit was so strong that, just as I turned eros into "just" sex, so I assumed afterward that what I had encountered was "just" the magic of birth. As the mind-expanding experience of birth drifted into memory, replaced by sleepless nights and dirty diapers, my old attitudes returned. The split between sex and spirit divided me until I approached the second half, when the price I had to pay for it rose sharply. To borrow Jung's phrase, it was "damaging the soul."

After almost two decades of lovemaking and three children, Shelley and I had thoroughly explored most of the possibilities of spirit-less sex. Within the walls of my personality and hers, there was little room for genuine innovation. The only direction we could move with each other was through those walls and into the world where sexual and spiritual meet.

Soul/Mates at Last: Uniting the Inner and Outer Quests

Slowly a new dimension entered our relationship. It became as important to be authentic as it was to have sex. Our first priority was no longer making sex work; it was enabling ourselves to become whole—or, to repeat Scott Peck's phrase, "to nurture one's own or another's spiritual growth." Sometimes it was Shelley, other times it was me, but often at least one of us would find ourselves hesitant to make love. With some patience and often some pain, we would discover that a wound, whether old or new, needed healing before we could be sexual. Sexuality become a kind of beacon light, shining its powerful beam into whichever one of us (and most often it was both) had soul work to do.

And so sexuality came full circle. Split apart from spirit in childhood, sexuality emerged in adolescence as a rebellion *against* the spirit. By the second half, it had revealed itself as a path *toward* the spirit. For the first time in our long marriage, each of us had the experience that when we touched each other, we were touching something sacred. A new gentleness, patience, and purity emerged in our bed. Orgasm, while still a vital part of our experience, no longer seemed the sole or even primary purpose of sex. In this erotic spirituality, or spiritual eros, we found nourishment for our souls that we needed as much as, if not more than, we needed sexual release. As spirit more readily entered our sexuality, the experience become more authentic—sometimes so authentic that it was unexpectedly derailed. When we begin sex with our shadow in the closet—that is, with one or both of us denying our deeper feelings rather than expressing them—sex is unfulfilling no matter how hard we might try. But when we bring our whole selves to bed, sex is more whole, and more healing and holy, than ever before.

For me, the journey into the land where sex and spirit meet has just begun. For every mystery that has been revealed to me, there are many others that I am sure I have not yet even glimpsed. What happens ahead on the quest is a story that, at least for now, I will leave to others to tell. But about this I am sure: *The inner quest for wholeness, and the outer quest for intimacy, are ultimately one.*

I firmly believe that this kind of healing and wholeness is emerging in many long-term marriages, and that this in turn will cause the rate of divorce to continue falling, as has already been reported by the National Center for Health Statistics. Indeed, preliminary statistics indicate the lowest divorce rates since 1974. Author Diane Medved similarly concludes that we are witnessing a "dynamic and palpable shift" away from divorce and attributes it to "graying 'baby boomers' who are, for some reason, becoming *more mature.*"[25] "The pendulum has begun to swing," concurred Ralph Earle, president of the sixteen thousand-member American Association for Marriage and Family Therapists at a recent conference. "What we're seeing with our members . . . is more emphasis on marriage *enrichment.*"[26]

The "maturity" and "enrichment" to which these specialists refer is the vital ingredient in the second half marriage—the capacity to move through pain into a deeper, more spiritually grounded kind of love. It is the discovery that there is another alternative besides being a martyr (endlessly bearing marital pain) and a coward (running away from it, only to repeat it with someone else). To take one's marriage into the quest and to enter that terrain, couples can neither permanently submit to, nor completely avoid, pain. On the contrary, they must find ways to make their marriage their spiritual path. This does not necessarily mean that they pray together or share the same religious beliefs. It does mean that they are willing to seek something more in marriage than the obvious economic and sexual ties, something more than just one female neurosis trying to live under one roof with a male neurosis. On the quest, they are two souls seeking a sacred marriage.

For the same reason we had to redefine the word *virgin,* so it it necessary to redefine the word *soulmate.* In its standard usage, the word implies that we are looking outside ourselves for another person who is a uniquely, perhaps profoundly, suitable companion. By *soul/mate,* however, I mean that *an outer quest for a partner for the second half of life (mate), and an inner quest to discover the unknown realms of ourselves (soul), are at last being joined.* Our mate becomes a guide to our own soul; and our soul becomes a guide to a new relationship with our mate. We are seeking not just a mate but a soul/mate who inspires us to encounter our own souls as well as a deeper love.

Since joy is harder to quantify than divorce, we have no accurate accounting of how many couples come this far on their quest.[27] After all the data are tabulated, we are still left with mystery. But those of us in the second half do not need statistics to tell us what we already know: Long-term love contains seeds of pain—and joy. Studies show that many do discover a depth of caring and meaning that is beyond anything they could imagine in their youth or early adulthood. Other studies show an "intense deepening of relationships" at the second half, based on true caring and compassion. According to John Pollack, a survey researcher who recently completed one such national poll, the second half for many can be "a period of caring rather than crisis. It's a time when people look forward to increasing closeness and compassion as opposed to, say, developing new relationships."[28]

New relationships—this is the key! We can turn this challenge into an outer quest or an inner one. Does "new" mean ending our "old" relationship with our mate or lover and finding another different face, body, and personality with which to be intimate? Or does it mean *re*newing our current love relationship so that deeper meaning and passion emerge?

Unfortunately, it is far easier to find models for the former than the latter. Our society inundates us with stories of tempestuous, cruel divorces.[29] Relationships that are renewed and reborn after many years almost never get headlines. If we divorce and remarry—once, twice, or more—our society offers us rituals by which to measure our changes. Our legal status changes. And, for some women at least, names change too. But the inner quest for renewal has no such demarcations. It is a private, lonely, and often uncharted journey. No minister will bless it. No court proceedings will examine it. No judge will decree it. No wedding anniversary, whether silver or gold, will truly do it justice. For it is recorded not in city hall but in our souls.

Until we know more about the marital breakthroughs as well as the marital breakdowns, midlife couples have blurred vision as we look ahead at our own future. As long as we listen to the headlines rather than our hearts, we will inevitably tend to associate "new" with the visible, tangible process of changing partners, rather than with the invisible and mysterious process of changing ourselves. The money, time, energy, and spirit that are sucked into divorce will continue to be diverted from the search for a soul/mate. And the children in our society will continue to be tossed back and forth, helter skelter, in the ongoing battle of the masculine and feminine shadows.

But we cannot afford to wait for the media to begin reporting stories of marital renewal. We cannot wait for society to change before we confront our repetitive infidelity, casual divorce, domestic alienation, bitter boredom, and the other symptoms of deadened relationships. We have to bring our quest not only to work and play but with us every night to our beds. We must take responsibility ourselves for recognizing that, when we feel disenchanted with marriage after several years, it is often because we are seeking a deeper spirit in our own lives. When our marriages no longer inspire enthusiasm (a word derived from the Latin, which means literally "filled with God"), it is because the sacred is missing in our lives.

In the final chapter, we will explore the quest for the sacred in the second half of our lives. But if we are to find it anywhere, we must seek in our homes, in our beds, and in our lover's eyes. We are divided into men and women not simply to reproduce (for that job is completed earlier in our lives), but also to seek a wholeness greater than ourselves. It is in the second half that we receive the invitation to another wedding—not to enter into marriage, but to enter the sacred marriage.

In the dance of generations, we are often seeking our sacred marriages just as our parents are facing their deaths and our children are facing their sexuality. Both the young and the old need us to be connected to the sacred: the old because the end of their bodily lives is rapidly approaching; the young because they need guidance and initiation into the meaning of adulthood. The young, eager for their first love, are counting on us. If we, the generation now in the second half, turn our backs on love's challenge, our betrayal of the quest is fully witnessed by the next generation.

Our soul/mates are asking us to remember our vows. Whatever words we spoke, whether in a holy building or on a grassy field, the vows are sacred. Whether we are married or divorced, the challenge of the second half of life is to learn to keep the promises we make—not just to our mates but to our souls.

Instead of denying that things have changed, it is time to admit our disillusionment; to recognize our urge to have "affairs"; to acknowledge the need for a "separation" from our old relationship; to "divorce" ourselves from apathy and bitterness; and finally to "marry" in the deepest, spiritual sense of the word. To survive this journey, remember:

Pay attention to your disillusionment. Illusions *are* dying. They want a proper burial. Mourn their loss. Cry together. Become curious about who this person you have married (or want to marry) actually is.

Have the ultimate affair with the ultimate stranger: your shadow. Encounter the part of yourself you do not know. Find out about the parts of yourself that have been hidden from view. Before you jeopardize your marriage by "falling in love" with somebody, fall in love with the rest of yourself.

Ask your mate for a "separation." Recognize that you both are different and more complex than either of you thought. Acknowledge the distance between you and the "kids" you once were. Face your mortality. Recognize your aloneness in the universe. Explore how you have changed. Put your old self behind you, at least for a while, so your new selves can have some room to grow.

With compassion and courage, face your "divorce." When you reach this fork in the road, each of you must make your choice. Do you want to live with this new and separate and mysterious being who has been called your wife or your husband? Will he or she support you on your quest? Or must you travel alone for a while, or with someone else? Take responsibility for your life. Choose your path.

When, at last, you are ready to open your soul, truly marry (or remarry) your soul/mate. Give yourself wholeheartedly to the one you love. Let them in. You have picked him or her—either your mate, or a new and truer love. So trust, and be trustworthy. You have no more excuses for hiding. Your relationship is a path to your soul. This mate will be the one who holds you when you die, or the one you hold. Let the light shine in to every corner of your beings.

Let your marriage enter the sacred. Let the sacred enter your marriage.

4

FINDING A VOICE
IN YOUR VOCATION
The Quest for a Calling

Our age has as its own particular mission . . . the creation of a civilization founded upon the spiritual nature of work.

SIMONE WEIL
The Need for Roots

When we get our first job in our late teens or early twenties, we know very little about ourselves. We may know our dreams and our ambitions. We may know our skills, insofar as schooling revealed them. But in terms of our occupations, we are novices. We do not know what kind of work satisfies us. We do not know about bureaucracy and office politics. And we do not know much about the pleasures or the pressures of paychecks. But by the time we reach the second half, we have been initiated into the world of work. After working for a decade or more, the thrill of the first paycheck is far behind us. We are looking for something deeper in our work now. It is not just a job, not even an occupation or a profession. More strongly than ever before, we feel the need to express our whole selves in our work. A vital part of coming into our own is finding our true calling.

The job we chose in our twenties rarely satisfies us in the same way after we reach the second half. Given the length of our life-spans, this should not surprise us. If we picked the wrong occupation, we feel the urgency of finding the right one before it is too late. If we picked the right one, we may feel that it has lost much of its meaning after two decades or more. And even if it is still meaningful, we may well feel the need to express a deeper part of ourselves that has come with maturity and experience. So in the second half, we urgently feel the need to listen to the inner voices in us that are trying to provide us with a midcourse correction toward more fulfilling work.

Our vocation is one of our voices. It comes from the same Latin root: *vox,* "voice," or *vocare,* "to call." In our thirties and beyond, we are looking for work that not only pays the bills but allows us to speak in our own voice. This is the cornerstone of a true calling.

In the second half, it is common to experience feelings of

dissatisfaction, alienation, and emptiness in our work. We feel inexplicably lost or, more precisely, abandoned. *Abandonment* means literally "to be uncalled," "to be without destiny." Derived from the verb *bannan,* meaning "to summon," abandoned is how we often feel during the darkest times in our quest when, listening intently for success, we fail to hear the summons. This does not happen only to the man in a gray flannel suit or to the woman executive dressed for success. It happens to even the most enlightened and adventurous.

For Eric Utne, it happened in his thirties. A successful magazine publisher, he had started with his wife Peggy Taylor—herself a gifted writer and editor—a new and commercially successful, Boston-based magazine boldly called *New Age.* But after several years, this lofty dream became hollow. He lost faith in what he was doing. He grew tired of what he called the magazine's "succession of enthusiasms, the parade of answers, every guru and human potential figure trumpeting themselves as God's gift to humanity." He and his staff would move from one enthusiasm to the next so quickly that they never stayed with anything long enough for the shadow to emerge. As his marriage unraveled, he made the decision to leave the magazine, and he began casting about for his calling. He went through a host of business cards so quickly that many were obsolete by the time they were printed.

Finally, just when he felt most abandoned, he realized that magazine publishing was what he wanted to do. But he wanted to do so with deeper wisdom and greater modesty. Having moved to Minneapolis, he started a simple newsletter with the plain and unpretentious title *The Utne Reader.* Its philosophy was based on the sound advice offered to Eric by Margaret Mead: "Never ask your readers what they want, because then you'll give it to them, and that will be entertainment. Ask yourself what *you* want, and then you will delight your readers." He followed her advice and created a forum where diverse, conflicting views could be heard on the cutting issues of our time. Instead of selling answers, the publication posed questions. Within a few years, *The Utne Reader* became one of the fastest-growing publications in America.

Although Eric reached this watershed in his thirties, many of us do so only in our forties or fifties. Sooner or later, we reach the point where, as psychiatrist Daniel Levinson puts it: "Internal voices that have been muted for years clamor to be heard." When, bubbling up from deep within us, we hear a voice calling us back to our dreams, we feel compelled, despite our fears, to listen. Each of our dreams is different. There is no movement to join, no cause to which we are being called in unison, no drummer whose beat we must all follow. The beat we must follow now is our own heartbeat, that mortal drum beckoning us to rediscover the immortal rhythm of our deeper selves, which some call the soul.

But to hear that drum, much less follow its beat, we have to do another kind of job interview. Our challenge now is not to dress up, rehearse our lives and sell ourselves and our résumé to a potential employer. Our challenge is to take off our tie or makeup, forget our lines, and dare to interview ourselves.

Self-Interviewing:
A Banker and an Ad Executive Tell Their Stories

Jan Niemi and Donald Marrs were not looking for jobs. They were already employed: Jan with a major New York bank, Donald with a top Chicago advertising agency. They had absolutely no reason to seek job interviews because they were, to all outward appearances, successes. What they desperately needed, however, was a "self-interview." They had to interview themselves about what they truly wanted.

For fifteen years, Jan had been crunching numbers at Citibank. Although she had been an English literature major at Cornell with a strong interest in the arts, the pressure of making a living had led her to a job in finance. But now she was increasingly bored. It was hard for her to imagine spending the rest of her life doing the same thing. Yet she had no prospect for another career and very little confidence that she could find one.

"I had worked at Citibank on the corporate side directly for the vice-chairman of the bank," Jan told me. "At first, it worked out all right. I wanted to live overseas, which in fact my job allowed me to do. But I had no intention of turning it into a long-term career. After spending several years in Italy and Greece with the bank, I returned to New York and found myself at the bank, year after year, in a high-pressure job. When my boss left to become president of another bank, I reached a turning point. Something had to change."

But of course, she was afraid. She was single and had no other income besides her salary. "If you leave your job, you're crazy," one of her friends told her. "You'll be throwing away security—and for what?" At first, Jan had no reply. She didn't know what she wanted to do. All she knew was that she could not go on doing in the second half what she had done in the first.

"What I was doing was sedentary, narrow, analytical. I realized I wanted to do something that was visual, creative, and active. I was tired of spending my time in recycled air in an office building doing something that was no longer challenging. I needed to be re-fueled. I could almost feel brain cells dying in the unused parts of my brain. Even the creativity related to my work felt like it was slipping away."

She consulted a specialist in the field, Neil Bull, who organized the Center for Interim Studies to provide people in transition with practical ideas about how they could make the professional changes in their lives that fulfill their heart's desires. Neil asked Jan what she really wanted to do "if she could have her dream." She hesitated because she believed, as most of us do, that her dream was impossible. After all, how could a New York bank officer possibly get a job with an art museum in Italy?

But finally, after much prodding from Neil, she shared her secret goal. "I'd like to work for a while in the Guggenheim Museum in Venice," she told him. "Venice is my favorite place on the planet. The museum is my favorite place in Venice. And I love art—I always have. But why would they want *me*?"

Jan knew that she had neither the experience nor the contacts she needed to get such a prestigious job. She also felt that, if she was taking time off, she should be pragmatically building toward a new career. But Neil advised her to follow her dream, at least for a few months. "If you follow your interests," Neil suggested, "maybe the rest will fall into place."

Neil Bull did not give this advice lightly. He had come to it only after years of seeking his own true calling. The son of a lawyer who always wanted to be a writer, Neil had witnessed in his own family the price we pay for not pursuing our dream. Throughout his career—first as an educator and then, in his fifties, as director of the center—he always made sure that his employment kept in step with his heart. Once, during his own "midlife crisis," he spent six months in his early fifties "wasting time" repairing a barn, completely uncertain about where his next paycheck would come from. In retrospect, he considers it one of the most important investments of time he ever made, because he emerged from the barn clearer and stronger than ever about finding his calling.

Now in his mid-sixties, Neil is just as determined as ever to find meaning in his work. He is as passionate about helping other people find their calling as he was about finding his own. "As I look at retirement, there are all these books supposedly written for people my age, and all they talk about are annuities, insurance, IRAs . . . always money! Dammit, you can't watch the stock market all day! These books neglect the most important question: what are you going to do all day?"

After interviewing Jan, the first call Neil made was to someone in Italy who knew the staff at the Guggenheim Museum. Intrigued by her unusual background, the key administrator at the museum gave Jan a six-week volunteer position that covered only the costs of her room and board. But he and his colleagues soon discovered what a rare find Jan was: someone who cared about art, but who also had business sense. When her short stay ended, they told her she was welcome to apply for a paying job.

When I spoke with her, it was two years later. She was just packing her bags to return to Venice for a second time around, this time as a full-time executive with the Guggenheim Museum.

Although quests for a true calling often have happy endings, they also involve pain. When Jan Niemi left Citibank and went to Italy, many of those who knew her believed the rumors that she had had a nervous breakdown or was otherwise "going off the deep end." It is true: She was in pain. But she was not breaking down—she was breaking *out* of a constricting job and breaking *through* her own lack of confidence. Although her story may be more vivid and dramatic than others, it is being repeated in infinite variations by thousands of others as they enter the second half. How these men and women decided to spend their talents and energies will not only determine their professional future, but will also influence the quality of all our lives.

As a vice-president at a Chicago advertising agency, which he proudly calls "one of the largest in the world," Donald Marrs's self-interviewing process began in the early 1970s, when he was offered an extraordinary career opportunity. The head of his agency asked him to help the top brass of General Motors craft a major advertising campaign that would help GM sell large gas-guzzling cars despite the pressure of the oil crisis. Quietly, without making waves, Donald turned it down. He heard the voice again when he was overseeing the creative development of an ad campaign for Philip Morris, shortly after he had quit smoking to protect his own health.

But Donald was not a crusader. He enjoyed his work, or at least he thought he did. He was a practical man. He had risen through the ranks and had been rewarded with financial incentives, and all his net worth was tied up in the company. He was in midlife, married (unhappily but loyally) with two children. If he left, where would he go? How would he support his family? What would he do? Although he heard the voices within himself questioning the value of his work, he was no fool. He was not going to throw away everything just to be a martyr to a cause. So he waited, hoping the voice calling him would simply go away.

But then, out of thirty-six offices around the world and over two thousand employees in their Chicago offices, twelve people were promoted to vice-president, and Donald was one of them. "I'd worked hard all these years, and this was the day one of the prizes I had been waiting impatiently for was finally to arrive. I had waited for this the way a high school athlete awaits his first monogram, or a senior officer anticipates his gold stars. . . . It had been a long trip, starting when I was a kid drawing pictures of cows in the fields, continuing as I worked my way through art school, and now culminating with my making it to the forticth floor of advertising. I felt like I had proven something to someone, but I couldn't remember who."

Having received the boon of success, he felt its double edge. It was liberating, "like planting a flag at the top of the corporate mountain." But as he sauntered up to the bar in the executive club on the top floor of their skyscraping offices, Donald could not help feeling struck by its "vague irrelevance." As he later tried to put into words what had made the moment so unsettling, he settled on the metaphor of mortality. "I had a nagging feeling that I wasn't going to be with these people much longer," he wrote, "as if I were seeing the group from a distance, and they were a mere memory. It must be what a premonition of death is like, a view of a picture that no longer has you in it." As his responsibilities increased, so did his inner tensions. Combined with the slow unraveling of his marriage, his feelings of professional homelessness bred an intensifying anxiety. He coped by taking a couple of Valiums before important meetings and by stopping by the bar after work.

A few months later on a business trip to Minneapolis, he and his creative team had prepared a pitch for Pillsbury, one of their major clients. With storyboards starring the famous Pillsbury Doughboy under his arm, he led his team into the crucial meeting. As his turn to make his agency's presentation approached, he felt nervous. He always did. But he assumed that, as always, he would find the right words to say.

> I opened my mouth, but instead of my voice growing stronger, it started weak and stayed weak. What I was saying sounded foreign to me, and ideas that had been important earlier were now dimming as I spoke. Finally my words trailed off into silence. My mouth dried up, thick with cottony phlegm. My shirt soaked with sweat, and the light in the room darkened to gray impressions.
>   I couldn't remember what I wanted to say. I couldn't even remember why I was there. And as I turned to look at the storyboards, they had no meaning either. My mind had been wiped clean.[1]

For a moment, Donald thought it might just be a bad dream. But then he saw mouths drop open, faces turning white. One of his team tried awkwardly to make a joke, but nobody laughed. Donald was frozen, helpless. No one knew what to do, he recalls, "because, after all, it was *my* meeting." Mercifully, the head of the Pillsbury team offered him a cup of coffee. Donald nodded and sank into his chair. He felt his

sweat-soaked shirt sticking to his chest. He tried unsuccess-
fully to swallow. When the coffee was handed to him, his
hands were shaking so much that he could barely get the cup
to his lips. He knew his old voice was gone.

Now Donald had no choice. He had to listen to this new
inner voice, which had been trying to get his attention. To
his credit, Donald followed his calling—and it led him to
change his career, his home, his marriage, and his
worldview. The man who lost his voice not only found it, but
as the heartwarming response to his book *Executive in Passage* underscores, he became a model for other executives
beginning their quests. He started his own small marketing
firm, using the skills he had learned in the first half, to build
a new career with more integrity in the second. "It began
simply with my trying to merge my ideals with my business,"
Donald told me, "but it went on and became a deep, ongoing search. It wasn't aligned with any dogma or anything. It
was just a natural unfolding, a process of maturation."

But if it's natural, I asked him, why doesn't everyone
break out of their occupational straitjackets?

"We're told that we quit growing," Donald replied bluntly
"but we don't."[2]

Transforming "Success":
From Ladder to Double Helix

In *The Heroine's Journey,* Maureen Murdock calls experiences such as Jan's and Donald's early career achievements
the "illusory boon of success." Whatever form this success
may take—an academic degree, a promotion, a spouse and
children and home—it makes us think that we are on the
road to achieving our goals.[3]

But then, the bottom falls out. We discover that our success is illusory. As evidenced by the title of Murdock's book,
second half career crises are not limited to male executives.
They haunt both men and women who reach the point

when, as Ram Dass describes it, "you can no longer justify your existence with achievements. . . . When you think you have won and find that you really haven't won anything, you start to experience the dark night of the soul."[4] We realize that we were successful in only one dimension of our lives. But in another dimension, we are still waiting to be born. To understand this dimension, we need another image of success.

Nothing has been more deeply ingrained in most of us than the old-fashioned image of a ladder. Father and son, mother and daughter, we cling to it. Step by step, we climb the rungs. Many climb up only a small distance; some rise quite high; a few reach the top. As a young person on the lower rungs, there was no question which way was up or down, no question who was above whom, and no question that higher was better than lower. But by the time we reach the second half, our sense of professional geography is more complex. Now higher up on the ladder, we can see farther. From this elevation, success no longer looks the same.

Even the covers of business magazines are now heralding the obsolescence of the ladder. "Farewell, Fast Track" blared a *Business Week* cover story, which proceeded to describe a scenario that corporate ladder-climbers know only too well. Having reached a median age of thirty-three, the 81 million baby boomers are beginning to "clog the ranks of management." Not only are there more employees grasping for the next rung up the ladder, there are fewer rungs. Middle-management ranks are thinning: One of every four such positions have been eliminated since 1980. Consequently, the "slow track blues" has become an epidemic. One recent survey of corporate management conducted by the recruiting firm Korn/Ferry International found that 70 percent were dissatisfied with the level of success they had achieved. No wonder American business is searching for ways to help managers "adjust to life in the slow lane."[5]

"There is a grudging awareness and acknowledgment that

there is a slowing down, that organizations are flatter, and there are fewer levels to go to," says Harold E. Johnson, Korn/Ferry's managing vice-president. "The younger managers I see are not very happy about it." Echoes a *New York Times* report: "Success in American business normally means scaling the ladder to the executive suite. But today more and more of the nation's leading corporations are encouraging executives to step off the fast track and convincing even business school graduates they can find rewards and happiness in lateral mobility."[6]

In management jargon, this is a polite way of saying that an employee has reached a professional dead end. The chances of going higher are slim. For those who are part of the demographic bulge of people born from 1945 to 1965, there is simply no way that all of them can keep moving up the career ladder until retirement. Somebody has to stop climbing. Cheryl Smith, director of career management at Pacific Gas & Electric, voices the employer's viewpoint succinctly: "We're trying to get out in front of this before we have tons and tons of people who are dissatisfied. We're saying: 'Wait a minute, wait a minute. It's OK to move laterally.' "[7]

But how does one move laterally on a ladder? Obviously, on a conventional ladder, it is impossible. So *Business Week* used as its cover illustration for the "Fast Track" story a bizarre drawing of a ladder that had no rungs at the top. Instead, rungs in the middle extended laterally. The employee can still move, but not up and down—only sideways.

It is not just demography, but also psychology and biography, that is causing the traditional ladder image to become obsolete. Life stories like Jan Niemi's or Donald Marrs's simply do not fit on ladders. Contemporary knowledge of the human mind and spirit underscores that many men and women in the second half of life are seeking something more, and deeper, than promotions to the next rung. As a page-one story in *The New York Times* business section reported, the loss of meaning is happening not only to billion-aires and millionaires but to ordinary mortals who are many rungs from the top.[8] So before we think in terms of a "lad-der" of success, let us be aware of what is wrong with that image.

The ladder image rigs the score. Money is not the only, or even the best, way to keep score. Once beyond poverty and hardship, money is *not* success. The more you have, the less it is a useful guide.

The ladder image implies success is just a step away. But it's not just around the corner. It's not even around the *next* corner. Because success is not a destination; it's a path. Find-ing our path is the key. Then every step is part of the pro-cess. Let go of the illusion of arrival. Love the journey.

Not going up, or going down, means you are going the wrong way. On the contrary, it is a vital part of our path. Accept mistakes and failures. Make them your guideposts. Mark the trail so others can take heed, but do not strive to eliminate all failures. They can teach us lessons that success never can.

If you've seen one ladder, you've seen them all. If you be-lieve that, you've lost the ball game before the umpire has yelled "Play ball!" Better to get lost than to follow someone else's path too far. No one else's path is just right for you. Although struggling through underbrush is tough, it is better than a well-worn path that leads to *somebody else's* idea of success.

The faster you climb, the higher you'll go. Perhaps. But this fast-track philosophy is also a recipe for burnout. If you go too fast, you actually may lose time—and more. If you exceed your own natural pace, you see less—and get lost more often. You also may find yourself alone because you have left your companions in your dust. Put simply, profes-sional success and its material rewards are only one dimen-sion of progress. The more we achieve in this dimension, the less it will matter in the second half of life. Indeed, we must let go of the illusion that the next rung will bring us happiness.

To replace the static, one-dimensional image of the ladder, I have found no alternative more compelling than the

double helix, the key to life itself. It resembles two intertwined staircases, held together by a series of flexible but strong bonds. One of the stairways symbolizes the external, visible world of achievement, accomplishment, and reward. The other symbolizes the internal, invisible world of feeling, relationship, and service. Pulled apart, either of these stairways alone is incomplete. Taken together, these two interconnected paths to the heavens strengthen and enrich each other—and the world.

In contrast to the ladder, the double helix symbolizes that *something else* is going on beside, beneath, and above our careers. No one would ever expect a child to stay in first grade for forty years. Yet somehow adults are often expected to stay in one job, or on one ladder, for decades. We have very little understanding of the unfolding that occurs during the more than half a century of work life that follows adulthood. Few institutions encourage us to change and grow professionally. On the contrary, most conspire to keep us where we are. The second stairway of the double helix is our reminder that there is a vital dimension of life *below* the "bottom line," a world of meaning that accountants cannot measure and contracts cannot define.

The transition from the ladder to the helix, however, is not automatic. If the only sense of direction we have is up-and-down our own ladder, leaving the ladder imagery will naturally trigger fears of getting lost or falling off. But those fears, if honored, can be our most valuable guide. They are signs that the underdeveloped parts of ourselves are about to awaken.

So listen to the voice, or voices, telling you it is time for a change. Listen to their tone, their cadence, their nuance. (Is it the voice of fear, offering you a way to escape? Or the voice of courage, challenging you to take a vitally important new challenge?) Distinguish between these voices so that you know which are there to befriend you, and which to distract you. Just because we hear a voice does not mean it should be followed. Our challenge is to decide which of them to heed, and when. And this requires taking stock of our lives.

Midlife Career Change, Part 1: Taking Stock

No one had worked harder throughout his life to stay professionally alive and growing than John Esty. After leaving the air force at the end of the Korean War, he proceeded to change professional venues almost every decade of his life. While staying within the framework of education, he spent a decade as a college dean, then head of a secondary school, until at fifty he found himself president of the National Association of Independent Schools. After a decade in that post, he knew it was again time to move on. According to conventional wisdom (as well his finances), it was too soon for him to retire, but too late for him to start a new conventional career. Besides, John felt that he had more lives to live.

However, his inner voices were not telling him what these new lives were. So he stayed put, uncertain when—or whether—he would ever make his move. A crucial turning point came when John attended the hundredth anniversary of the secondary school he had headed during the turbulent sixties. To his surprise, a building was being dedicated in his honor. As the plaque was unveiled with his name etched in stone, he felt overwhelmed. It was fulfilling to be recognized at last for the contribution he had made. But at the end of the ceremony, one person after another came up to him and, with the best of intentions, congratulated him.

"It's so nice that you're still alive," said one.

"You're not even dead yet," said another.

"Ah, John, it's so wonderful that they didn't wait till you were gone," said a third.

Driving home from the dedication ceremony, John felt dazed. The day's event, which he might have assumed would bring him joy, left him feeling queasy. He felt as if he had somehow overstayed his welcome. Things were happening to him now that were supposed to happen only to dead men. He had the surreal feeling that he had just attended his own funeral.

What do you do after your funeral? John wondered. It was a question that made his mind reel and forced him to take stock of what he wanted to give to, and get from, his work. It made him seek his calling once again.

Taking stock means recognizing that our time is finite, the second half of our lives is a gift, and our responsibility is to listen for our calling. As Murray Stein puts it, "I cannot specify what the gift of the soul to you will be at midlife. I

can only suggest that, when it is presented, it be received." [9]
We are not talking here about a calculated repositioning of
yourself in the career marketplace. We are not referring to
the free-wheeling, self-centered "yuppie" worship of maxi-
mizing salary and profit participation above all else. These
cerebral career projections are often conceived as if a human
life could be reduced to a business plan.

The rite of passage we are exploring is *not* merely a shift
from one desk to another. As Joseph Campbell put it so
powerfully: "The call rings up the curtain, always, on a mystery of transfiguration. The familiar life horizon has been
outgrown; the old concepts, ideals and emotional patterns
no longer fit; the time for *passing the threshold* is at hand."[10]
On a deeper, mythic level, this is what is usually occurring
when we seek midlife career change. We are not just switching jobs; we are pursuing our calling. And this requires passing across a threshold into a deeper dimension of ourselves.

Listening for deeper voices, drawing visual images of life's
complexities, imagining inner awakenings—all this is easier
to say than to do. Many of us think we are being "called,"
but everyone can make a mistake—particularly if we are
taking ourselves too seriously. One day, pulling into the
parking lot of the Baptist church in Wilmer, Texas, Bill Moyers recalled that this was the very church where as a young
man he heard a voice inside him urge him to go into the
ministry. Responding to the call, he had enrolled in the
Southwestern Baptist Theological Seminary and was or-
dained as a Baptist minister. But now, after more than a
quarter century in politics and the media, Moyers chuckles
at his naïveté.

"I thought it was a call to the ministry," he said. "But it
turned out to be a wrong number."[11]

But was it really a wrong number? Were those years in the
ministry a mistake? Or were they in fact preparing Moyers
for the second half of his life, a time when he would reach an
audience far larger, and far more effectively, than most of

his seminary classmates? In fact, I believe it was the *right* number after all. Training for the traditional ministry prepared Moyers for the modern telecommunications pulpit that he has occupied with such extraordinary distinction and integrity.

Clearly, listening for the Call, and decoding it, requires all our intelligence and intuition. It does not happen one day, and then—poof!—we forever after have our voice. On the contrary, the quest for a true calling must be renewed and deepened throughout our lives.

If we do not begin to take stock sooner than retirement, we will find ourselves adrift at sixty-five. Many eyes will then turn to you expecting that, as if by magic, you will suddenly have hobbies, travel plans, volunteer activities, or other new challenges and diversions. But from where will these interests spring? What seeds have been planted? In what soil have they taken root? In our forties or fifties, has rainwater or sunlight nourished them?

Thrown overnight from workaholism to leisure-mania, we will understandably feel completely disoriented. If we follow the path of cruise boats and bridge games, we may soon suffer from what Eda LeShan calls the "retirement blues." But if we refuse to be "put out to pasture" and recommit ourselves to working just as hard as before, we may get a bad case of the "no retirement blues." (As Alex Comfort quips, "Two weeks is the ideal length of time to retire.") But the real challenge is not to choose between the two extremes of work-as-usual and retirement but to combine the vocational and nonvocational stairways of the double helix in ways that further our quest for wholeness at this vitally important turning point in our lives.[12]

For some, what has been missing in the first half is ambition, and so the second half calls forth a deeper dedication to work and achievement. But for the vast majority, the first half was a time when we overidentified with work. After interviewing 230 successful career people, psychologist

Douglas LeBier concluded that most of them had lost their identity in their career. Indeed, for some people, identity and job were so enmeshed that LaBier found, "They are almost equivalent." Unfortunately, this is not a conscious, purposeful expression of oneself through work but rather a subordination of the self to its demands. As a result, a new cadre of therapists is emerging who specialize with analyzing not our family neuroses, but our work traumas.[13]

Idealists—usually with a spiritual orientation, or a relatively high income, or both—encourage us to find our calling without regard for any reward to be gained or any fame to be acquired. Only when we have freed ourselves from outer influences of all such outer considerations, according to the idealists, can we hear the inner voice that tells us clearly what to do. Practically speaking, however, freedom from such external pressure is hard to obtain in the second half of life. We have responsibilities that cannot be so easily thrown off. So we have to find a way of hearing our inner voice while still in the fray.

Nevertheless, the idealists have a point. If our voice is drowned out by the siren of reward or fame or by the overpowering drumbeat of raw ambition, our true calling will elude us. This is why the second half is so crucial—the siren and the drumbeat may have stilled, allowing the inner voice at last to be heard. My father, for example, kept the same job from the time he got out of the army to the time he "retired" (that is, was told by his corporation that he was no longer allowed to work). But what he expressed through his work as a medicinal chemist throughout these decades changed dramatically. "In my thirties and forties, I worked to prove myself, to advance in my career, to compete against my colleagues, to assure my place in the corporate world," he told me. "But in my fifties and sixties, when I did my best work, those earlier motivations didn't consume me anymore. Now I wanted to do something worthwhile. That's why I focused my energies on the cancer field." Consequently, as his son, I received something that money cannot buy: I saw my father find his calling.

Although taking stock may lead us to seek a second half career change, that outcome, as my father's career illustrates, is not preordained. Whether to remain in one's old job or switch to a new one is secondary, because it is possible to find a new voice within the same job description. An editor at a major New York publishing company, for example, found in her early thirties that she was feeling the need to express a different side of herself—one more connected to the community around her. The spark inside her was lit when she learned that thousands of books were destroyed by companies like hers simply because warehouses were overstocked. Yet the public schools were so underfunded that many schoolchildren rarely had a book to call their own. She proposed a program that, if implemented by the mayor's office, would assure that these surplus books would not be tossed into the incinerator but instead given to New York City's book-starved schools.

Similarly, Jim Hubbard was a successful commercial photographer who enjoyed his craft. But placing his work in museums and magazines did not express a part of himself that wanted to serve the world around him. One day he began working with a homeless boy, providing him with a camera and teaching him to record his world. Before long, Jim was working with a group of homeless children, empowering them through the magic of photography to observe their lives—and to share them with others. Their unforgettable images were first exhibited in New York City and eventually found their way into the pages of *Life* magazine.[14] So Jim did not only observe his world; he helped to improve it.

Such stories are not as dramatic as ones in which the heroine leaves Citibank to go to work at a museum in Italy, or the hero leaves his ad agency to find his true calling in California. That such romantic journeys may captivate does not mean that staying in banking or advertising is necessarily wrong. After all, for some people change itself is cowardice. Rather than persevere and finish anything, they are already moving on to the next great adventure (and usually leave a mess behind for others to clean up). Perseverance and continuity are vital; without them, "change" and "growth" are nothing more than polite misnomers for narcissism and escape.

So let us not portray those who embark on career change as either heroes or villains. There is no single right answer. Jan Niemi was listening to her inner voice when she decided that continuing to work at Citibank, despite its generous pay and opportunity for travel, was killing a part of her. But for a struggling artist, alone and penniless in his garret, going to work at Citibank might be just what he needs to bring new energy into his life. The key quality that is missing as we begin the second half of our lives is wholeness: regenerating the parts of ourselves that have been un-, or under-, developed in the first half. It is those parts of us that have been lost in the shadows that are now seeking the light. When these parts of ourselves speak out, as Daniel Levinson observes, our challenge is to listen more *attentively* to these voices and then to decide more *consciously* what part they will play in the second half of our lives. Here is a simple exercise that may help you do this.

Draw a circle in the middle of a page. Inside the circle, write down which qualities you are able to express through your current work. Now, on a separate piece of paper, write the qualities that you want to express through your work in the second half of your life. Lay the two pages side by side. One by one, decide which of the new qualities that you want in your life can be expressed through your current work. Write them *inside* the circle. Those you cannot express through your current work, write down *outside* the circle. Put your Taking Stock diagram up on a wall, in a place where you will see it regularly. Live with it for a while. Move words around as your thinking clarifies. It will help you decide how, and when, to make your move.

Getting ready to make your move, however, requires taking stock of something much more concrete. Sooner or later, we have to decide what to take along and what to leave behind; what to acquire and what to give away. Taking too much weighs you down so heavily with people and possessions that you are exhausted and your supplies depleted long before you reach your goals. Taking too little leaves you isolated, hungry, and empty-handed before you get to where you're going. The only way to avoid these twin dangers is to think clearly about what you need to take with you on the quest.

If you find yourself with too much clutter, you are not alone. Many people in the second half are reaching what Peter Siris, who analyzes retail and consumer trends for UBS Securities, calls "a fundamentally different stage" of our lives. "The party's over," says Siris point-blank. "The baby boomers, who led the spending binge of the past three decades, are reaching midlife." According to Siris, as well as others who chart the interplay between economics and demographics, those who are entering the second half are changing their spending patterns fundamentally. "It's not just that they're cutting back. They are trading down. For thirty years, retailers have upscaled ahead of the consumer. Now, the consumer may be *down*scaling ahead of the retailer."[15] Particularly for the part of the baby-boom generation that took for granted the expanding postwar economy of affluence, it is hard to come down to earth again. (As one chastened yuppie confides: "You come to realize that you will never achieve the standard of living you had in junior high school."[16])

The question of what we need for our journey through the second half of life is best answered, not by recalling other times or other places, but by imagining ourselves setting out on a journey into the wilderness. "When your pack is fully

loaded, it will represent your attachment to the life you are
leaving behind," write two veteran leaders of "vision
quests," Steven Foster and Meredith Little. "All of us require some material goods in order to stay alive. The question (and a very *big* question for Americans) is: *How much?*
The weight of your pack is the weight of your 'karma' (what
you must pay as a consequence of living the way you do).
Do you really want to carry that much?"[17]

Since the more we have, the more we have to carry, entering the second half often requires lightening our load—not
just physically but also psychologically. Like trekkers into
the wilderness, those of us on a journey into the second half
inevitably ask ourselves: What do I *really* need?

"It's a simple question," points out Susan Valaskovic, a
member of the National Organization of Professional Organizers, "but most people have never thought about it. Dis-
organization is just an aftereffect."

"Aftereffect?" I asked her, slow to catch her meaning.

"Yes," she said patiently, in the tone of someone who has
retrained many objectaholics. "Possessions are just an aftereffect of who you are and where you are going. When people don't have a strong center, often they think they *are* their
possessions. The stuff around them becomes more important
than who they are. In the later stages of life, people often get
stuck because they have too much stuff around them. The
reason people get old is because they get weighed down by
all their stuff."[18]

Susan and her colleagues are not Puritans. They do not try
to make their clients live like Mother Teresa. They do not
advise their clients, as Jesus advised Zacchaeus, to give half
their belongings to the poor. But they do agree with what
Jesus said in Luke 12:15: "A person's life is not made up of
things he owns, no matter how rich he may be." They help
people find balance—not the self-sacrificing, often self-destructive, asceticism of the rootless vagabond, and not the
voracious, all-consuming shopaholism of the overconsumer,

but a natural, personal balance between the material and the spiritual. Finding this "voluntary simplicity," the "avoidance of exterior clutter, of many possessions irrelevant to the chief purpose of life," can not only lighten our step but sometimes even en-lighten our minds.[19]

Again, another brief stock-taking exercise may be useful. Before continuing, draw another circle in the middle of another blank page. Inside the circle, write the possessions that you need on your quest; list those you don't need outside the circle. Don't give away or sell anything—at least, not yet. Just put the diagram up somewhere and live with it for several weeks. When you're sure you've got it right, *then* take action. The most common outcome is that you discover that you possess many things you do not need, but that there are a few tools for the second half that you urgently do need. It is time, therefore, for a different kind of housecleaning, one that requires going not only into your closets but into your soul.

Midlife Career Change, Part 2: Making Your Move

Even after taking stock of where we are professionally, making a move from one career to another is hard to do alone. We are too close to our subject. It is therefore important to identify our allies—those who will support the changes we are trying to make in our work life. The ally serves as a comforter—*and* a confronter. Allies may be real, physical beings, like a mate or friends; or inner voices that come from deep, psychic sources. You will have both kinds of allies before your quest for a calling is over.

Writers or teachers who do not know us personally can offer wise counsel in their books or workshops. But since they do not leave the page or the podium, they are not true allies. What we need at this point in our journey are flesh-and-blood companions who are committed to our personal welfare and growth. To protect yourself while making job changes and career shifts, you may understandably find yourself not disclosing thoughts and feelings (as well as interviews and explorations) to co-workers or even mentors. While keeping sensitive information to yourself is important, it is equally important to have trusted allies who have the whole truth, as best you know it. Otherwise you will find yourself without informed counsel during one of the most difficult times on your quest.

One of my best allies has been my friend Ken Druck, a psychologist, management consultant, and author whom I have known for years but with whom I had rarely spent much time. Between his career and mine, his two daughters and my three sons, his out-of-town speaking engagements and my business trips, there was no room left for friendship. We never managed to snatch more than a few hours together every couple of months.

When we finally found ourselves on an overnight trip together, we realized that we never gave a second thought to the time-consuming trips that contributed to our income or our careers. But to find even thirty-six hours for friendship alone required extraordinary discipline. As we began peeling away the layers of the first halves of our lives, we recognized that putting success before friendship was something we had learned a long, long time ago.

"In school, starting about the second grade, I developed learning problems," Ken recalled. "I didn't think well visually. As a result, I fell further and further behind. Other kids would answer questions that I simply couldn't understand. The teacher would call on me, and I would hardly ever know the answer. I felt stupid, and foolish, and embarrassed. By the time I reached junior high school, I had learned how to compensate for my disability. I did better in school and became a star athlete as well. My self-confidence improved. But those years left their mark. I had developed a compulsion to prove myself, to prove that I was as good as or better than other kids. It was a compulsion that would later become a strange kind of success addiction."

As I listened, I realized that I was part of Ken's problem. "I was one of those kids who always got good grades and made fun of kids like you," I confided. "When I was doing schoolwork, I always felt competent, smart, in control. What a contrast that was to how I felt at home! There I felt the confusion of living in a household that was often tense and lonely. So I tried to find refuge in achievement. I tried to spend more time in my head and less in my heart. I cut myself off from my feelings. That's how I persuaded myself I was happy. That's how I made myself feel like a success."

The time together was so healing that Ken and I pledged ourselves to becoming allies, helping each other stay true to our calling. We promised to support each other to stop letting work squeeze out the other things in life that mattered more, and to help each other make the career decisions that truly served our own unfolding.

Don't assume your ally must be someone new. It may be someone you already know but take for granted, like your physician. John, a vice-president at a major TV network, was being run ragged by his boss, who criticized him at every turn. John became tense, began losing sleep, and developed high blood pressure. "I was losing weight, smoking . . . going to hell in a handbasket," he told a group of us one night, during a meeting in Hollywood focusing on the stresses of careers in the industry. "But finally I opened up to my doctor about it. He looked at me and said: 'Come on, John. Your boss is just another guy. Just another guy like you. He's not God.' As soon as he said that, something snapped. I knew he was right. I knew there was a force higher than the head of my department." Fortunately, John's story, like Hollywood stories should, has a happy ending: "My boss got canned; I got promoted. And the rest, as they say, is history."

What John's doctor did is what allies do best. They tell the truth. They can help us clarify our vocational choices *before* we jeopardize our current job or begin seeking alternatives. This clarity will increase the chances that we actually know what we are looking for—and where to find it.

Ultimately, of course, no ally can teach us as well as our own experience. If you think you can enrich your current job or find a better one, there is ultimately only one way to find out—test reality. Having gained some perspective and having grounded that new perspective in strong alliances, you are now prepared to try out some small concrete changes. These first changes should be probes, experiments. You are testing several new approaches—to work, to relationships, to relaxation—in order to see what works.

If you throw yourself too quickly and at too great a risk into a new endeavor, it can overwhelm you. You may feel such urgency about it working out that you feel it *has* to work, in which case, you aren't experimenting at all. You have just moved from one cage to the next. So explore several alternatives. "You don't have to jump off a cliff," advises Neil Bull of the Center for Interim Studies. "You can tiptoe out of what you're doing into something new. See what's out there without burning a lot of bridges."

This time of reality-testing is the time to make your mistakes. As jazz saxophonist Coleman Hawkins said, "If you don't make mistakes, you aren't really trying."[20] Mistakes are how we move past our old limits and enter new territory. To succeed, you first have to dare to fail. This cliché is worth repeating because we are constantly bombarded with success stories and rarely told about the "failures" that fertilized them. Everyone knows about the phenomenal success of *Megatrends* and *Megatrends 2000,* written by business consultant John Naisbitt and his wife Patricia Aburdene. But few know that, before these best-selling books were published, Naisbitt's business consulting venture failed and he filed for bankruptcy.[21]

Most people do not realize how often one finds, behind an

extraordinary success, a dazzling failure. In his first half of his life, Bill Pilder (who is now fifty-two) took his vows as a Roman Catholic priest, fully intending to dedicate his life to the church. But by the age of twenty-seven, he had left the priesthood. He had "failed" as a priest, but that was only the prelude to finding his own voice. After intensive Jungian analysis and self-searching ("as is often the case," Pilder says, "it took me in directions that were in no way foreseen"), he fell into a position with a small company, and for the last fifteen years has been working as a career counselor with large and midsize companies. Since then, he has helped hundreds of men and women pursue their true calling through a unique blend of dreamwork, counseling and career planning.

"Joseph Campbell's phrase 'Follow your bliss' has become a kind of icon in our culture," Pilder told me recently. "But to find a practical way to follow your calling is extremely difficult. Much of organizational life is a spiritual wasteland. It's a wasteland because people are not allowed to be in touch with their personal life. They can express who they are away from work, but most that I meet in corporate life do not feel they can express that connection at work. They feel they've got to get out of corporate life. I think this is not only dangerous for them but also for these organizations and our culture."[22]

While experts advise us to dare to fail, to make mistakes, and to take risks, we must not forget that our neck is at risk, not theirs. With the help of our allies, we must decide what level of risk we want to take—and when is the right time to do it. Sixty-three-year-old Richard Bolles, whose job-hunting book *What Color Is Your Parachute?* has helped hundreds of thousands of people find their calling, stresses strongly with people in the second half of life that risk is a personal choice. "There are manageable risks and unmanageable ones," Bolles counsels. "Taking a shower is a manageable one. Stepping out of a window on the top floor of a ten-story building and hoping to survive is an unmanageable risk." Moral: Taking risks does not mean being foolhardy.[23]

Testing reality is not the same as ignoring reality. You will get no medals for going broke, and you will not be considered a hero for becoming unemployed. What makes the decision so difficult is that there are times in life when, paradoxically, seeking security is dangerous. Since companies are now cutting away deadwood and many are being hit by "workquakes," just staying put may not be safe at all. As Bolles points out, "coasting" can be one of the riskiest strategies, particularly late in one's career.

Our culture is not kind to people without money, particularly older people. The notion, "Do what you love, the money will follow," is catchy. But even Marsha Sinetar, who wrote the book by that title, admits that the phrase oversimplifies. It does not explain *when* the money will follow. "There is a waiting period" between finding a calling and making money, Sinetar acknowledges, which is "different for different people."[24] But how long actually is it? And how, in the second half, do we feed ourselves and our families in the meantime? Practical, day-to-day realities compel us to move beyond abstract strategies for job change before we can be sure that the risks are worth taking. Only then can we make our move.

But how do we know when the moment comes? Sometimes it hits like a thunderclap. You will feel as filmmaker Spike Lee (who made the movie *Do the Right Thing)* put it about his chosen craft: "I feel that's what I was put on earth to do."[25] But for most of us, lightning does not strike. On the contrary, the voice inside calling us is almost drowned out by the clamor of competing voices saying: "I have responsibilities. . . . I need a constant cash flow. . . . I'd better be realistic." This is the time when your efforts to take stock of your situation and to identify your allies proves vitally important. This is the time to tune out the clamor and listen to the inner voice.

That voice is telling you that your job is not right for you now. Not anymore. You need something different. You need a different way of living. Other parts of you want to be expressed. One way or another, you need a new way of making a living (that is, making a life). You want to be fired (that is, freed). You have to quit (that is, begin). You have to step down (that is, step forth). You have to resign (that is, enlist). You have to leave (that is, arrive).

These parenthetical reframings are not elegant. But we simply cannot allow the old language to be used unchallenged. The old language is loaded in favor of staying employed and against moving on. Who would not want to be considered a "loyal" employee rather than a disloyal one? Who would not want to be praised for "persevering" and "hanging in there" rather than "bailing out" or, even worse, "chickening out"? This is what makes letting go of the old so hard: The new is not yet in place. This is where the risk is greatest, and the reward most elusive. But our calling will elude us until we let go and jump.[26]

No one would have ever guessed that when Riane Eisler, a little refugee girl from war-torn Europe, found her voice, she would have a vital message for the postwar generations entering the second half in the 1990s. She had grown up with only tragic heroines (from Joan of Arc to Madame Bovary and Anna Karenina), who died before they reached the age of forty. Like so many immigrant children, she was starstruck from an early age and wrote stage plays that were never produced. She became a lawyer in the entertainment industry, then a Hollywood adviser to the stars. She too "had it made"—except that she was desperately unhappy. "I found myself in my mid-thirties," she recalls, "without a script for the rest of my life."[27]

She was desperately dissatisfied with her life because her career was not a calling. It seemed empty. "Success" meant becoming a senior partner, which to her meant helping these very wealthy Hollywood people "count their money and massage their egos." Riane didn't want to do that. In fact, she says, "what had previously seemed glamorous now repelled me."

Following years of anguish, she quit her job, ended her marriage, and overcame her addiction to smoking, all in the period of a few months. "I was driven by desperation," she says now. "I had two small children. I was violating every conceivable norm. Finding your own voice, your own vision, is extremely difficult. All we have is the internalized voice of the external authority. You know that you are going to get severely punished if you don't listen to that internalized voice. You have heard that you must be God-fearing. Or, if you are a woman, you must fear your husband—or impoverishment, if you leave him."

Despite her fears, Riane let go. She and her husband divorced, and she left the law firm. Then, while trying to be a single mother and start her own practice, her parents died. Out of the crucible of this pain and loss, she found her voice. Through her speaking and writing, she began sharing her image of true male-female partnership. She spoke in a language that women (and many men) could understand. She realized that her pain was not just her own. It was the pain of breaking loose from a social structure that pitted men and women against each other. "All this pain, I don't think it's inevitable. The kind of pain we have to go through in order to be true to higher, more evolved and empathic selves, is not natural. It's more painful than it has to be because it threatens our social structure. So I am not saying 'Go find pain. It's good for you.' I don't believe that. It's there because of the old scripts that we carry with us."

But, she adds, blindly throwing out the old will not work. "Just switching to a new job, a new relationship, is not the answer. From my own experience, there was no question of staying in that job or in that marriage. Then divorce and job relocation were not as simple as they are today. So I had to be clear. I gave it years and years of thought. The kind of decision that I made doesn't take as much agonizing now as it did then. Now it's easier. That's good—but it also means we have to be careful."

Her advice to others is the same she gave herself: "Take the risk. Sometimes you have to let go of something before knowing where it leads. I didn't have a clue that I would be doing what I'm doing now. Have faith that what seems like disconnected pieces will in fact turn out to be part of a puzzle. I spent a year while a suburban homemaker reading ancient mystery cults. There seemed to be no rhyme or reason for doing this. But years later it tied directly into the archaeology for *The Chalice and the Blade*"—her ground-breaking book calling for true partnership between men and women.

In a workplace built for men, women often face particularly difficult obstacles in finding their own voices. They are understandably tempted to adopt the lexicon and tone of their male counterparts rather than find their own. My sister, Dr. Jeannette Gerzon, a career counselor at MIT, recently delivered a talk at Radcliffe College on the challenges women face in working with men. During the talk, she shared a poem she had written called "A Voice":[28]

> Where is her voice?
> Where is the voice with which to speak?
> Where is the voice with which to say the words
> that belong to this one?
> This one who has been unknown.
> This one who has been buried behind the many walls.
> What is her sound?
> For what does she stand and raise the sword of truth?
> To what music does she dance?
>
> Where is this voice that is her voice?

When any of us, man or woman, finds our voice, we become agents of transformation. By finding our voice, we make our contribution, however small or large it may be, to our time. While many of us would prefer to have a long, illustrious obituary rather than one that is short and boring, that is no way to measure a calling. What the obituary reports is our role. Callings belong to the soul.

Trained as an actor to play the many roles that made him famous, Dennis Weaver has articulated better than anyone I know the difference between role and calling. In part, he credits his training as an actor for helping him. "As an actor, you convince yourself that you're someone," he told me as we talked in his home office. "If you're good, you even convince the audience. But inside you know that you are really something more, something else. I may be playing Chester, or McCloud or Buck James—but I know I am really Dennis Weaver. I think the same thing applies to real life. We need to watch out for becoming too attached to things, goals, titles."

Dennis fixed his gaze on me as if he knew how much I needed to hear what he would next say: "You, me, each of us —we are playing a part in this world. I try not to be attached to it anymore. Sure—I'm going to play my part with all the energy, imagination, and skill I can. But I always remember that it is not the inner reality. Where people go wrong is that, the more they get from the world, the more they want. They can never quench their inner thirst. They forget to make the inner search, to learn about their own inner reality."

Dennis is not naive about the harder realities of life. In fact, he dedicates much of his time to dealing with the harsh conditions in which many people live. "I'm involved with a program that feeds more than a hundred thousand people every day because I know going hungry isn't good for you. But happiness also depends on your own attitudes—on what you bring to the world. For most of us, what's missing is not something outside us, but ourselves—our own sense of being, our souls. That's what gives our life balance, a center."

To help you find your center, where your calling will continue to unfold, remember to check the dial on your radio. How long has it been since you've listened to your own station rather than somebody else's? How long has it been since you've interviewed yourself?

You must not only hear the call, but heed it. A calling is not a free ride. The right path may be just as steep and rocky as the wrong ones were. The difference is, this time you are headed where you are meant to go.

Don't decide too quickly that it's a "wrong number." Yes, it may seem like a wrong turn now. It may seem as if you "wasted" your time. But you're not on the mountaintop yet. You can't see the whole terrain. The step you are now taking may turn out to be the most important of your entire journey.

Work isn't everything. Few people on their deathbed say they wish they had spent more time in the office. ("God respects me when I work," wrote the Indian poet Rabindrinath Tagore, "but He loves me when I sing.")

Money isn't everything. It's not even a good way of keeping score. Money measures only what the bank can hold, not the heart. (That's why Thomas Jefferson, in the Declaration of Independence, changed the last word in the phrase from "life, liberty and the pursuit of *property*" to *"happiness."*)

Success isn't everything. (In fact, wrote Arthur Miller in his memoirs, "The quickest road to failure is success.") Neither work, nor money, nor success is what we are seeking. That is, after all, why we are on our quest for wholeness.

5

GROWING WHOLE
The Quest for Meaning

I'm eighty-seven and during the month I've taken GH3 it's made me feel younger and full of vitality. I was worried before that I would have to go to a rest home. Now I'm confident that I won't have to go because of GH3. Thank you.

P., S. Dakota.

Although I am in very good health at age seventy-three, I decided to try GH3 upon the recommendation from a friend who told me that it was the very best thing that ever happened to him. I have been taking it for two months now and I feel even younger than before, especially my sex drive.

J., Washington.

When my GH3 runs out before I reorder I feel down and out. Please rush my order.

Mrs. J. M., Mississippi.
Testimonials from an ad for GH3,
an "anti-aging" formula

We are growing older. How we feel about that process of aging profoundly influences our experience of our lives. Is aging a blessing or a curse? A decline or an ascent? An enemy or a guide? Our answer to these questions is important because in the second half of life, they shape our destiny.

"For me to go under the knife is a scary thing," says an actress who I will call Carol, whose face you have seen often on television. "But I'm sure my time will come. I've always known from the age of twenty-five or so that I'd have work done on me. I would look at older women and think that their lives were over just because they had wrinkles. I'd see two women in their forties out for lunch, having a good time, and I wouldn't understand how they could be happy. After all, they were so old."

Now that Carol is thirty-eight, she finds herself stepping into her own stereotype.

"In your later thirties and forties, people start to look at you differently. The beautiful twenty-five-year-old actress . . . she's full of *potential*. When you're my age, you're not. They might consider you a 'good actor,' but they know you won't be a star." I could have asked her who "they" are, but I know. She means producers, agents, other actors; she means herself. So far, all she has had are a few thousand dollars' worth of collagen injections. She shows me the places on her face and lets me touch them with my forefinger. I could see traces of wrinkles, but only if I leaned up closely, as close as a lover—or a camera.

Carol loves acting and does not regret going into entertainment, but she nevertheless feels the pressure of aging. "The most successful people in the entertainment industry are the plastic surgeons," she says. "It's not just our vanity that keeps them busy. The audience *wants* us to look good.

For them, movies are a mirror. The way they see it, if Liz Taylor still looks good at her age, so do they. There are a lot of women in their forties now who are thinking, 'I still look good. After all, so-and-so is forty-four, and she looks fabulous.' Well, after forty thousand dollars, *of course* she does!

"My best friend Sheryl says her mother has spent her inheritance on her face. Sheryl's so mad that she refuses to spend a penny on cosmetic surgery." Carol pauses, wondering if I get her point. Then, with much more tenderness than when she touched her face, she lays her hand on her stomach. "My C-section scar is what gave birth to my son. I used to think it was ugly, you know, and felt sort of ashamed of it. But as I get older, I sort of like it now."

Since Carol is a strong actress, she is aware there are also positive professional consequences of growing old. Until recently she always played the ingenue, or what she calls "the Juliet role." But now, she tells me, she is looking forward to playing more mature roles, like the middle-aged mother Arkadina in Chekhov's play *The Sea Gull*. "Arkadina is a much more interesting role," Carol muses. "She has such history, such depth. She's not just a young girl—she's a woman."

I admit to being puzzled about how Carol can look forward both to playing a middle-aged woman *and* to getting a face-lift. She laughs at my naïveté. "Even if I play that role, I still don't want to look *old*. I want to look *good*." Clearly the two, in her view, are incompatible. That "looking old" is the opposite of "looking good" is not just Carol's opinion. It is the deeply ingrained bias of the entertainment industry and its consumers—that is, you and me. This is why it is so hard for fine actresses, such as fifty-seven-year-old Shirley MacLaine, to find scripts. "Let me tell you something I've discovered with the scripts I'm getting now," MacLaine complained. "There are parts for twenty, thirty, thirty-five, maybe forty-year-olds, and then there are scripts for women sixty or so." For the women in between, she says, "Nobody knows what to do."[1]

Younging versus Aging:
Behind the Scenes in the Beauty Business

When I ask Carol to introduce me to the doctor who has done the work on her face, she tells me that she sees Dr. Arnold Klein. "He does Madonna, and Cher," she explains. "Remember the Meryl Streep–Shirley MacLaine movie *Postcards from the Edge*? Two men are talking about MacLaine, and one of them says 'She looks so good.' Then the other one says, 'She goes to Dr. Klein. Everybody does.' So he'd be great for you to interview."

"There's no question that changes have occurred since I entered the profession," Dr. Klein, a specialist in collagen injections who is also a professor at UCLA, explains to me a few days later. According to Klein, in 1975 there was no injectable collagen. By the beginning of the 1980s, approximately five thousand people had been injected using a technique that Dr. Klein helped develop. By 1990, the number had risen to half a million, and it is still going up.

"Narcissism has become acceptable. After all, there's no commandment: 'Thou shalt not be narcissistic.' Studies show that people achieve more, and feel better, when they look better. Face-lifts, nose jobs, having your lids done— you don't have to hide your head in shame today if you want to look better. This town is filled with buildings in which people are exercising, trying to look better and live longer. It's become a way of life. So cosmetic surgery has blossomed. It's as acceptable to have your eyelids done as to have your gall bladder removed."

Dr. Klein wants just what his patients want: to stay fit and young-looking. "I'm forty-five. I still want to be a kid. *I* don't want to be old. *You* don't want to be old. So we're redefining what *old* means. We're changing the way we look.

I have a patient who's ninety-four." As if adding a final, irrefutable point, he continues: "Remember, there are a lot people who are single in our age group. They're back in the dating pool. They want to look good. They want to present themselves as well as possible because first impressions are important.

"We're used to looking at ourselves. We see a line form between our eyes, called a frown line. We see a line form at the corner of our mouths, called the drool line. But the reality is not the line. The reality is what the person *thinks* about the line. The reality is not what you look like. It's what you *think* you look like. Now I think a certain degree of narcissism is very healthy. It's having self-respect. It's feeling good about yourself. But taken to an extreme—like anything—it's not good. I try to help my patients differentiate between the healthy and the unhealthy."

Does he ever say no to a patient who wants unnecessary surgery? "Of course. People can be over–cosmetically surgerized. Unfortunately, if I say no, they will go on shopping until they will find someone who'll do it. You shouldn't have to take out a second mortgage to be able to afford a surgical procedure. But there are people who get addicted to surgery. They go too far. You can spend forty or fifty thousand on cosmetic surgery, if you want to. If you're going to spend that much, though, you might as well spend some of it to have your head examined."

Is he concerned about our culture becoming too afraid of aging? "You bet I am. People's lives aren't naturally over when they're old. In Japan, they consider them national treasures. We don't. People don't seem to understand that standards of beauty change. It all depends on how we see things."

Men and women at ever-younger ages are opting for a wide variety of cosmetic interventions. This trend toward early, and possibly premature, surgery concerns even some promoters of such procedures. Dr. John G. Penn, chairman of public education for the American Society for Aesthetic Plastic Surgery, recognizes the danger of moving in with the scalpel too soon. If the skin is still fairly young and taut, stretching it (which is plastic surgery's primary technique) could leave the skin looking unreal, almost glassy in its smoothness. "Some lines, like smile lines, give the face character," Dr. Penn philosophizes. "You don't want to stretch the skin so much that every line, all individuality, is taken away."[2]

Look at my picture on the back cover of this book. See the lines around the eyes; on the forehead; cutting across the cheeks. Which are signs of aging that should be eliminated? Which convey "character" and "individuality"? Which of these crevices merely make me look old—and which of them bear witness to my yearnings and triumphs, my struggles and my sorrows? And who among us has the wisdom of Solomon to lift the scalpel?

Although I do not share Dr. Klein's enthusiasm for cosmetic surgery, I do agree with his view that "it all depends on how we see things." How we see aging, and how our society sees it, is a question that goes to the very heart of our quest for wholeness.

In a laboratory in Milwaukee, housed on the unassuming campus of the Medical College of Wisconsin, an experiment has been unfolding over the past few years that, once again, promises the Fountain of Youth. As of this writing, a synthetic human growth hormone (hGH) has been administered scientifically to more than fifty men. (A much larger, three-year study involving thousands of men and women is about to get under way at St. Thomas Hospital in London.) Unlike the control group, participants in the study who took hGH reported greater strength, reduced body fat and cholesterol levels, and increased lean muscle mass—in short, they look and feel like they did when they were younger. One seventy-two-year-old participant told reporters that wrinkles were disappearing from his face and hands, that he could open jars again for the first time in years, and that he could now enjoy gardening for hours without getting tired.

Although hormones and other strengthening agents such as steroids have been generating controversy for years, the preliminary press release for hGH received a hero's welcome and opened a floodgate of speculation. "Human Growth Hormone Reverses Effects of Aging," trumpeted *The New York Times.* "The Hormone That Makes Your Body Twenty Years Younger," hyped *Longevity* magazine. All articles included the necessary caveats, duly noting that the anti-aging effects were temporary, that there might be increased cancer risks, and that other negative side-effects could not be ruled out. But that did not stop the journalists from using phrases like "bodies moving backward through time," "second youth," and "safe and effective anti-aging formula." The men who were admitted to the study by answering a local newspaper ad, wrote one journalist, "got the chance to do what other people only dream about—retrieve lost youthful vigor."[3]

Another anti-aging wonder drug that has been causing a stir among longevity-watchers is deprenyl, which first came into legal use as a treatment for Parkinson's disease. According to its advocates, including the physician who developed it, deprenyl not only retards the advance of this debilitating disease, it retards aging itself. "We now have a safe, selectively acting drug that for the first time can slow down the most rapidly aging neuronal machinery in our brain," says physician Joseph Knoll, who calculates that taking deprenyl twice a week could add another fifteen to twenty years of normal life, thus making the average lifespan closer to ninety-five than seventy-five. "Now it is stupidity not to take deprenyl after age forty-five."[4]

Among those who agree is Canadian physician Morton Shulman, a former member of parliament who founded Deprenyl Research Limited, which has the Canadian rights to distribute the drug. He is so enthusiastic about deprenyl's anti-aging powers that he takes it regularly, as do many of the company's employees ranging in age from thirty-five to sixty-five. "We're supposed to be an ethical pharmaceutical company," the comptroller, Ed Foster, told me when I checked if the account I had read about this was true. "So it is a little embarrassing for it to be reported that we are taking this for anti-aging purposes."[5]

In our lifetimes, we will see many more reports of anti-aging drugs such as hGH and deprenyl. As time passes, we will have more facts and less hype. Scientists specializing in the relatively new field of biogerontology will find better and better methods for retarding, halting, and perhaps in some ways actually reversing the aging process. And as they do, their scientific breakthroughs will become *our* ethical dilemma. We will have to decide whether to age or to "young." We will have to choose whether to let nature take its course, or whether to intervene to alter that course.

Superficially, the chemistry involved is easy to understand. Certain chemicals in the body have now been correlated with aging. The levels of some of the compounds that promote youthfulness, such as growth hormones, decline as we age. The levels of others that promote aging, such as monoamide oxidase (MAO), increase as we age. So scientists have basically two methods for altering the aging process: artificially increasing the chemicals that keep us young, or artificially blocking or inhibiting the chemicals that make us age.[6]

Clearly this is a step well beyond collagen and cosmetic surgery, hair implants and liposuction. This research could lead to methods, not for making us *look* young, but for making us *stay* young. No doubt they will be expensive and have unintended side-effects. Nevertheless, they will be popular. And you and I will face the choice of whether, or when, to join in the race to find the fountain of youth.

If we invite a medical swordsman to ride in wearing his white coat and improve upon God's work because we consider aging the enemy, a naturally occurring "cancer" to be surgically eliminated, then we are solving one problem and exacerbating another. A medical advance will camouflage a spiritual retreat.

If we join what Eda LeShan refers to as "a mad panic to remain young and gorgeous forever," our waistlines may not sag as much, but our inner life will be in shambles.[7]

An article promoting face-lifts for people under fifty advises baby boomers to use surgery in order to " 'skip' middle age"[8]—as if this period of the life cycle were a disease to be avoided. Our minds can hide from the truth of physical aging and let us pretend that we will be around as long as the Rock of Gibraltar. But our bodies, the flesh of life, will not let us lie so easily. They insist on reminding us of aging. So the solution, according to the scalpel-users, is to change the body, to make it look the way the mind thinks it should.

Even if we spend the remaining decades of our life fighting aging, we know how the war ends. No matter how hard we struggle we are not Men of Steel or Wrinkle-free Women. We are flesh and blood. Unable to win, all we can do is try to forestall losing as long as we possibly can—which is not the point.

The point is: There is a difference between *staying* young and *coming* into your own. Those who wish to stay young may wish to "skip middle age." But those of us who are coming into our own want to live it to the fullest and learn everything it has to teach us.

Why Aging Slowly Is Not Enough

I am waiting in my doctor's office, ready for my annual checkup. I look up on the shelf and see a book about aging. I pull it off the shelf and browse through it. The chapter titles —"Diets to Lighten the Years," "Plans to Keep You Young," "Exercises for Vim and Vigor," "Tips for Beauty and Fitness"—intrigue me. Impressed, I begin reading. The editors have gathered the best, most up-to-date health tips for the second half of life. I leaf eagerly through the book, pleased to have found such a useful resource.

I must have a copy of this book, I think to myself. I check the title. It is called *Aging Slowly.*[9]

In the pit of my stomach, I suddenly feel a dull ache. My reaction to the book sours—but why? Is there something wrong with the title? Making aging more comfortable and more healthful is obviously worthwhile. I responded so positively to the book precisely because it was offering me hope and reassurance about the quality of the second half of life. I certainly don't want to age quickly. So why would the phrase "aging slowly" make me recoil?

I turn to the book's preface to search for clues. The executive editor of the volume writes that it is "full of fresh ideas, practical tips and, best of all—*inspiration.*" Inspiration? That is precisely what I do *not* feel. Imagine a book on plumbing or electrical wiring claiming to offer inspiration. As I leaf through the book, I find informative and useful suggestions about physical self-maintenance—but inspiration? Inspiration to do what? Forestall midriff bulge? Reduce cholesterol levels in the blood? Evade the surgeon's scalpel? Postpone our funeral?

If we view ourselves as a machine, "aging slowly" is an excellent summary of the goals of the second half of life. Viewed as humanoid gizmos, aging *is* meaningless. Of course we want to slow the process down. To a machine, the only purpose is mere functioning: "I operate, therefore I am." Like Hal, the robot in the outer-space drama *2001,* our only goal is to survive as long as possible. Forget having a soul or any such gibberish; our existence revolves around our "on-off" switch. All we care about is our AA batteries, our cardiac motor, and the control panel encased in our cranium. And life is nothing more than shelf space at Toys Я Us!

Of course we are not just machines, but human beings—right? But then why do we so often treat ourselves, and people older than us, as if we were machines? If something positive is happening and we are actually growing as we "grow old," then why is there no book about it on my doctor's shelf? If there is something positive happening, then why are we trying so hard to make it slow down—or stop? Why do we hear so much about *staying* young and so little about *growing* old?

Of course living to eighty-five is preferable to sixty-five. But what are we doing with those years? Isn't there more to the second half of life than holding back the tides of time? Isn't there a deeper purpose to this time of life than just trying to prolong it? The purpose of a baseball game is not to play as many innings as possible. The purpose of a symphony is not to postpone the final note. But if the purpose of aging is not merely to do so as slowly as possible, then what is its purpose? If, as Dr. Klein observes, everything depends on "how we see things," then how, in fact, do we see aging?

Because we have grown up in a youth-oriented culture, we face both an opportunity and a danger. The opportunity clearly is that we can look and feel younger longer than our parents' generation. The danger, however, is that we will forget the value and meaning of aging. Popular culture reveals a deep cynicism about aging, a cynicism far deeper than our wrinkles. Even our contemporary comedians, from whom we might expect some unconventional wisdom, are bitterly conventional when it comes to aging. Through the thin veil of their humor, we see the sad truth that for them (or for their graying gag writers) aging is pointless.

On the very first page of her meandering and melancholy memoir *The Joys of Aging and How to Avoid Them,* Phyllis Diller begins with the capitalized premise that YOUNG IS BETTER THAN OLD! For the remainder of the book, this zany comedienne, who does scores of nightclubs each year in front of primarily elderly audiences, itemizes the drawbacks of old age. Finally, a few pages before the end, she says: "Let's take a look at some of the highlights of aging." At the top of the next page is the headline HIGHLIGHTS OF OLD AGE, followed by a blank page.[10]

Although more thoughtful, Bill Cosby's view of aging is equally bleak. In his best-seller *Time Flies,* he draws a hilarious self-portrait of his own physical decline. When Cosby began thinking about death and immortality, he decided that if he wanted to live forever, he needed help "either from a divinity or from a drugstore." Apparently, "Kryptonite Cosby" (as he calls himself) chose the latter. While the "average person wonders about the weather," Cosby has more cosmic concerns, such as "when Macy's will be getting in artificial hearts." Page after page, all Cosby can do is lament the passing of the Young Athlete and the arrival of the Old Paunch. Despite some great one-liners, his book is one long litany of decline.[11]

The funniest by far is Dave Barry, whose best seller about turning forty is filled with side-splitting tales. But when he homes in on the aging process itself, it is, unfortunately, just more of the same:

> Is there something you can do about aging? You're darned right there is! You *can* fight back. Mister Old Age is not going to get *you,* by golly! All you need is a little determination—a willingness to get out of that reclining lounge chair, climb into that sweatsuit, lace on those running shoes, stride out that front door, and *hurl yourself in front of that municipal bus.*
>
> No, wait. Sorry. For a moment there I got carried away by the bleakness of it all. Forget what I said. Really. . . .

And on he stumbles through liposuction, face-lifts, male pattern baldness, and dentures until, at the very end, he reveals the great consolation prize: We can become old geezers, otherwise known as "crusty old farts" who are "expected to be eccentric and crotchety and generally weird."[12]

The hollowness of the comedians' message about aging is perhaps best summed up by Diller, who gaily promises her readers that, even though she "chug-a-lugs Geritol," she "will show you how to become part of the Pepsi Generation." Stripped of all subtlety, this is our culture's conventional wisdom about getting old. Our job is to resist, delay, outwit, or outmaneuver it, to camouflage it cosmetically, or if all fails, to remove it surgically. In other words, our job is to slam on the brakes.

If this bitter, one-dimensional view of aging were limited to comedians' monologues, we could simply dismiss it as nightclub humor. But it pervades much of our culture and surfaces when we least expect it.

"Will you get black balloons?" asked my friend Jean as I was planning my fortieth birthday party, an occasion that has special meaning in our culture.[13]

"Why black?" I asked.

"Oh, just about every birthday party for the big four-oh I've been to has had them."

"I don't understand. Why black?"

"It's a joke, you know. Funeral. Death. The end. Get it?"

Later I happened to be at a drugstore, and out of curiosity I looked at the birthday cards.

The cover of one card, published by ACME Greetings, showed a full-grown man in a business suit and the caption: LIFE BEGINS AT FORTY. On the inside page, the man is standing on the ledge of a building ready for a suicide jump. The copy read: "ALONG WITH: cosmetic surgery, bladder trouble, high fiber diets, liver spots, hair replacement treatments, sitz baths, eczema, senility. HAVE A HAPPY BIRTHDAY, *anyway*!"

Avoiding other macabre cards, I reached for one that read enigmatically: *"Now that you are turning forty . . ."* I opened it and it continued: *". . . you will never have fun again for the rest of your life."*

The comedians' flat humor, the joking comments from my friends, and the sardonic humor of these greetings cards—

these are some of the ways our culture obliquely recognizes that men and women in the second half are encountering their own mortality. They reveal that we are obsessed with what we lose as we age, and ignorant about what we gain. Caught up in the absurdity of aging, we are oblivious to the growth and transcendence involved in the process. Our goal seems to be to slow down this ruthless "enemy" as long as we possibly can.

No wonder those in their thirties and forties begin to exhibit so many signs of anxiety about aging. As Landon Jones observes in his portrait of the postwar generations, the price we paid for our freedom was anxiety.[14] We don't know where we are going. We have forgotten what it all means. What is the second half of life *for*? When we grow old, how exactly do we *grow*? Does a society *need* its older members? If so, why? Are they just a nuisance, an irritation, a burden on the productive members of society? Are they just another needy group, toward whom the younger population can feel pity, or at best compassion?

In this and the following chapter, we look unflinchingly and truthfully in the eyes of our own aging. In our youth-oriented culture, a culture which our generation helped create, our first challenge is to unlearn the fundamental lie that *to be "young" is to be whole, and to be "aging" or "old" is to be impaired or broken.*

An anti-aging lexicon has emerged that, despite its veneer of homespun common sense, is ultimately destructive to us all:

"Think young!"
"Act young!"
"Look young!"
"Stay young!"
"You're just as young as you feel."

Although often well-intentioned, these phrases contain the seed of our culture's fundamental lie, which is so ingrained in us that we do not recognize it. Once we embrace the lie, once it becomes part of us, we begin to deny our own growth. We begin to identify with the *puer aeternus,* the "eternal youth," the young man or woman we once were (or imagine we were). We identify with how he or she felt, looked, made love, played ball, danced, dressed—everything! We remain stuck in time. We begin to define happiness, not as being here now, but as being there then.

Open a magazine. Look in a store window. Turn on the television. Walk down the street. Get your hair cut. Buy a dress. Watch people at work or at play. Go to a yuppie party or a working-class bar. Everywhere, men and women are trying to look young. After spending our teen years trying to look older, by the end of our twenties we are doing just the opposite. Models and athletes in their late twenties talk of being "over the hill" as if there were nothing of value on the other side. Youth wanes, and fears of aging set in. And so we spend two billion dollars on various remedies to ward off aging, and tens of billions more to disguise it.[15]

Conservative or liberal, male or female, executives or blue-collar workers—we all are confronting what George Will calls "juvenophilia."[16] Since 80 percent of television actors are between twenty-five and forty (compared with only 20 percent of the viewing public), we inhabit, in Stephen Levine's words, "a strange land where one is punished for being old."[17] So we begin to search frantically for "20 Ways to Wipe Away 10 Years," as one magazine article about longevity put it, so that we won't "slowly go to pieces like a time-release capsule."[18]

The further we move away from that ideal of youth, the more we feel something is wrong with us. We interpret every wrinkle, every sign of our unfolding self, as an assault on *who we really are*—that is, eternally young. Like generals preparing for battle, we marshal our troops. Fortify our immune system with vitamins, our digestive system with acidophilus and bran, our skin with collagen! Strengthen our muscles with weight-lifting and our cardiovascular system with aerobics! Pump ourselves with hormones, and preserve ourselves with deprenyl!

Whatever inherent value scientific advances against the ravages of age may have, many will leap on the rejuvenation bandwagon because, in their hearts, they believe aging is meaningless. Unfortunately, the same rule applies to our relationship with time, as to most other relationships: If we treat time as our enemy, it ultimately becomes one, which is why the metaphor of war is used again and again to describe aging. A recent article about the unsuccessful search for an effective antiwrinkle agent concluded that, in "the war against aging skin . . . the wrinkles seem to be winning all the battles."[19]

Hating aging is, in fact, self-hatred. This is not only psycho-logic, but soul-logic. Such hatred forces us to enter what John Bradshaw, the well-known specialist on addiction and codependency, calls "a maze of paths to eternal life studded with strictly juvenile standards and objectives, where we wander until we lose our souls."[20] We criticize ourselves for "looking old" because we no longer look like we're twenty-one. "There are generations of women who feel alone in the world," says sixty-six-year-old Frances Lear, founder of *Lear's* magazine. "They truly feel like outsiders when advertisers show antiwrinkle creams on seventeen-year-old faces. It's insulting."[21] And once the self-hatred takes root, it can only grow. If wrinkles are ugly, then are not receding hairlines ugly too? And don't forget sagging skin and dark spots; they're ugly too. And why stop there? Why not label as ugly anything—or anyone—that reminds us that our bodies are not immortal?

Deep into his research on aging, Dr. Ken Dychtwald was startled at how deeply ingrained our anti-aging bias is. He "quickly learned something very interesting about how Americans want to think about aging: they *don't*." To sell a product to people over forty, Dychtwald learned, the last thing you do is mention that it is for people over forty. As one ad executive said; "How many women want to walk into a drugstore and say, 'Do you have that shampoo for women over forty?' None."[22]

Particularly while I worked during the eighties in Hollywood, I witnessed firsthand a set of people, chronologically well into midlife, who were striving desperately to be forever young. Based on shared denial, this well-dressed and fast-moving group makes a fetish out of looking and acting as if they were collectively still in their mid-twenties. Music, dress, attitudes, styles, exercise—in every respect, they are so "with it" that they actually fool themselves into thinking time has stopped.

If you doubt that this is a powerful undercurrent in our culture, read Stanley Ellin's short story "The Blessington Method," in which a multimillion-dollar conglomerate builds its empire by contracting to eliminate quietly and without bother those troublesome, elderly parents (or parents-in-law) who can be such a burden on their children. In fact, read almost any of the modern fiction about aging from Saul Bellow to Carol Bly to John Sayles, and you will see through the compassionate eyes of our finest writers the desperate struggle for dignity by the old among us.[23]

But asking ourselves to identify with what is old as well as what is young involves an even deeper challenge. It requires us to reflect on our destination.

A "Nearer-Death" Experience: Breaking Through Denial

One day I am combing my hair after a shower. I notice a scar on my forehead just below my hairline that I had not thought about for years. It was caused by a traffic accident when I was twenty years old. My friend who had been driving veered to the left to avoid on oncoming bus. It slammed directly into him, crushing his body and killing him instantly. I was thrown out of the car, and my head was smashed

against the pavement. I remained unconscious until someone found me and took me to a hospital, where they oper-
ated on my head. As a result of that operation, I had a scar
that at the time was well above my forehead and totally
hidden beneath my thick wavy hair.

Now, staring at that scar, which is plainly visible on my
wrinkled forehead, my hand involuntarily stops combing. I
gaze for a long moment in the mirror, as if at a stranger. The
scar is startling evidence that my hairline is receding. In five
or ten years, I think, I may be bald. I picture it, and immediately I feel fear—not of baldness, but of the process of aging
that it represents. But then I lower my gaze and look directly
into my eyes. By some strange alchemy, fear suddenly shifts
to gratitude—and mourning. If my friend had veered right
instead of left, I would have died and he might have lived.
He would then be standing in front of a mirror, staring at *his*
receding hairline. Even now, a quarter of a century later,
this experience of my own near-death continues to teach me.
The scar takes on a different meaning. I no longer see it as a
sign of aging but as a sign of life.

As I studied the second half of life, I was struck by the
similarity between what happens at midlife and what happens to those who survive actual "near-death experiences"
(NDEs). After undergoing medical emergencies or accidents
that brought them perilously close to death, those who have
undergone NDEs report value changes in their lives that are
strikingly similar to those experienced in the second half.
These value changes include

- a greater emphasis on intimacy and authenticity in
personal relationships;
- a deeper appreciation for nature and the beauty and
interconnectedness of all life;
- a decreased interest in material rewards and professional ambition; and

- a generally heightened awareness of the spiritual dimension of life.

As one near-death researcher summarized: "Most NDErs also state that they live afterward with a heightened sense of spiritual purpose and, in some cases, that they seek a deeper understanding of life's essential meaning."[24] As we have seen, this is strikingly similar to the transformations we have witnessed among those in the second half.

When I first began writing this book, I noticed that virtually none of the books about health and longevity (including *Aging Slowly)* used the D-word at all. There were eloquent paragraphs about living longer, endless pages about vitamins and aerobics, elaborate chapters about cholesterol and bran. But death? Not a word!

In my twenties, I read Ernest Becker's Pulitzer Prize–winning book *The Denial of Death* and prided myself for outgrowing my childish notions of life everlasting and accepting the reality of human mortality. I braced myself to encounter what Becker called "the real dilemma of existence, the one of the mortal animal who at the same time is conscious of his mortality."[25]

The "facts" of death (which, one quickly learns, are too mysterious to be reduced to facts) were a bitter pill to swallow. At the time, I had not even heard of Elisabeth Kübler-Ross or the stages of dying. Nor did I know that denial (Stage 1) is common, and that acceptance (Stage 5) comes only after deep, often painful transformation.[26] All I knew was that one believed either in everlasting life or in returning to dust. Swallowing this bitter pill seemed to be part of growing up, the intellectual equivalent of playing tackle football. It proved I was tough, but it gave me a superficial sense of superiority over poor fundamentalist souls who imagined themselves posthumously walking on clouds listening to harp music. I prided myself on having accepted the existentialist rigors of finding meaning (or meaninglessness) within the realm of life itself. It was all a very convincing, bravura performance.

Unfortunately, I had missed the point. I knew *about* death, but only in my head. I accepted death with an open mind, but a closed heart.

The second half of life is not a question of theology. Our beliefs about the hereafter are not what ultimately matters. What matters is whether we live out our beliefs with an open heart. Or as Stephen Levine puts it in *Who Dies?:* "Death is not the enemy. The 'enemy' is ignorance and lovelessness." But my still-young heart was closed to these truths, shut tight to protect myself against the host of fears surrounding death. Intellectually accepting the finality of death had not made me more compassionate or forgiving. It had not made me less fearful or judgmental of myself and others. It had not opened my eyes to the deep and fragile wonders of the sacred. On the contrary, I was still rooted firmly in fear.

I know that my heart remained closed to death well into the writing of this book. I remember one day, before leaving for my office to work on this chapter, I was slicing a ripe melon. I was in a hurry to write during the early hours before my workday began. Cutting through the hard rind, the knife entered the soft green flesh of the melon and continued into the soft pink flesh of my forefinger. My finger began to bleed heavily. I quickly reached for an ice tray from the freezer hoping that cold would stanch the flow. Several large drops of blood fell onto the tray. I tried to wipe the blood off, but it had frozen instantly on the frigid surface. Like the blood drops, I too was frozen. I had seen my blood before, always liquid, flowing, warm, and red. Suddenly, there it was: hard, cold, brownish, and immobile.

But I was not about to let myself be deflected from my schedule by a little blood. I regained my poise, applied the ice to the cut finger, and raised that hand up to limit the circulation. After several minutes, I put on a bandage and went to my office, now even more in a hurry to get to work.

But when I lowered my hand to the keyboard to write, the bleeding resumed. I could not put my hand down on the computer keyboard without red drops falling on the keys. So, finally, I had to stop. *Full* stop. I sat quietly in contemplation. I could not work on this chapter about aging and death until enough blood had flowed.

According to psychological researchers, my epiphany with the melon happened right on schedule. In the second half, our awareness of mortality changes. Some place the crucial age at thirty-five; others at forty to forty-five. But all agree that in the second half our awareness of aging and of death unmistakably penetrates more deeply into our consciousness.[27] Whether this awareness will be a negative or positive force, one that undermines life's meaning or enriches it, is up to each of us.

The poet Hermann Hesse was thirty-nine when his father died. It was only then, for the first time in his life, that this sensitive and reflective man opened his heart to death.

> Until now I had thought little about death. . . . But it was only now that I saw its reality and grandeur, the way it stands over there as our opposite pole and waits for us, so that our fate may be fulfilled and the circle of life completed. Until now I had lingered in love at the beginnings of the path, which is my life, and the end of this path had never stood clearly before me.

In midlife, Hesse no longer identified more with the beginning of life than with its end. For the first time, he felt that his life was "bound and appointed at *both* ends."[28] At the heart of our quest is this dawning realization, that we stand on a high-wire, equidistant from both ends of life, the beginning as vivid and real in our minds as the end.

We do not age in a vacuum. Behind us in the life cycle are our children, whose visible growth is a dramatic reminder of the passage of time. And ahead of us are our parents, whose aging we cannot ignore. When we are in midlife, they are nearing life's end. We must confront the death not only of our own parents but of our mate's and friends' parents as well. And so, after years with few, if any, funerals to attend, we find ourselves unable to avoid them any longer. And at their funerals, we envision our own.

Like Hesse, we often do not become conscious of the connection until death comes knocking on *our* door. I remember when my kids and I watched as Shelley anxiously left to get on an airplane to be with her father, who was slowly dying. When she arrived at his bedside, she looked into her father's eyes and saw his life waning. Tubes in his nose and mouth, IVs in his arms, Samuel Kessler could not move. For his entire life, he had been a tailor. His hands had moved incessantly as he sewed the cuffs and fitted the jackets of his hundreds of customers; his feet had never stopped as he searched in the men's clothing store for just the thing his customer wanted. But now he was motionless. His pale arms lay still beside him. His right hand lay limply, clasped in his daughter's. She wanted to stay with him longer, but she couldn't. He might recover, and he might not; either way, the doctors said, the process might take weeks. She had to tell him that she was going home to her children. When she told him she would be leaving soon, their eyes met. She could see him strain to sit up, as if trying to kiss her. But he couldn't. Suddenly, she felt his hand tighten around hers, and his eyes rimmed with tears. He was saying good-bye.

Shelley never saw her father alive again. But his death, the first and so far the only one among our children's grandparents, continues to this day to echo in our home. After his death, Shelley's own entry into the second half quickened. The spiritual questions that had hovered at the edges of her life took center stage. She was propelled into the second half.

As I worked on this book, a colleague told me the story of a doctoral candidate in her late thirties who was working on a book about midlife. She had finished a draft of her dissertation and was flying home for the holidays with it in her briefcase. She died in one of the plane crashes that you and I read about in the newspapers. It turned out that her "midlife" was, in fact, the end of her life. By the time we reach our forties, all of us know at least one person, and probably many, for whom this was the case. In this sense, "aging slowly" is not only meaningless, but an illusion. As Lewis Thomas wrote in *The Lives of a Cell:* "The vast mortality, involving something over 50 million of us each year, takes place in relative secrecy."[29] Death surrounds us. It is omnipresent. Only our level of attention changes.

Since I am still years away from what the actuarial tables predict of my time of death and both my parents are still alive, I am still a beginning student when it comes to dying. But during the last decade, my lessons in mourning began.

The board of directors of a company I founded was chaired by Harry Hollins, a brilliant, independent-minded former Wall Streeter well into his seventies, whose failing health was already in the early eighties of growing concern to all of us who loved him. The rest of the board was younger than he, including three extraordinarily vital and creative people in their sixties: a journalist-sailor who won the transatlantic singles competition at the unprecedented age of sixty-five; a nun-turned-artist whose paintings popped up unconventionally all across America from billboards to gas tanks; and a businessman who played an instrumental role in getting John F. Kennedy elected in 1960 and who continued to be a courageous participant on the cutting edge of social change for the rest of his life. Yet by the end of the decade Harry was still alive, but his three younger colleagues had passed away—two of them after long battles against cancer, one from a sudden heart attack.

Struck by death's unpredictability, I was working on this chapter when the call came: Harry was dead. Even before the ink was dry, death had taken yet another friend and mentor. Before I turned thirty, I had experienced virtually no losses. Now I felt surrounded by gravestones. And they are but a foreshadowing of the many, many farewells in the decades to come.

Unless our eyes and our hearts shut tightly in denial, the second half is a "nearer-death" experience. In the second half, not only do our mentors and parents die, but a part of *us* dies.

We don't need a heart attack to confront death; it is built into midlife. Virtually everyone I interviewed for this book referred to their suddenly heightened awareness of their own mortality in their late thirties or forties. Time and time again, men and women at this age shared with me stories of how they encountered death—not the abstract, philosophical concept discussed in college classes, but the visceral, gut-wrenching experience of personal mortality. At midlife, death is on our minds, and it should be.

Although the challenge of facing death in the second half is unavoidable, there are many ways to respond. You may wish to befriend death. Or, like Dylan Thomas, you may consider death an adversary and "rage, rage against the dying of the light." You may portray death as your savior, the entrance into an everlasting life free of pain and fear and filled with light and love. You may accept it intellectually but deny it emotionally. But whatever your beliefs may be, you can no longer dismiss death as, in Susan Sontag's memorable phrase, "an offensively meaningless event."[30]

One of the most direct ways to seek death's deeper meaning is to spend time with the dying, as Robert and Marilyn did. As newlyweds in their forties, they decided to work with a hospice program, which provides care for the dying both in and outside hospitals. I asked them what they had learned from the experience.

"Awe and helplessness," Robert began. "You can't spend time with those who are dying and not feel some mixture of those two emotions. You are in awe because death isn't an idea anymore, not just something to think about. It becomes as real as life itself. Until I joined the hospice program, I still felt self-conscious about how vulnerable I was in relation to my own death. But it opened a doorway to understanding how to live. When faced with someone who was dying, I had this urge to fix them somehow, to make them feel better. If I said the right thing, I could help them relax—or give them some peace. I had to learn what a burden that kind of helpfulness could be for them. To take care of *me,* they would have to relax or be open. Finally, I realized that I was helpless. I couldn't do anything, except be fully present with them. Share the moment. Share in *their* reality."

"That's the key, isn't it?" Marilyn added. "It's the key, not just to hospice work, but to living: to be able to empty ourselves enough of all the games we are usually playing so that we can really be with someone. The people I worked with, and their families, were all very different. But they all taught me to see more clearly that much of the time I was with people, I wasn't *truly* with them. I was with my anxiety, or my awkwardness, or my uncertainty more than I was with them. Learning to see that helped me to change that. And it's made all the difference in the world."

As I listened to them speak, I could feel the love between them. Although each had been married before, I felt confident that this marriage would work. They could stay married "until death do us part," in part because they had accepted death and the state of full presence that comes with that acceptance. This cannot happen if we are trying to age slowly. It comes only when we dare to age deeply.

Aging Deeply: The Meaning of Growing Older

Even as we open our hearts to death, part of us naturally wants to stay young-looking, filled with energy, unbothered by the ravages of time and the inevitability of death. But another part of us is aging, and changing. Our young selves,

like a caterpillar becoming a butterfly, *are* dying. By the end
of our forties, the secretion of human growth hormones has
ceased. As we lose the energy-rich biochemistry of youth,
another more mature metabolism takes over. It is only natural to think of death at this time—not because we are becoming morbid or melancholy, but simply because we are
alive and aware.

Now in his seventies, Marvin Barrett has a hearing aid in
both ears, is balding, moves slowly, and occasionally cannot
remember names. It is obvious that he is old; what is not so
obvious is that he is growing. This is even more remarkable
when you consider that he "died" seven years earlier.

Several years before our interview, Marvin was locked in
a struggle with cancer. Perhaps as a result of radiation treatments, he suffered a heart attack. "They tell me I was dead
this afternoon," he wrote later in his touching autobiography *Spare Days,* but adds: "Not all that dead." But he was
dead long enough to experience the classical near-death images of tunnels ("like the shoot-the-chutes at Riverview
Park"), dazzling lights ("but not blinding"), and then the
return to the land of the living. At the time, he was "not
ready to go all the way. So I am back. Spinning. Uncertain.
My legs shaking."

Now seventy, he looks back on that day in the operating
room with the perspective of a man who had accepted death
—accepted it, then been given a reprieve. "Death seems less
intimidating now than it did when I was young," he confides
in me, even though at my age he knows I cannot fully understand. "That's true with many of the people my age with
whom I have spoken about it. I was more nervous about
dying when I was twenty than I am now." He chuckled at
the irony: when death was far away, it scared him; now close
at hand, it has become a companion.

"The media only seem to be interested in the old age
freaks," he said, referring to the men and women his age
who attract attention because they act or look half their age.

"Yes, they're cute, those old folks dancing and prancing around. But cuteness isn't everything." Marvin was rebelling against the notion that the old people who look "young," or who go dancing every night, are necessarily aging well, while those who look or act "old" are aging badly. After returning from the dead, this mechanical and materialistic view of life strikes him as quite silly.[31]

Certainly Marvin is not sedentary. He is preparing to write another book, swims a quarter of a mile every day, and continues to serve on the boards of several organizations. But he takes pains to stress that he is proud of being old, not ashamed. He is proud of the deepening of his mind and the ripening of his soul that would have been impossible even ten years earlier. He is not a likely candidate for wrinkle-reducing collagen injections or cosmetic surgery. On the contrary, he is quite at peace with how he looks. For Marvin as for us, learning how to live has gone hand-in-hand with learning how to age—and how to die.

"One of the psychological problems in growing old is the fear of death," Joseph Campbell told Bill Moyers in their dialogue at George Lucas's Skywalker Ranch. "People resist the door of death." But, Campbell said, death can be the ultimate teacher. "The problem in middle life, when the body has reached its climax of power and begins to decline, is to identify not with the body, which is falling away, but with the consciousness of which it is a vehicle. This is something I learned from myths. What am I? Am I the bulb that carries the light, or am I the light of which the bulb is a vehicle?"[32]

In his poetic, philosophical language, it may be hard to feel the power of Campbell's question in our guts. If so, listen to a woman (age sixty-nine) who is reflecting on her own aging:

> I see my arm with the skin hanging loosely from my forearm and not believe that it is really my own. It

seems disconnected from me; it is someone else's. It is
the arm of an old woman. It is the arm of such old
women as I myself have seen, sitting on benches in the
sun with their hands folded in their laps; old women I
have turned away from. I wonder now how and when
these arms I see came to be my own—arms I cannot
turn away from.[33]

This reflective woman is watching her body (what Campbell
calls the bulb) aging and, ultimately, dying. At the same
time, she is becoming more aware of the light of consciousness within her, which is more alive and aware of itself than
ever.

If we identify with the body rather than with consciousness, then aging means nothing more than decline and ultimately death. It is meaningless only because, through the
lens of our myopic materialism, we have screened out its
meaning. In the second half, this worldview becomes fatally
flawed. Following in a long tradition of religious wisdom,
Campbell argues that, even though the bulb itself wears out,
the light is eternal. As the body ages, our awareness of the
light within can intensify. If we approach our bodies as a
vehicle of consciousness, then our challenge as we age is to
identify with the consciousness. Then, advised Campbell,
"you can watch this body go like an old car. There goes the
fender, there goes the tire, one thing after another."

Like Campbell, a champion runner in his youth who lived
actively and creatively until the day he died, most of us intend to live as long and as vitally as we can. Resisting death
makes good sense. All those who love life will do so. But
resisting *awareness* of death, when we reach the second half,
makes no sense. For how can we plan a journey if we have
blinded ourselves to its destination? How can we find meaning in aging if we are blocking out any awareness of where it
leads?

Of course we want to take care of our bodies. But to take

good care of them in the second half of life requires what Jean Houston, who is charting some of the unexplored terrain of the second half, calls *deconstruction* and *reconstruction*. At a recent series of weekends whose participants were mostly in the second half, she said matter-of-factly to her audience: "Many people in this room are already over the hill in terms of 150 years ago. Most of you, if we could put you back 150 years, would be dead." From her point of view, we are not just alive in the second half, we are engaged in a "whole new order of emergence." In her work, she has witnessed transformation in people over sixty which she describes as so phenomenal that she compares it to the kind of growth that is normally associated with the first year of childhood. Speaking specifically to her workshop participants who were over seventy, she encouraged them to think of being back "not in a second childhood, but at a second level of complete development. Some of you are literally in the womb."[34]

Images such as these free us from the mechanical, no-win game of aging slowly. They introduce the notion that aging is not only physical decline, but some kind of search, a quest. Guided by this question—"What does it mean to age deeply?"—concern for nutrition, exercise, bodywork, and other kinds of physical self-care can play a vital, sometimes catalytic role in furthering our quest. If we are lucky, we are called to the quest when we still have time and energy to explore it fully.

After spending her mid-thirties mired in chronic fatigue, aches, low-grade fever, and depression, Debbie found herself on vacation in Hawaii staying at one of the larger tourist hotels. All the medical treatments and diagnoses had been useless. She felt so hopeless that she felt as if she were starting to die. Looking through the directory of hotel services, she decided to treat herself to a massage. An old Japanese man with huge gnarled hands gave her an acupressure massage, which means that he focused on the points in her body that coincide with the meridians in which traditional Chinese acupuncturists place their needles. Afterward, Debbie felt immediate relief from all her symptoms, a respite that lasted several weeks. She not only felt better physically, but for the first time in months she felt alert and excited about living.

Intrigued, she decided to look into acupuncture more deeply. Over her husband's objections (he felt that more traditional medical approaches should be followed), she committed herself back home to ongoing acupuncture treatment. She was startled to discover that, although she had been involved in psychotherapy for several years, she had far more powerful psychological insights and breakthroughs while lying on the acupuncturist's table than she did on her therapist's couch. "One day," she recalls, "I was overwhelmed by an ancient sadness, a legacy of pain handed down to me from my mother and my grandmother. I was overcome with deep, racking sobs. It was the same anguish that I had been struggling with for years. But now I felt it pass through me. It was as if I had been living in a fog for so long that I didn't even know it. It wasn't until it lifted that I knew what it meant to see a clear sky."

For Debbie, it was a kind of death. She would never feel the same again. Her heart had been opened. Although brief periods of sadness and melancholy would engulf her again from time to time, the chronic illness and depression was gone. She was amazed that it all happened without words, and without warning. The experience did not fit within any of her categories. Why should a body therapy have such a profound psychological and spiritual impact? What exactly were these meridians of energy that acupuncture needles rechanneled? What had blocked her life energy for so long? And now that it was being released, where would it lead?

Now fifty years old, Debbie has not found answers to these questions. But she has found her path. She is deep into her own training as an acupuncturist and is as aware as never before that her quest is at the heart of her life. When she read Murray Stein's *In Midlife,* she recalls, "it was a tremendous relief just to have it named. Instead of feeling isolated in my own pain, like some kind of crazy person, I realized I was experiencing a vital dimension of human life, a dimension that I never knew existed."

Debbie's story illustrates that, particularly at midlife, aging has a soul dimension. Learning to live also means learning to die. The walls that divided us in the first half of our lives must come down. Like the Berlin Wall, they have outlived their usefulness. We may keep pieces of them as souvenirs, but their time has passed. It is time, as one older woman confided to a researcher, to "accept age. Accept aging *as a process of my own being.*"[35]

On the wall of the room where I cried in Shelley's arms hung a poster featuring a photograph of Albert Einstein. Underneath his mane of swirling white hair was printed in bold black letters a statement he had made toward the end of his life: *"Is there not a certain satisfaction in the fact that natural limits are set on the life of an individual, so that at its conclusion it may appear as a work of art?"* (In almost identical words, Ernest Becker makes almost the same observation: "in order to have a truly human existence there must be limits."[36]) It is fitting that Einstein, who taught us so much about the universe, also points us toward the importance of aging deeply. For ultimately, no matter how many equations humankind invents to describe the properties of energy and matter, space and time, our quest is for meaning. Without it, the rest does not matter.

From the perspective of mentors such as Einstein, Becker, Houston, and Campbell, aging and death do not undermine life's meaning; they actually *give* life meaning. Like artists, we are compelled to make choices within limits. Just as a painter has a canvas of limited size and a sculptor has a limited amount of clay, we human beings have limited amount of time. With it, we can create beauty, love, and meaning—if we dare! In every era, artists and mystics and

seers echo Einstein's observation. As the poet William But-
ler Yeats wrote upon entering the second half:

> Begin that preparation for your death
> And from that fortieth winter by that thought
> Test every work of intellect or faith.

Or as a contemporary poet, the rock musician Bonnie Raitt,
put it on her comeback album *Nick of Time,* which won her
a Grammy at the age of forty: "Life gets pretty precious
when there's less of it to waste."

But what is "precious"? According to the technicians, it is
longevity itself. The rejuvenating synthetic hormone hGH
was welcomed so warmly in the public imagination because
humankind has been waiting for it for centuries. What Ponce
de Leon could not find in nature, genetic engineers at
Genentech, Inc., and Eli Lilly & Co. made in their laboratories. These companies, poised on the leading edge of
anti-aging research, are trying to make possible through
pharmaceutics what, according to Freud, human beings have
unconsciously always wanted: everlasting life. The human
organism, argued Freud, is fundamentally unwilling to believe in its own demise. "No one believes in his own death,"
he wrote in his World War I essay "Thoughts for the Times
on War and Death." "In the unconscious, everyone is convinced of his own mortality." (Or as Bill Cosby quipped,
"Immortality is a long shot, I admit, but *somebody* has to be
first.")

But is death not part of life? ask the philosophers, many
of whom recoil at this brave new world of the longevity
technicians. When our hearts are closed to death, are they
not also closed to the process of life that leads to it? The
notion that the denial of death takes no toll on our appreciation of life is contradicted by all available evidence. Trained
by Kübler-Ross and having worked with the dying for years,
Stephen Levine is often asked how he knows when to stop

trying to promote healing in a dying patient and when to begin preparing them to die. "This question," he writes, "once again comes from a partial understanding. In reality *the opening to healing and the preparation for death are the same.*"

This is confirmed by the most compelling and comprehensive book on preventing heart attacks. *Dr. Dean Ornish's Program for Reversing Heart Disease* was written by a cardiologist who wanted to title his book *Opening Your Heart*. Unfortunately, the book's publishers wanted a more straightforward title. By doing so, they sacrificed not only poetry but spirit. For Dr. Ornish's entire book (which became a best seller and at this writing is in its seventh printing) is a testament to how the emotions of a closed heart (isolation, bitterness, anger, hatred) not only diminish life but increase the likelihood of premature death.

This is not just his opinion, but the result of extensive research that is only now available. When I asked him what its impact would be on the generation now entering the second half, Ornish replied: "People listen now who previously would not. We use state-of-the-art, high-tech equipment to prove the power of ancient truths. Aging is inevitable, but we now have new choices. It used to be a bypass or death . . . angioplasty or death . . . lifetime medication or death. Now we know there are often other choices that *work*. Changing your life-style—what you eat, how you exercise, how you manage stress—correlates with the health of your heart."[37]

Unlike so many other self-help books, Dr. Ornish's frankly addresses our unconscious wish for immortality and refuses to feed our denial of death by making outlandish promises. "None of us is going to live forever," he repeats often in his book. Instead, he focuses on the real issue: How we can feel more free and more joyful. "Altruism, compassion, and forgiveness—opening your heart—can be powerful means of healing the isolation that leads to stress, suffering and illness." Ornish makes an eloquent case, at once scientific and spiritual, that developing the biblical virtues in the second half of life may not only keep you alive longer but may also give your second half meaning. This, not a wrinkle-free face, is the reward for aging deeply.

When we say that we want to "stay young," we really mean that we want to become whole. And we cannot be whole if we are denying the part of ourselves that is no longer actually young. *Of course* you want to live a longer and healthier life. So do I. As we have seen, we can do much to take care of our bodies so that the second half of life invigorates and sustains us. But I am deeply suspicious of a view of aging that fundamentally disrespects the process of growing older. Strategies to retard aging that lead to frenzy and fear, to obsessive diets and frenetic workouts, and to a cult of youthfulness that denies the rhythms of life is not progress. Of what value is a long life if it is lived without self-respect? Of what value is a wrinkle-free face if it masks despair? Of what value is aging slowly if we deny its depth of meaning?

"When you're in your sixties," the actor Paul Newman mused, "you look at things differently from when you're fifty." This is why he was in such a hurry to turn his idea for a camp for terminally ill children into reality: He did not know how much time he had left. Age made him focus on what meant most to him, including sharing his love of life with those who had even less time left than he did.[38]

Loving life is natural. The desire to drink fully from its cup is healthy. The challenge in the second half is to do so consciously, as Newman did—that is, without denying death. If we do not meet this challenge, we fall prey to those charlatans and demagogues who would profit from our naïveté. We also fall prey to that more dangerous con artist inside ourselves who is always too ready to persuade us that we are not good enough, or beautiful enough—or young enough—to be loved.[39]

So we must all be vigilant in our response. On the one hand, we must be open to the exciting, life-giving breakthroughs in science that will prolong our lives *and* maintain our health. Insofar as these breakthroughs allow us to age deeply on our quest for wholeness, we are truly blessed to be alive at this moment in history. As a generation, we may well live longer, healthier lives than any of our predecessors, and for this gift of life we may be truly thankful.

But on the other hand, we must not become casualties of the anti-aging epidemic. The virus of aging slowly is itself aging us. We are getting old trying to stop it. If we were genuinely youth-oriented, we would take care of the young and invest in their education and growth. Instead, we witness today what one critic calls "an attempt by the middle-aged to commandeer through nostalgia fads, freakish styles, hair-blowers, skin-oils and inarticulate slang, the supposedly happy condition of youth."[40] This is not a love of youthfulness, but a jealousy of the young. Instead of providing them with inspiring models, we envy them. By so doing, we send them the debilitating message that, after youth is passed, it is all downhill. Instead of passing this lie on to them, it is our responsibility to tell—no, to *live*—a deeper truth: that aging has meaning.

Old is not a dirty word. If you wish, slow your aging process as much as you can. Stay alert, healthy, growing. You may not want to show how old you are. But be sure to show *who* you are. In bumper-sticker language: Slow it—but show it! Until we accept death with an open heart, our own souls will be as strangers to us. So let's talk about it, befriend it. Awareness of it won't kill us. Perhaps this awareness will even help us grow. This is what the quest is for: not aging slowly, but deeply; not staying young, but becoming whole.

6

HONORING THE SEVEN GENERATIONS
The Quest for Interdependence

A large part of the despair, loneliness and confusion of those individuals now undergoing midlife crises is that they have no map that suggests post-normal, post-adult *stages of life.*

SAM KEEN

Consider what you want to do later in life while you are still young. If you associate enough with older people who do enjoy their lives, who are not stored away in any golden ghettos, you will gain a sense of continuity and of the possibilities for a full life.

MARGARET MEAD

John Anderson, age 75, passed away suddenly on Easter Sunday in a Fort Lauderdale nursing home after a long illness. He is survived by his wife, Mary, who lives in Vero Beach, Florida. He is also survived by four sons: John, of Grand Rapids, Minnesota; Frederick, of Albert Lea, Minnesota; Harry, of Columbus, Ohio, and Daniel, of Mt. Vernon, Illinois, as well as their wives and eight grandchildren. . . . Also by a brother James, who resides in St. Paul, Minnesota, and a sister Frances, of Newton, Massachusetts. Mr. Anderson began his career in the electronics industry in the early 1920s and was founder and president of that corporation until his retirement in the late 1960s. Memorial services will be held on Thursday at the Lyndale Avenue Congregational Church in Minneapolis. There will be no reviewal or visitation.[1]

This obituary, similar to thousands that appear in daily newspapers in towns like yours and mine, is not only about one man's death. It is also about the demise of elders and the loss of community. For John Anderson passed away not amidst others who saw him as an elder of the tribe, but as a patient in Room 407 of a nursing home. He did not pass away surrounded by the community in which he had participated for three-quarters of a century. He died alone.

If we are still far from our expected deaths, it is tempting to see this situation through our parents' eyes rather than our own. But it will soon be our dilemma too. In whose arms shall we die? In whose room? In whose care? What will survive us? In whose memory will we live? Will we feel connected to the next generations, or estranged and alone? Where will our children be? Our friends? Our community?

We may pose these questions at any age, but in the second

half of life, they matter more than before. Whether the generations are interdependent not only influences how we age
and die. It runs straight through the landscape of the life
cycle.

• Whether we have a crisis or a quest depends in part on
the social context of our lives. Do we have models of people
older than ourselves who inspire us? Are we sustained by a
network of deep friendships that will support us even if we
dare to change?

• Whether we can open our hearts to aging and dying
depends in part on our connection to the rest of the life
cycle. Are the lives of those older than us bleak and lonely?
Are they treated with respect and honored for their wisdom
—or shunted aside?

• Whether we care well for our bodies depends in part on
what we are taught, and the examples that we follow. As we
age, does our community provide us with information, facili-
ties and incentives to become fit—or to fade away? Do we
find understanding and care from those around us—or indifference? Compassion—or stereotype?

• Whether our marriages in the second half grow or die
depends in part on how the culture around us interprets
love. Does it invigorate long-standing love by helping us to
understand its unique challenges and its rewards? Or does it
undermine such love by ignoring its special qualities and
stereotyping marriage as uneventful, if not boring?

• Whether we find a voice in our vocation in the second
half depends on what work our communities let us do. Are
the elders allowed to choose the work roles that enable them
to participate as fully as they can in productive life? Or are
they involuntarily retired, or even victimized through age
discrimination? Do they feel entitled to a decent way of life,
or do they live in fear of dependency and impoverishment?

If we have not realized it before, then in the second half it becomes painfully and joyfully evident: We need generational *interdependence* as much as we need generational change.

The native Americans recognized the importance of honoring the "seven generations": before us, our parents, grandparents, and great-grandparents; after us, our children, grandchildren, and great-grandchildren; and last but not least, ours. These seven generations were the human cornerstone of community. Those who wanted to represent the whole community or to speak of its welfare had to consider the needs of all.

Authentic community—that is, community that honors the interdependence of all seven generations—ensures that the young are initiated by adults; that infants are tended by parents or other loving caretakers; that those in the second half are supported by others in carrying out their responsibilities; that the old are respected and their skills utilized. Authentic communities do not isolate the old in ghettos for the elderly, or warehouse the young in impersonal, understaffed child-care centers or schools that neglect them; they do not leave young mothers trapped home alone with infants, or create jobs that prevent working parents from being with their young children. Authentic communities do not place education at the bottom of their budgetary priorities and do not frighten the elderly by jeopardizing their finan cial support systems.

Authentic multigenerational communities tend to *every* stage of the life cycle because they know that, ultimately, this is the only way they will flourish. When the community is weak or absent, we all stumble forward, lurching through the life cycle. When it runs strong, life flows with greater meaning.

As John Anderson's obituary shows, however, the threads of community are unraveling. Although I am just over half the age when he died, I know the anxiety he must have felt in his last years. Children move away. A wife or husband dies. Suddenly, we are alone. If we do not have a community, we must fend for ourselves. And if we are too old or frail to do so, we are then utterly dependent on the resources and care of well-meaning relatives or, failing that, institutions and bureaucracies. Just when we most need to be supported and held, we are isolated. Just when we most need the security of having a home, we are housed in a unit. Just when we most need to be known, we become a number. Just when we most need to be remembered, we are forgotten.

These are not sociological assumptions, but personal experience. My mother, divorced, lives alone in Florida. Shelley's mother, widowed, lives alone in Detroit. Their children are scattered from Boston to San Francisco, from Chicago to Los Angeles. None of their offspring lives within a hundred miles of their homes. Our mothers have chosen to be where they are; they do not want to move. But they are lonely, isolated, and vulnerable. To what do they belong? To what do *we* belong? Where is their community? Where is *ours*? What can we do for them now? What can we do for ourselves in preparation for reaching their age? How can we care for them as we ourselves hope we are cared for?

Generational interdependence is not some magic panacea that will make all our troubles go away. It is not "out there," like some kind of product, which we could buy if only we could find it. It is in the hands of people like us who decide day-to-day what we value and what we do not. The fate of the life cycle, like that of marriage, depends on how we balance valid yet conflicting needs: our need to be free and independent individuals, living life for our own fulfillment; and our need to be connected and interdependent with the larger community. Though both needs must be honored, the voice of community often calls out more loudly because it is the one we have shortchanged in the first half.

As we outgrow the narcissistic definition of ladder-climbing success, we are in fact committing ourselves to the success of something larger—our families, our colleagues, our community, perhaps even the world. If we are raising a family, we have seen that parents alone cannot safeguard a child's future but that community supports are vital. Furthermore, if we have confronted our own mortality, we know that it is only as members of a community, "defined in part by its past and its memory of its past," that we will be remembered.[2]

Whatever our religious beliefs, we know as human beings that we live on in others' memories of us. At the end of our lives, we want to be remembered not only by those who are our own age but by others throughout the life cycle who have touched and been touched by us. This, ultimately, is what community means: the web of human connection. Birth, puberty, coming of age, marriage, parenthood, midlife, elderhood, death—as different as the stages of life are, they share an important element. *Each needs the others.* At certain times of life, the interdependence of the stages of life is obvious. For example: Babies need parents to give birth to them and care for them; the old need someone to care for them and, ultimately, to bury and to mourn them. This is why community is so vital: It enables every stage of the life cycle to do the growing that is uniquely theirs.

Bringing together youth, adults, and elders under a common roof is not somebody else's job. By the time we have reached the second half, it is ours. So let us hold ourselves accountable. It is all too easy to blame enormous social trends or intractable social problems for the lack of generational continuity. It is hard, and much more vital, to begin bringing the generations together.

As we explore generational interdependence, we will do so not just through our eyes but through the eyes of elders. I am still only in my forties. I can look ahead at the life cycle's second half, but I cannot look back at it in its entirety. For this I will rely on men and women older and wiser than I.

Seeking Our Elders: The Hub of the Life Cycle

Through a cold winter wind, two white men slowly approached the cabin on the land of the Onondaga Nation in upstate New York, home of the Six Nation Iroquois Confederacy. A gray-haired native American man—Oren Lyons, faithkeeper of the Turtle Clan—opened the door and let them in. He knew why these outsiders had come, the writer with his tape recorder and the photographer with his camera. But why should the Iroquois bare their souls, he wondered, and reveal their tribal lore to these white men, whose ancestors took their land? Why should the native American now let them take all that is left—their sacred stories and ancient wisdom?

Before Oren Lyons spoke, he examined the faces of the two middle-aged white men in the light of the kerosene light. "Why come to us?" he asked sternly. "We're the toughest nut to crack. You think we turn our elders over to anyone who walks in the door? We guard them like pure spring water."

Steve Wall and Harvey Arden were at first startled by his harshness, but they held their tongues. Steve and Harvey were not tourists. They told Oren that they had committed themselves to recording the stories of the Old Ones. For Steve, a native North Carolinian who had grown up to become a well-respected photographer for *National Geographic,* UPI, and scores of other publications, the desire to record the native Americans' stories came when a Cherokee medicine man lamented that the elders were dying and their wisdom was not being passed to the next generation. Steve had traveled through the years to over forty countries, his camera always focusing on the human condition: What makes a community? How does it hold together? What is its glue? The old Cherokee's fear had touched Steve's heart, and he decided with Harvey to put their words and images down on paper—before it was too late.[3]

"The glue in America is getting very thin, if in fact we still have any," says Steve, when I asked him why he began his modern photographic trek through Indian country. "I've lived with native Americans, learned more than anything I could ever have got from history books. They have a very strong sense of family, of clan, including clan mother. After he came to trust us, Oren explained, for example, that there is no such thing as illegitimacy within his community. Every child has a mother. She is a member of the clan, which is a kind of extended family. So every child is automatically a member of the clan. Everyone belongs. Everyone has a place."[4]

It became clear that it was not just Steve's concern for native Americans that motivated him, but his concern for America itself. He lamented that the torch of wisdom was not being passed through the generations in the white and black neighborhoods of his hometown of Charlotte, and in the other hometowns throughout America. Drug use, divorce, juvenile crime, teenage pregnancy, social isolation, disregard for the elderly—these and other social problems were rampant in his hometown. He was drawn to tell the stories of the Old Ones, not just to preserve native American culture but to heal his own. Like so many other Americans entering the second half, he was sensing a vacuum.

"Where would you go," I asked Steve, "if you wanted to interview the elders of *your* clan?"

"I don't know. I really don't," he replied sadly, in his slow drawl that, even in this fast-talking era of MTV, still survives in the American South. "When I was working with the elders of native America, I asked myself that question. I thought about where I would go if I were looking for the elders of Anglo-America. Would I go to a bank president? No, he knows about money, but not necessarily about wisdom. No matter who I thought of, their role seemed fragmented. I don't think we have real elders anymore."

When I asked him why, Steve spoke of death. "Within the

traditional circle in native America, there is no fear of death. Life is the caterpillar, death is the butterfly. But for us whites, we are afraid of death. The elderly symbolize our fear. So we don't want them around. They are bad news. We want them put away somewhere.

"I was very fortunate in having a grandmother who was a guide for me," Steve went on. "She taught me to follow my heart, not just abide by the system. We could be looking to a much brighter future if we knew that some older people have real lessons to pass on to us. We do have some elders out there, with stories to tell us. But we may need a revolution of some kind to get our bearings straight before we'll listen to 'em."

Fortunately, Steve and Harvey listened well. They gathered more than a dozen interviews with native American elders into a beautiful, large-size volume of photographs and interviews, which was issued by a small Oregon publisher. Despite almost no advertising and publicity, *Wisdomkeepers* ran through its first printing of fifteen thousand within three months. Just as Steven and Harvey were seeking elders, so evidently are thousands of others.

In a way, each chapter of this book is a reflection of my own search for elders—men and women, usually older, who can guide the way. In the pages of this book, you will find countless elders who have shared their wisdom with us— about our hearts and our health, our marriages and our jobs, our lives and our deaths.

Consider the results of a 1990 poll by *New Options,* the political newsletter whose circulation is heavily weighted toward those now entering the second half. Editor Mark Satin asked the newsletter's readers to vote for the most influential book of the eighties. The authors whose books were in the top ten were in many respects very diverse—half men, half women; some scholars, others journalists; some more culturally oriented, others more political. But they had one common feature. Despite the fact that the voters were primarily under fifty, the top ten authors were, with one exception, all over fifty. (The exception was Jonathan Schell, author of *The Fate of the Earth,* who was only forty-eight.)[5] In a wonderful twist of fate, the generation that had coined the phrase "never trust anyone over thirty" now cherishes most the guidance of authors over fifty! As we mature, we are able to grasp the greater truth that we need the old, just as they need us.

Particularly as we enter the second half and feel the finiteness of the human life-span, we yearn for the interweaving of the threads. Childhood, youth, early adulthood, midlife, elderhood[6]—we want them to form a fabric that is stronger than any of the threads alone. No thread is more important than another. Just as water and air and earth are all essential, just as an artist cannot paint a rainbow without a full palette of colors, so we cannot live our lives without all the generations—including our elders. True elders have a wisdom that we need. We must cherish them.

We must "guard them like pure spring water"—not for their sake, but for our own.

Elderhood: The Thread of Wisdom

To strengthen the fabric of the life cycle, we must first, as weavers know, recognize and appreciate the separate skeins of yarn for their unique colors, textures, and strengths. We must be able to call them by name. And we cannot. We seem to be in a quandary about what to call the later phases of adulthood. Old people? Senior citizens? The aged? The elderly? Golden-agers?

No one has struggled with this dilemma more than Gerald Hotchkiss, whose magazine designed for this age group was first called *Harvest Years,* then switched to *Retirement Living,* and renamed itself *50 Plus* before settling down with the long-winded *New Choices for the Best Years.* According to Hotchkiss, none of the various names for this age group is acceptable. "Mature people don't like any of those words," Hotchkiss says. "At one point, I asked readers to give us a new name. They couldn't come up with a good term, either."[7]

"When I hear people talk about people my age, it makes my stomach turn," says Richard Gunther, a businessman in his mid-sixties who has researched peak performance in his age group and feels passionately that the old are underestimated. "Senior citizens, the aged, the elderly—it's like they're already sliding us out the door. The terms used to describe us sound like the culture's really saying: 'Let's stick them in a room and watch them die.' "

The problem is not merely linguistic. Even if we found an acceptable term, we would not know to whom it applied. As Simone de Beauvoir accurately observed, we don't even know when we have actually reached this stage because it has no rite of passage.[8] Certain privileges and penalties apply as one enters this stage of life. Positively, one becomes eligible for certain social benefits; negatively, one can be removed from one's job or become a victim of job discrimination. By the age of sixty-five and usually well before, it is clear that the term *midlife* simply does not do justice to one's circumstances. One has entered a new stage—but what is it? Does *old age* do it justice?

No, it doesn't. Instead, *elderhood* is what this final stage of the life cycle should be called. It immediately conveys a fundamental and forgotten tribal truth. Elders know something that those of us in other stages of the life cycle need to understand; they possess something that the generations following them need. Within their bodies and minds, at the core of their very beings, true elders embody the gift of life. Just as newborns archetypally symbolize hope and new beginnings, those who are closest to the end of the life cycle symbolize wisdom and wholeness.

A society might debate the pros and cons of respecting "senior citizens." It might squabble over how well it needs to care for "the aged." But the term *elder* immediately states its own case; it demands respect, just as *youth* or *adult* does. It sends a signal to the rest of the life cycle that, whatever the frailties or hardships of the old might be, *the elders must hold their rightful and respected place within the tribal council.* They must have an honored place not because of charity or compassion, pity or affirmative action, but because elderhood, like the other spokes on the wheel of life and death, is vital to its turning.

Sixty-six-year-old Rabbi Zalman Schachter-Shalomi is working hard to repair the broken wheel of the life cycle. In seminars from Arizona and Florida to Pennsylvania and New York, he has presented his basic training program called "From Aging to Saging." It is all part of what he calls the Spiritual Eldering Project, an effort to awaken among America's elderly an awareness of their "true calling." They are not worn-out parts to be discarded, he maintains; they deserve a place at the tribal council.

"With our longer life-spans," says Rabbi Zalman, "we can shape ourselves into the kind of elder we want to be. We can maximize the bliss that we find in our condition. But you can't find the bliss unless you understand the condition." The rabbi argues that, just as children need adults, so do those in the middle of the life cycle need elders. In order to live fully the middle decades ("between forty-two and sixty-three," as he puts it) we need a vision of elderhood—of how we want to spend our late sixties, seventies, eighties, and beyond. We human beings are made "to look beyond one phase of life into the next phase so that [our] orientation in life can be right. . . . You can't develop the October, November, or December of our life," he concludes, echoing photographer Steven Wall, "if you don't look at death."

Like the "Elder Hostels" initiative and other innovative programs, Rabbi Zalman's seminars help participants rediscover what Oren Lyons and the Iroquois have tried never to forget. We cannot sustain the life cycles without elders, and we cannot respect elders without sustaining the whole life cycle. If a community "desires to live on spiritually," wrote psychiatrist Robert Coles in the conclusion of his best-selling book *The Spiritual Life of Children,* "then it looks upon the ancient man, who belongs both to the past and to the after-world, as its embodiment."

The connection between elders and community is not a lofty abstraction. It is a medical fact. When researchers probed the rising rates of elderly suicide, for example, they discovered that the key variable is not physical or mental illness but isolation. Loss of daily contact with other human beings actually alters bodily rhythms and produces depression, which in turn can lead to suicide.[9] This is not an isolated research finding but a consistent pattern in investigations of the aging process: Social isolation leads to higher rates of illness and mortality. *"Anything that promotes a sense of isolation leads to chronic stress and, often, to illnesses like heart disease,"* concludes Dr. Dean Ornish. "Conversely, *anything that leads to real intimacy and feelings of connection can be healing* in the real sense of the word: to bring together, to make whole" (emphasis in the original).[10]

All over the world, research findings demonstrate conclusively that social contact and support keep people healthier and alive longer. Scientists at the Ohio State University School of Medicine have found that those who are lonely have lower immune functioning. At the Medical College of Wisconsin, Dr. James Goodwin studied 256 healthy elderly adults and found that those with friendships and consistent social contact had lower blood cholesterol levels and higher immune function. At Stanford, doctors found that women with metastatic breast cancer who had regular support group meetings had twice the survival rate of those who did not. A decade-long study of 150 middle-age men in Sweden proved that the more isolated were more likely to die of coronary heart disease. In countless studies, the message is the same:

In the second half of life, community is not a luxury but a vital necessity.[11]

Wherever a society collapses or dies, you will notice that the life cycle has been disrespected. One, and sometimes many, strands in the generational web have been neglected, damaged or destroyed. Conversely, when a society flourishes, you will find that the life cycle has been honored. Each stage has been cared for and provided with some kind of initiation into the next. To bind the generations together, to nurture them all, and to enable them to rediscover the natural synergy in the human life cycle—this is a crucial part of our quest for wholeness.

Throughout this book, the stories we have told and the references we have cited are in fact the footprints of men and women in the second half who have passed on their wisdom to us. One such elder was Margaret Mead. She was an anthropologist—not a profession designed as a platform for public recognition, much less a launching pad to fame. Yet she became a celebrity in the best sense of the word—celebrated by the public for her gift to the larger community. Her face could be found on everything from sugar packages to decks of feminist playing cards to the walls of restaurants in college towns. She was a regular columnist in a mass circulation women's magazine and inspired thousands of women, including *Passages* author Gail Sheehy. She not only deepened our understanding of the purpose of the second half of life, she was a model—idiosyncratic yet compelling—of the quest.

Like Campbell, Margaret Mead lived her almost eighty years with extraordinary zest. Transcending narrow gender roles, she combined "masculine" and "feminine" qualities with charisma. In the Roaring Twenties, when young women like her were getting married and having babies, she was off to the South Pacific studying the diversity of cultures. When many of her contemporaries were living out their sex-role stereotypes, she was observing them in other cultures—and her own—and challenging conventional wisdom about the meaning of gender. On the eve of World War II, she had her first and only child at thirty-eight. She was one of the few women of her time who set the pattern of late motherhood that was to become so common among later generations. As fiercely committed to motherhood as she was to her career, she did not let her professional ambitions stop her from mothering, nor did she let the tug of motherhood stop her from renewing her work in the second half of life. As she reveals so clearly in her memoir, *Blackberry Winter,* her quest intensified as she moved through the adventure of her second half.[12]

Although a bibliography of her academic work spanning fifty years would fill a hundred pages, her passion as well as her prose in the second half of her life were directed increasingly toward Main Street rather than academe. A frequent guest on the *Tonight* show and a regular columnist in *Redbook,* she was once asked by a *Family Circle* interviewer about Western society's approach to retirement. "The practice of early retirement is terribly wasteful," she replied with characteristic bluntness. "We are wasting millions of good years of good people by forcing them into retirement. . . . They don't know what else to do but die."[13] And so she became one of the most articulate proponents of linking the two ends of the life cycle, for she was concerned that the seven generations were in danger of losing touch with each other and therefore with themselves. For a program developed in conjunction with the bicentennial of the United States in 1976, she helped develop a model book called *How to Interview Your Grandparents.* "It is the reverse of a baby book," she explained. "The [young people] make up the questions simply by thinking of what they wanted to know about the past. The older people adore being asked. They stop complaining that nobody is interested in them or that 'nobody listens to me anymore. . . .' And the young people find that what they have to say is fascinating."

There are many other wise guides who, like Campbell and Mead, have deepened our understanding of the cycle of life. Whether we call them "elderheroes,"[14] "pathfinders,"[15] or as I prefer, simply elders, they are offering us valuable advice and counsel. They are our "wisdomkeepers." They are not asking to be revered. They ask only that we help guide those who follow as they have guided us. As Wendell Berry writes: "The teachers are everywhere. What is wanted is a learner. . . . [The teachers] are waiting, as they always have, beyond the edge of the light."[16]

So now, cast a quick glance over the preceding pages of this chapter. Simply register the names: native American leader Oren Lyons . . . businessman Richard Gunther . . . philosopher Simone de Beauvoir . . . Rabbi Zalman Schachter-Shalomi . . . physician Dean Ornish . . . anthropologist Margaret Mead . . . writer and farmer Wendell Berry. By calling them elders, I do not mean that they have a monopoly on the truth, or that their lives were models that we should copy in every respect. But I do mean that they, and the hundreds of others who appear in the pages of this book, have lessons to teach us.

Children and Youth:
The Momentum of the Life Cycle

"Before I got married I had six theories about bringing up children," said John Wilmont, the Earl of Rochester. "Now I have six children and no theories."

If the above statement makes you think that the following pages are only for those of us who have children, think again. For the truth is that what parents have the opportunity to learn in the second half of life from their children is learning with which all of us, whether we are parents or not, must reckon. Indeed, what the young can teach the old is a vital key to the quest for wholeness. Elsewhere in this book I share experiences that I had with my two younger children that taught me important lessons. But my oldest son, Shane, who is now seventeen, is preparing to begin his own life in the world. When our children reach their own coming of age, they can, if they wish, teach us as much as our elders can.

Like any parent, I had a vested interest during the first half of my life in thinking of myself as a good parent. I took pride in doing a good job. When we are childless or when our children are still too young to articulate *their* truths, we can persuade ourselves (and sometimes them) that we are right and they are wrong. When our relationship with them proves problematic, we can bask in our own wisdom and experience and view them as the problem. During the years when I was in training as a family therapist, I witnessed many families in which the parents were all too quick to present me with their children's shortcomings but slow indeed to itemize their own. Unfortunately, at a weekend workshop for men that I attended with Shane, I learned that I shared this myopia.

When the time came during the workshop for Shane and me to stand inside a circle of men and speak our truths, Shane used the safety of this orchestrated space to level with me about how I had hurt him during his childhood. With passionate precision, he showed me that many of my actions that I felt had demonstrated my love and support for him were, in his eyes, self-serving efforts to prove to myself that I was a "good father." It would be a violation of his privacy, if not my own, to recount the specifics of what he said. But I can report that virtually every father in the room, as well as many sons, were moved to tears by the devastating yet liberating accuracy of his critique.

As painful as it was for me to hear the darker, negative side of his feelings about me, it was ultimately inspiring, as only the truth can be. For he was calling me toward wholeness. He was asking me to treat him as a young man, not a child—that is, to treat him with greater authenticity and integrity. The time had to end when I could shade what I did or said with the excuse that it was "for his own good." The time had come to say exactly what I felt—nothing more, nothing less.

Because of that eye-opening, heart-opening confrontation with my own son, which was followed by hours of cleansing conversations, I have learned that my strategies for child-rearing were often designed not to nurture them but to protect myself. His courage and honesty in expressing his own pain and anger enabled me to experience more clearly my own. In this way, the strengths that I had helped him to develop came back full circle to strengthen me. His own growing maturity catalyzed mine.

I had invited Shane to join me in this men's workshop because I felt his need to be initiated as a man. I knew that this can best be done not by a father (or mother) alone, but by a community of adults. Unfortunately, in our culture, it is often not done at all. Just as the passage *out* of adulthood into elderhood has no rite, neither does the passage *into* adulthood from youth.

Adulthood means more than a social security number and a driver's license, more than a diploma and a paycheck. But exactly what *does* it mean? As my generation's "Don't trust anybody over thirty!" slogan indicated, adulthood to us seemed remote, strange, and frightening. We had no idea how to get there, or how to even recognize when, or if, we arrived. From what we had seen of adulthood, we were not convinced it was a place we wanted to go. The men were afraid of becoming the "organization man" or the "man in a gray flannel suit"; the women were afraid of becoming victims of what Betty Friedan called the "feminine mystique." We came of age at a historical juncture of accelerating change that made us feel abandoned by our elders. Yes, our elders gave us SATs and College Boards, driving tests and fraternity or sorority games, boot camps and baby showers. But *as a culture,* our rites of passage were fragmented and hollow. Our elders were absent or unacknowledged. We turned to each other, and to our popular culture, to be initiated into the next stage of life.

"Anthropological literature is filled with accounts of how the Hopi Indians or the Arapesh of New Guinea nudge their youth into adulthood with help of myths, symbols and invitation rituals," observed one reviewer of Robert Bly's *Iron John.* ". . . But one could read a towering stack of ethnographies without encountering the suggestion that perhaps the same necessity holds also for us. Primitive people may need myths and rituals because, well, they are primitive, aren't they? We, being rational, need none of that. Just give us the facts and the truth shall set us free."[17]

Before the young have even passed around the first quarter of the turning of life's wheel, they encounter the consequences of being without such a communal rite of passage. They do not know how to get from youth to adulthood. There is no bridge. The rite of passage they seek cannot be reduced to one-liners, or packaged in curricular "modules," or sandwiched between home room and geometry. And when we think in our adult arrogance that we know what they need and how to give it to them, we betray not only them but our own quest. Ultimately, they want what we want: a chance to explore the mysteries of their unfolding lives and an opportunity to pursue their quest. What they bring to their quest is the fiery energy of youth. They have questions. They seek answers. And they want them *now.*

Because Shelley is head of an innovative high school program that deals with the inner development of young people, I have been privileged to hear teenagers speak directly and eloquently about what is actually on their minds and in their hearts. When asked what they wonder about and what really concerns them, junior high students wrote:

Who likes me?

I worry about my brother. Does he really hate me? Do I
really hate him?

Why are parents so un-understanding?

How should I act around friends that hate my other
friends?

Do my friends really like me or are they faking?

Why does my best friend always get angry when I get a
better score?

How do you know if you love someone? What is a good
time to lose virginity?

Why do parents fight over the smallest mistake?

Why isn't there peace in the world?

I wonder about AIDS and about evil in the world.

Why does everybody except me do good at everything?

Why do I get periods of depression?

Why are people mean to each other?

And from students in high school:

How can some people like me so much and others not
like me at all?

Do we all really have "a purpose," or do we live just for
the sake of living?

What am I going to ask myself when I'm about to die?

Do I believe in God?

How long am I going to live?

Why do people use drugs for excuses?

Is a long-term relationship necessary for sex?

How important are looks?

What goes on in people's minds when they do cruel
things to one another?

What happens when we die?

Is there a physical God, or did we just make Him out of
our need?

> If there is a God, why is there so much Bad on
>   Earth?

I think of these questions whenever I am asked to speak to a
high school or college audience. This list makes clear that
they do not need adults—much less elders—to "make them
think." They are *already* thinking.

The yearning of the young to feel the wheel of life in all its
wholeness is powerful. It is why, I believe, a European-born
professor who had been a student of Sigmund Freud became
such an unlikely hero on the Harvard campus during my
student years. Erik Erikson had no Ph.D.; he was called a
lecturer, not a professor; he spoke English slowly and with a
heavy accent; his presentation was neither dynamic nor charismatic. Yet, as one of my Harvard contemporaries, Howard
Gardner, observed: "Though neither senior in status, not a
compelling speaker . . . he had within a few years become
a major figure, *if not the major intellectual force,* on the Harvard campus."[18]

The last time I saw Erikson during my college years, he
and his wife Joan were sitting in an armchair in my apartment. She sat on the armrest, holding his hand. Our apartment was filled with our fellow classmates who had just completed Erikson's course on the life cycle. I watched them
from the other side of the room while holding the hand of
my girlfriend, who had also taken the course. Almost half a
century separated them from us. Yet they had communi-
cated to us, who were a third their age, a sense of our own
future. He enabled us to believe that the half century or
more that lay ahead of us was not predestined to be a mechanical repetition of patterns imprinted on us in childhood.
Those years were—or at least *could* be—an adventure of
mind, body, and spirit leading into extraordinary new terri-
tories. From the sight of this extraordinary couple, we received something far more valuable than a college education
—a living vision of an ever-unfolding, ever-deepening life

cycle of which all the generations are a vital, interwoven part.

If Erikson had not existed, we would have had to invent him, because he gave us back the vision that Freud had taken away. The warmed-over Freudianism that had swept America persuaded our culture of the vital importance of children's psychological development, but it said virtually nothing about adults'. The implication was that grownups had been formed in childhood—and therefore had finished growing. But according to Erikson, character was not finally formed in childhood. We were not "grown up" at the age of twenty-one. On the contrary, the entire human life cycle was a series of interwoven, interdependent developmental stages that together determined the quality of our lives.

In his book *Identity, Youth, and Crisis,* Erikson stressed that the late teens and early twenties are a crucial time when our sense of self crystallizes into an "identity" that is more than the sum of its childhood parts. But that is only the beginning of the adult journey. Next comes a period characterized by a tension between *intimacy versus isolation,* when we try to forge new deep bonds with others outside our childhood families. Then follows the challenge of *generativity versus stagnation,* a period spanning the first decades of adulthood, when jobs are found, homes established, children conceived and raised. Erikson's final stage of adult development he dramatically called *integrity versus despair.* During these final decades of the life-span, as we confront our own death and that of those we love, we face the challenge of holding our lives together meaningfully even as they are about to end. Moving beyond the dependency of childhood and the independence of early adulthood, we discover the mysteries of the second half.[19]

Rough and general as Erikson's descriptions are, these stages of life constituted much-needed landmarks on the path ahead. They were a moral as well as a psychological compass that provided an inner sense of direction. While everyone around us spoke of career ladders and sound investments, here was a man who reminded us that one of the responsibilities of adulthood is to grow—psychologically, ethically, socially, and spiritually. Even in their eighties, Joan and Erik were still writing about the vitally important role of elders in our society.[20]

Respect Your Elders and Then Become One

A fifth-grade girl named Ginny is walking home from school one day when she encounters an old woman on the sidewalk who seems disoriented. The white-haired lady, who is talking to herself and seems quite agitated, is desperately clutching a little piece of paper in her hands. After hesitating to get involved, Ginny asks her if she needs help. Although the woman speaks incoherently, Ginny learns that she has taken a wrong turn and that now, despite the little map she is holding, she is completely lost. Ginny manages to calm the old woman down and lead her home. But as Ginny starts to leave, the grateful woman grabs Ginny's arm and begins to pour out her gratitude, saying that God had sent Ginny to her and that she would thank Him in her prayers.

"I wasn't sure, at first, if she was serious," Ginny recalls. "But I looked at her, and she had tears in her eyes, so I knew she was. I was going to tell her it was an accident we'd met, but I decided not to."[21]

Robert Coles concludes his book *The Spiritual Life of Children* with this story precisely because it was *not* an accident. It was a precious moment when the wheel of life was turning as it was meant to. But how often today, in our fear-ridden and hurried metropolitan world, do young people ignore the needs of the old? And how often do adults neglect the young?

When the distinguished black educator James Comer was a boy, he would walk to and from school knowing that at least four or five adults' eyes were watching him. If he misbehaved, he knew his parents would hear about it. Those eyes belonged not to relatives, not even to friends, but to other adult neighbors who considered themselves part of the Comer family's community. Now, says Comer, most children walk by strangers. Once they leave their parents' care, they are on their own. As Jane Jacobs observed over a generation ago, when a neighborhood dies, a child on the sidewalk is no longer watched by anyone. In the calculus of real estate, the needs of the life cycle are of low priority.[22]

Generational interdependence is being stretched to the breaking point by forces that we are only beginning to understand. Half a century ago there were *ten* working adults for every American over sixty-five. Today there are *five* workers for each older citizen. If current demographic projections hold into the mid-twenty-first century, the ratio of adult workers to retirement-age persons will be little more than *two* to one. As we age, fewer and fewer younger adults will be supporting more and more older adults.[23]

While these demographic and economic facts have many implications, one impacts directly on our second half: *We must be better prepared to take care of ourselves.* Indeed, polls show that those under forty-five years of age expect to get little benefit from social security and other programs for the elderly. For economic reasons, if not for psychological and spiritual ones, we are compelled to find a more creative, productive, and self-reliant vision for the second half. "Today's vision of being old *has* become dysfunctional," says the coauthor of *Generations,* Neil Howe. "In the next century, the elderly—and that means us baby boomers—will have to be more willing to abandon our claim on economic resources."[24]

The very notion of relinquishing entitlements will strike many as absurd. After all, the name of the game is to get as big a piece of the pie as we can for any interest group to which we belong. This is what the elderly today have tried to do and to some extent, they have succeeded. After all, the standard of living of the over-sixty-five population is now as high as it is for the nonelderly. Their incomes are about the same as those under sixty-five. Their poverty rate is lower (11.4 versus 13 percent). They are better housed (75 percent are homeowners, versus 61 percent of the nonelderly). And they have better health insurance coverage. If this is "discrimination," it is certainly not primarily economic.[25]

Discrimination against the old runs so deep that it cannot be so easily measured by economists' data. It is a discrimination not of dollars, but of esteem. The elderly have successfully lobbied to gain a vast array of economic entitlements, but the price they have paid is to be undervalued as human beings. They are seen not as elders, but as a "special interest" group that has tried to carve its initials on the federal budget. Some in Washington see them as the enemy, using their status to put a stranglehold on the shrinking funds available for human welfare programs. From such a polarized view, it is the elderly *against* the young, since a dollar spent on Medicare and Social Security is a dollar that will not be spent on schools or Head Start.

While advocates for other groups besides the elderly have reason to be concerned about generational equity, turning one age group into an enemy of another is a political strategy that will quickly backfire. In fact, economically as well as spiritually, the generations are utterly interdependent. As expert testimony to Congress made clear a few years ago, it is in the *self*-interest of older Americans to support educational and other programs that invest in the young. Unless the young are well educated and grow up to be not only productive but also creative members of society, the economic base on which the old depend will most certainly erode. Unless we invest more in the young, our "closing years [will be] filled with poverty and social unrest because a very large fraction of the work force, which is itself a declining proportion of the population as whole, *will be unable to support themselves, to say nothing of others.*"[26]

Just as it is in the economic self-interest of the old to invest in the young, so it is in the spiritual self-interest of the young to invest in the old. It is the elders who initiate us into the second half. It is they who are forerunners on the quest. If this transmission of wisdom does not occur, every generation has to learn the same truths over and over again. "A culture which does not venerate its elders has no inherent cultural lineage," observes Jack Zimmerman, an innovative sixty-year-old educator who has developed rites of passage for adolescents. "It is disconnected from its own ancestry. The hard-won spiritual wisdom of their ancestors is lost and has to be rediscovered all over again."[27]

So it is extremely short-sighted to view the elderly merely as an interest group battling for their piece of the economic pie. Fortunately, by the time we reach the second half, we have the maturity to see in the social fabric the invisible thread that binds the life cycle together: *The growth of each depends upon the growth of all.* The more successfully one generation enters the next stage, the more it enhances the ability of those before and after it to enter theirs. The young are within us; so are the old.

Respecting our elders does not mean turning them into gurus or becoming mindless followers of any gray-haired orator who claims to know the secrets of the universe. Neither do we need a gerontocracy in which, as in China, the very old stagnate the vital processes of social change and thereby force the young to become revolutionaries. Respect does not mean blind obedience. On the contrary, it means respecting ourselves enough to listen to them and then to follow our *own* quest. Only then will we become elders ourselves.

When we are still in our teens or twenties, we can revere leaders on the one hand or deride them on the other. We can speak of leadership as if it were another generation's problem. At that age, those who run for the highest offices are by law required to be our parents' age, not ours. But by the time we reach the second half, mocking those who govern the tribe strikes a hollow chord. We are their age now. As we move into life's second half, we find ourselves called to lead the young. Whether or not we seek this responsibility, it is ours. Although we may criticize the performance of the leaders in our community for not acting as true elders, our tone must change. The challenge is not only to find elders, but to become them.

As far back as A.D. 1000, the chief of the Iroquois called the Peacemaker brought together the chiefs of the several warring tribes and greeted them with this invocation: "Think not of yourselves, O Chiefs, nor of your own generation. Think of continuing generations of our families, think of our grandchildren and of those yet unborn, whose faces are coming from beneath the ground."[28] The leader's responsibility is to embody integrity, or wholeness, which means not only the living but the dead and unborn as well. Although they cannot vote, they are still part of the tribe. Only when their spirits are honored can we truly embrace all seven generations.

Today, one thousand years since the Peacemaker spoke, the tribe is much larger. Its members are no longer of the same skin or language, but of every nation and culture on earth. The tribe resides not on a reservation, but on a planet. And so humankind now needs elders who can create common ground where all the tribes can come together. So we cannot afford to simply walk in our fathers' and mothers' footsteps. Many of their footprints have already been washed away. We must look farther back, beyond the parents and grandparents, to the perennial wisdom of our ancestors, and to the future needs of our children's children.

This is true elderhood. And it is to this challenge of leadership that we now turn.

7

TAKING CARE OF YOUR HOME
The Quest for Integrity

This we know: The Earth does not belong to man, man belongs to the Earth. All things are connected like to blood that connects us all. Man did not weave the web of life, he is merely a strand in it. Whatever he does to the web, he does to himself.

CHIEF SEATTLE
in a letter to U.S. President Franklin Pierce, 1855

As I have attempted to come into my own in the second half of my life, my quest has taken me to many gatherings around the world, to places where the individual quests of men and women encounter some of the global realities that will shape our journeys whether we like it or not. One of the most exciting—and frightening—of these gatherings took place in the dead of winter in 1990.

Along with several hundred religious leaders, political figures, scientists, and activists, I arrive in Moscow for a global environmental conference that Gorbachev himself is scheduled to address on the final day. Like most newspaper readers, I have known for many years about the environmental crisis. But I have never before sat for so many days and listened to so many experts from so many different places make the same bleak arguments. Speaker after speaker, from virtually every corner of the world, has reached the same conclusion. Even if we begin to change our ways immediately, the biological forces that will cause the deterioration of the ecosphere to continue for years to come have already been set in motion. We are destroying the planet not by the nuclear war we always feared, but by the way we live when we are at peace.

The speakers at the conference, of course, disagree about many subjects. But regarding the deterioration of the biosphere, there is, unfortunately, little debate. Capitalist and Communist, religious figures as well as political leaders, delegates from East and West and North and South—they all agree that:

- Forest coverage is receding.
- Deserts are growing.
- Soil cover is eroding.
- Warming "greenhouse gases" are increasing.

- Ozone is being depleted.
- The number of species is decreasing.
- Fresh water supplies are dwindling.
- Per capita grain production is falling.
- The number of people is still climbing.

Lester Brown, who heads the Worldwatch Institute, which monitors these trends, foresees the fabric of human life unraveling within forty years if we do not change course. He believes we have a four-decade opportunity to turn these dangerous trends around and keep this planet fit for human habitation. "By the year 2030, we will either have achieved an economy of environmentally sustainable development," warns Brown, "or we will have failed."[1]

If I have the life-span that actuarial tables predict, 2030 is about the time that I will die. My children will be in midlife, and my grandchildren will just be entering adulthood. What Brown is saying to our generation is that *the second half of our lives is a crucial turning point in human history.* According to Brown, unless we change the way we live on this planet profoundly and rapidly, the natural world will be fatally wounded by the time we pass from this earth. He is telling me, and you, that if we live the second half the way we lived the first, those who follow us will find a wasteland.

"Whether we want to or not, our life-style will change," Lester Brown told me later. "The question is: will we change how we live quickly enough to sustain human civilization? Or will we let environmental degradation and economic decline feed on each other? If we do [the latter] it will lead to social disintegration. We know that our own economic system is environmentally unsustainable. Our challenge is to convert into a system that can last, and do so in our lifetime. I can think of no challenge more exciting or more important."[2]

Simply put, the question that Brown and other experts on

global ecology are asking us is this: *Will we also care about the planet on which our quests depend?*

Protecting Our Quest = Protecting Our Planet

As we go through midlife and into our later decades, what is happening to the planet? How does the condition of the biosphere impact on our own lives? And how do our fears about how it will impact on our children's and grandchildren's lives affect us?

To become the kinds of leaders the earth needs, we must expand our concept of the quest. The previous chapters have been intimate. Body, marriage, work, aging, generations—these are personal matters indeed. But politics? For most of us, no. Whether the word refers to national affairs or global diplomacy, we tend to associate *politics* with Washington, D.C., or with Moscow, Paris, or Tokyo. "Politics" is something we read about in the newspaper or watch on TV. Rarely does it happen to us. It is something that is done by others, in other places, for purposes that are often unclear and, even worse, uninspiring. So for many of us, we almost instinctively recoil at the word *politics.*

In this chapter, however, I ask you to approach politics in a different way. In keeping with the spirit of our quest, I ask you to reflect on your *personal connection* to politics. What does it have to do with your everyday life? With your health —and your children's? With your sense of meaning and purpose? With your visceral experience of power or importance? With who you *are?*

This more personal, visceral kind of politics matters to each and every one of us. Whether you are a Democrat or a Republican, independent or just indifferent, you have no choice but to be political on this level. It is part of being human, and certainly part of being in the second half. By the time we have watched several political administrations come and go, we are veterans. We know how the game is played.

Unless we are professionally involved in politics (which few of us are), we watch the game from the bleachers. But something important has changed since we were children or young adults: The players are now more or less our age. We no longer see the "older generation" at the microphones, standing in front of the White House or the Capitol. We see our peers. Naturally, we begin to feel more responsible for what is happening to us, to the next generations, and to the planet.

Whether or not we have children, we have reached the age of parenthood. In the seventies, I wrote a book subtitled *The Politics of Parenthood* because I realized that the act of becoming a parent (to which I was about to commit myself) was a political act. Our baby would be influenced in the womb by radiation and toxic substances resulting from corporate and government policies; affected in childbirth by medical practices, drugs, and hospital regulations; shaped in infancy by the quality of the food supply; molded by an educational system under state and federal control; instilled with images and values by mass media; and raised in a family buffeted by economic and political pressures. Being a good parent, I realized, would not just require changing diapers and being a breadwinner. It would mean taking responsibility for the myriad forces that would shape our child's life.[3]

Becoming old enough to be a parent (not to mention old enough to be a senator or president) naturally makes us feel more engaged. It feels increasingly irresponsible, even foolish, to discuss the state of our nation or the world anymore as someone else's problem. After all, I write these words at an age when John F. Kennedy was president of the United States of America. I have friends and acquaintances my own age who are senators, congressmen, governors, and presidential candidates. I know what they are doing with *their* power. Our similarity in age compels me to ask: What am I doing with my power? And, as I do so, I trust you will ask yourself: What are you doing with *yours*?

As this question hits you, I can well understand that you might now be afraid that I am about to tell you what to do. After all, dire warnings about the fate of the earth are not new. They are usually the predictable prelude to some self-appointed activist telling us in tones of self-righteous authority what we should do. The worse their predictions, the more entitled they are to persuade us to change our behavior. Then they will proceed to enumerate the fifty ways we can "save the world," or the one thousand and one ways that we can "protect the planet." In other words, they will tell us where *our* quest should take us.

Although I respect these activists and in many ways include myself among them, I cannot adopt their strategy or their tone in this book. To do so would violate the spirit of the quest. In the context of this book, such admonitions and exhortations would sound patronizing. They would be a negation of one of the most important truths that we have learned together—that our quest is not someone else's responsibility, but our own. It is we who must ask *ourselves* what our mission or Calling shall be. Not only the answer we find, but the personal power we invest in the question itself, will be the heart of our quest.

Mortal Power: Becoming Earth-Centered Leaders

Power is seductive. It feeds on itself. Those who covet it are often not the ones who should have it; those who get it are often not the ones who deserve it; and those who are without it are often the ones who have the most to give. So for all my life, I have looked for men and women who are humbly grounded in their own mortal power. In this chapter, you will meet some whom I have learned to trust and who have, in turn, introduced me to others who are equally trustworthy.

But sadly, I must report how few such men and women I have found who are prominent in politics. Indeed, as a profession, politics is held in lower esteem than ever. When asked who their heroes are, for example, young men and women rarely name politicians anymore (and when they do, they feel compelled to dip back into history). Except in election years, business leaders, movie stars, pop musicians, and self-help gurus draw far larger crowds than politicians. And even when it comes time to vote, a right for which others around the world struggle and even die, more Americans than ever are staying home.

Political scientists and sociologists have long lists of reasons to explain this apathy. But one reason above all relates to our quest in life's second half: Politics lacks wholeness. The goal of politicians is to appear as if they were made of Teflon (nothing ever sticks to them, much less hurts them). They almost always describe their records as flawless (they have never made a mistaken vote or error in judgment). They are advised by their managers never to cry (doing so has lost more than one election); never to admit emotional turmoil or even ambivalence (which is depicted as synonymous with weakness or vacillation, not depth); and never, absolutely never, to seek (or admit having sought) psychological counseling or guidance of any kind. Most of those who have been entrusted with such power behave as if they were invulnerable, infallible, immortal. They must act, in other words, as if they were almost perfect in rectitude, godlike in judgment, and emotionally as stable as a rock. Only their spouses may be in pain, and not surprisingly in such marriages, they often are.

By cutting themselves off from their own wholeness, they undercut their own capacity for compassion—for the people they claim to serve, for the planet that nourished them, and for the future that has been entrusted to their care. Though they may call themselves public servants, they act like masters, motivated by ambition, not service. As a result, politics provides us with few elders who can speak with moral authority.

Sometimes, however, even the most powerful are rudely awakened by one of the most powerful teachers of all: their own mortality. Lee Atwater was George Bush's youngest intimate campaign adviser. He contributed to the 1988 campaign against Michael Dukakis some of its most effective—and ugliest—tactics. Well past the election, he continued to defend his behavior and showed no signs of remorse for the tasteless as well as unethical means he had used to defeat the Democratic opponent. But then he learned that he was suffering from a life-threatening brain tumor. After weathering a particularly dangerous time, he wrote: "The doctors still won't answer that nagging question of mine: How long do I have? Three weeks. Three months. Three years. I try to live as if I have at least three years, but some nights I can't go to sleep, so fearful am I that I will never wake up again."

Not long before he died, the outgoing Republican National Committee chairman apologized for the first time for the dirty campaign tactics he had used to defeat Democratic presidential candidate Dukakis, including his infamous remark that he would make the public think that Willie Horton, a convicted rapist and murderer, was Dukakis's running mate. After his near-death experience, his outlook had changed.[4] As Jung put it, what was true in the morning of life had become in the afternoon a lie.

I firmly believe Atwater's awareness of mortality made him *more* powerful, not less. For the first time, I respected him. (So did Dukakis, who acknowledged that Atwater "had the courage to apologize. That says a lot for the man.") He spoke with integrity, because his encounter with death altered his constituency. Before his illness, as a young and ambitious man still in his thirties, his constituency had been members of the Republican party who vote in current presidential elections. After his terrifying encounter with death, he entered the second half. As he faced his own imminent death, his constituency became more timeless. He measured his behavior not in terms of electoral votes in 1988, but in terms of ethical values that would last long after he, and we, are gone. He cared how he would be remembered. For the first time in his life, he became grounded in his mortal power —that is, power grounded in wholeness, not blind ambition.

On our quest, we have worked diligently toward our own wholeness: healing our deep wounds, seeking our soul/mate, caring for our families, committing ourselves to a true Calling, respecting the aging process and our elders, and honoring the seven generations. But now, if we start trying to lead a life based on wholeness, we discover that it is not highly valued in our society. Our political leaders do not speak to us as whole men and women. They are not—indeed, *cannot* —be whole because they must act as if they have no wounds (except from war). Instead, they must "package" or at best "present" themselves. They speak not from the heart but from calculation. They embody not sincere enthusiasm but media poise. They consult not the gods but their pollsters. They are grounded not in compassion but in ambition. Behind the image that is fed to the public, a soul still survives. But they cannot risk allowing it to surface, except in thirty-second "spots" that reduce whatever wholeness they may actually have to professionally crafted guile.

At the heart of American politics, according to veteran political media consultant David Garth, is this fundamental contradiction. "One of the clichés in this business is that by playing it down the middle, by not taking chances or taking risks, you won't expose yourself," he explained to me. "You won't make yourself vulnerable in front of the public. You don't get in trouble. And so you don't lose votes. But everybody is yearning for something to believe in. And it's hard to really believe in someone who is just out for the numbers and playing it safe."

Having worked with candidates for a quarter century, Garth has watched with growing concern the evolution of current voter apathy. Although he believes the suspicion toward politicians that is so prevalent in the post-Vietnam generations is partly justified, he feels it has "snowballed" to the point that candidates of the future would be well-advised to practice authenticity. "Press scrutiny is so close that you're going to be seen. As that camera comes up close, it's going to catch you up when you are not being real."

Just as a therapist knows his patient's problems, so Garth knows the politicians' neurosis. "When candidates are trying to make it, they're absorbed at first. But when you get older, when they've been elected for the first or second time, that's when they often start to lose their center. They begin to feel like they are walking through a charade. They get lost in their own images. They begin to fall apart inside. Some of them don't see that it's happening. But even some who recognize it don't know what to do about it."[5]

During a recent trip to Eastern Europe, Michael Rowan, the former president of the International Association of Political Consultants, was startled to realize that these newly liberated nations elected as presidents poets, playwrights, writers, and scientists. "Not since the days of Jefferson, Adams and Madison," wrote Rowan in *Campaigns & Elections,* the professional journal of his group, "have the great writers, philosophers and thinkers of the United States also been its political leaders.

> "In fact, it is a rare event in the United States to have a political leader even celebrated by a poet, the way Walt Whitman wrote about Abraham Lincoln, or the way Robert Frost spoke about John F. Kennedy on Inauguration Day, 1961. Other than the authentic biographers, what serious writer has taken as a subject a political leader in the United States? I can't think of one."

Concluding that "leadership in the United States has been eviscerated," this veteran political consultant admits that his profession must shoulder some of the blame for helping style to triumph over substance and salesmen to push aside statesmen. The majority of the public does not even vote and, Rowan confirms, "the cynicism toward politicians is profound."[6] No wonder two best-selling books on American politics are called *Why Americans Hate Politics* and *Parliament of Whores.*[7]

My cynicism too is profound. So, I suspect, is yours. We wait for a man or woman to emerge who will enable us to trust again. We wait for a campaign that inspires rather than repels. We scan the horizon for a political movement that makes us feel empowered, not betrayed; elevated, not debased; enriched, not compromised. We are surrounded by grasping politicians when what we yearn for is elders—men and women who express a vision that goes beyond their own images, beyond the next election. We seek true elders.

Perhaps this is why the words of Chief Seattle, which opened this chapter, now seem to be appearing everywhere. During the last few years, I have seen so many times the words of this native American leader (after whom the city in the Northwest was named) that I began to consider it some kind of New Age eco-cliché. I finally stopped and listened one day when I was taking refuge in a friend's home in order to find time to write. I noticed on the wall a framed portrait of a dark-skinned man with long black hair. I stepped closer and read the headline: "Chief Seattle speaks." It was a picture of Chief Seattle, and on it was superimposed in small type his entire letter to President Pierce. In the fine print at the bottom was the credit line: "Produced by the Silicon Valley Toxics Coalition." To raise money to protect their valley from industrial poisoning, the citizens' action group had turned to the native American leader who died long before the personal computer was ever invented.

Intrigued about why an Indian leader who had been dead for over a century would now be resurrected, I decided to retrace the story. Calls to the Toxics Coalition led me to Ted Smith, a forty-five-year-old lawyer whose quest had led him to Chief Seattle, he said, "quite by accident." He was taking his kids on a field trip to a park called Coyote Hills on the outskirts of their hometown of San Jose, just south of the San Francisco Bay area. Because the parkland included a restored Indian village, park attendants had available various materials relating to native American traditions. Ted picked up some of them and read them while riding home on the bus with his kids.

As he read, he was amazed at the prophetic vision of this uneducated chief of a tribe in the far Northwest. Ted found it hard to believe that, well over a century ago, Chief Seattle had foreseen the consequences of the way white people were taking over his ancestral land. "Continue to contaminate your own land," he wrote to President Pierce, "and you will one night suffocate in your own waste."

"How true it all has become," muses Ted. "My family lives in an area that the residents used to call the Valley of Heart's Delight. It was an agricultural paradise with a population of one hundred thousand. Now over a million and a half people live in the Silicon Valley, and just what the Chief predicted has happened: We have contaminated our own bed."

Now, five years later, Ted works with the Silicon Valley Toxics Coalition, a nonprofit grassroots advocacy organization that works with neighborhood groups, elected officials, and corporations to clean up the valley, with a particular emphasis on protecting water supplies. He became a full-time environmental activist, he admits, not for abstract political reasons, but for very personal ones. "I have children now, and that has made a big difference. It's not just *my* life that's important. It's theirs too. There's stewardship involved here. It's a sacred responsibility."

He paused, clearly unfinished. Then he added:

"One other thing affected me as deeply as Chief Seattle's words. It's an old Kenyan proverb: 'Treat the earth well. It was not given to you by your parents. It was loaned to you by your children.'"

Since hearing Ted's story, I have encountered Chief Seattle's words again and again. Perhaps so have you. But I wager that neither of us will so easily encounter the words of the Chief's adversary, U.S. President Franklin Pierce. The reason for this, I believe, is quite simple: *Chief Seattle was thinking about us, the seventh generation. President Pierce was not.* In other words, the Chief is one of our elders. The president was merely a politician.

Of course we expect environmentalists nowadays to cite the ecological wisdom of native American leaders. But more and more, the words of elders like Chief Seattle are entering into the mainstream of American life. I could not have been more surprised, for example, to find a native American prayer echoing Chief Seattle's theme showcased in a critical speech by the president of the Rockefeller Foundation. A graduate of the Kennedy Administration and staffer of New York City Mayor John Lindsay, a former budget director for the State of New York and head of the New York Port Authority, often mentioned as a potential Cabinet member, Peter Goldmark was so surrounded by the trappings of establishment power that he put me immediately on guard. But I was moved to trust him by a poem he shared with me, which I quoted in the opening pages of this book. ("If life is a day, in mine it is after one / If life is a year, August has come.") I was startled, not simply because the power-broker was also a poet, but because he was so poignantly aware of his mortal power.

Shortly after taking his new and challenging job, he was asked to make one of the most important speeches of his career. On the 2,700-acre Rockefeller Estate in Pocantico Hills just outside New York City, many of the world's richest men and women (ranging from Japanese business tycoons to Prince Aga Khan) gathered in the fall of 1989 to commemorate the one hundred and fiftieth anniversary of the birth of America's most famous capitalist, John D. Rockefeller. It was partly a private party for fourth- and fifth-generation

family members (eighty-eight descendants in all) and partly
a conference to philosophize about philanthropy. Approaching fifty, surrounded by the powerful family who had put
much of their wealth in his custody, Peter knew it was an
important moment in his life—or as one of his old friends
put it, "a truth-telling moment." It was a speech that would
show something about who he was as a man, and what he
stood for.

As *The New York Times* reported the following morning,
October 29, 1989, Goldmark's speech called for a "new phil-
anthropic strategy to help alleviate poverty in the third
world and protect the imperiled global environment," and
he received a standing ovation from this wealthy international elite. As head of a foundation known for its scientific
achievements and political connections, he could have cited
the words of scientists or economists, politicians or philosophers, environmentalists or academics. But instead he used
as his primary text an Iroquois prayer to which he returned
repeatedly throughout his speech:

> There is a law—a law of time and nature.
> If you do not listen to the law,
> there will come a time of suffering,
> And the law of nature will seek retribution.
> Let us bring our heads together as one.
> So be it that way.

> There is a single law for all.
> Man is not the ruler.
> The law applies to all,
> The law applies to the four-leggeds,
> and to the wingeds, and to humans.
> Let us bring our heads together as one.
> So be it that way.

The law works in twos:
The sun and the moon, the day and the night,
Male and female, birth and death.
All the suffering of our mother the earth
Has been brought by man.
Let us listen to the law of natural things.
Let us bring our heads together as one.
So be it that way.

There in the citadel of capitalism—in the very home of the man who (along with Getty, Carnegie, Mellon, and a very few others) represents the white, established elite that conquered North America—echoed the ancient prayer of the people that the Rockefellers and their white brethren had conquered. Now the custodian of some of their riches is turning for insight to their victims, who in retrospect had a wisdom that the well-armed conquerors lacked.

Just as Chief Seattle's tone was different from President Pierce's, so the tone of the prayer is different from that of speeches by our political leaders. Those who invoke the prayer refer to something greater than themselves and greater than America. They do not close with a perfunctory invocation of divine blessing. On the contrary, the entire message and theme is grounded in nature. The law to which they refer is not man-made but timeless.

Peter was drawn to the invocation for just this reason—it evoked what is most timeless and precious. If the earth were the size of a basketball, then the zone of life that surrounds it—the zone that sustains everything that is human—is approximately the thickness of the film you put in your camera. This is why some ecologists actually call this zone, not the biosphere, but the "biofilm." It is *that* thin—and *that* fragile. And yet we have treated it as if it were indestructible, created only for our pleasure and our profit. If, as Chief Seattle said in his letter to President Pierce, "to harm the earth is to heap contempt on its creator," then we have spat in God's face.

Unlike any of the speeches in most presidential elections, the Iroquois greeting in Peter's speech survives. It was here hundreds of years ago; it will remain hundreds of years after we are gone. It remains, not just in the memory, but in the heart. It lasts because it is not just a political tract, not just a social commentary, not just a psychological analysis, and not just a religious prayer. It is all of these and therefore greater than the sum of its parts. It has integrity.

Eager to learn more about the prayer, I traced it back to its source, an Iroquois elder who recited it at a conference in Utah on global warming, which Peter had attended. After making several phone calls to track down the source, I was finally referred to a number in upstate New York that was answered by a man whom we encountered in the previous chapter, Iroquois faithkeeper Oren Lyons.

"First of all, we don't call it a prayer," he explained patiently, when I told him of the unusual setting in which those lines had been invoked. "It's a greeting . . . to be spoken. It is the standard way of opening our meetings. We're in our midwinter meetings, and I actually heard this greeting twice already this morning. It's an acknowledgment of the powers that prevail. It's as old as our nation is, and no one knows how old that is. It's instruction we were given. When we gather, we start this way because it sets the context of the discussion. You're not a leader, not a follower . . . you're a person in the context of creation. So when you sit there, you're not overblown with your own importance because you're just part of creation. It serves to remind us of who we are. We understand that, in international meetings, it has impact. Even the flowers lift their heads and the animals stop. Everybody listens because it is a greeting."

When I asked Oren if he could send me an authentic version of the invocation, he said that would be impossible. "We don't write it down. Never have. We don't write it down because then people start analyzing it and interpreting it. And that's not what it's for. It's a greeting. It's a litany of respect—that's what it is. And that is what is required: respect for the earth. All of the laws that you make should follow this spiritual law. If you follow it, you won't have these problems. Unfortunately, human beings have their own agendas. We don't want to listen. We want to complicate things."

When we forget our mortal power and lose our integrity, true leadership is impossible. Leaders who are not humbly grounded in their mortality are, in effect, posturing. They are pretending to have a power—an immortality—that they in fact do not have. They cannot call us, their tribe, together as one because they are split. They cannot close with the invocation "So be it that way" because they do not know in their hearts the way it is. Because they are lying to themselves, everything they say to their people, no matter how well intentioned or well researched, is also a lie. They are not speaking to us as whole, mortal human beings, and so we do not respond from our depths to their words.

As we seek wholeness in the second half, we seek leaders who are whole. "Authenticity may be the only tool we have left to get us through the bullshit," concludes Garth bluntly. "It's the only thing that can break through the mass of information that is being sent out. We have learned that you can't believe what people say; you can't trust what you see—at least on TV. *So integrity is all we have left.*"

No wonder that efforts to develop alternatives to conventional politics or to rejuvenate the two major parties always include an ethical dimension. The outside challengers—whether independents such as John Anderson, Democrats such as Jesse Jackson, or Republicans like Pat Robertson—often evoke ethical values because they smell, as does the public, the hollowness at the core of public life. In one of the most thoughtful behind-the-scenes strategy papers exploring political "strategy for progressives in the 1990s," two young political analysts focus on precisely these ethical issues. "There is something truly debased about the present state of public life in the U.S., the sheer level of corruption in public office, and the lying by public officials. While it is naive to expect of government what one might expect of a friend (loyalty, kindness, generosity), it does not seem unreasonable . . . to expect that government officials not intentionally mislead the public, abuse the public trust, loot the treasury, or engage in basic malfeasance that are now routine, and routinely unpenalized. This is the stuff of cynicism. And it is the stuff of powerlessness, for that is the destination of cynicism." What is missing from conventional politics, they conclude, is wholeness.[8]

As the preceding chapters bear witness, there are many paths that lead us toward integrity and wholeness. But the ecological crisis requires that we understand the even deeper meaning of these words. Clearly our quest has taught us that, since before our conception, the world is in us and we are in the world. Its oxygen feeds our lungs. Its gravity holds us. Its water and soil sustain us. Its plants and animals nourish us. Without this life-giving sphere, we do not exist. Or as Joanna Macy puts it in *World As Lover, World As Self,* the most recent book by this advocate of "deep ecology": "We can place [the self] between our ears, and have it looking out from our eyes or we can widen it to include the air we breathe . . . the oxygen-giving trees and plankton, our external lungs, and beyond them the web of life in which they are sustained."[9]

Since we are part of the environment and it is part of us, "we" cannot save "it." That would presume that we are separate from it, which we are not. We cannot save the world without saving ourselves. When we take care of our home, we take care of ourselves and vice versa. So we will not take care of "the planet" out of a sense of ecological etiquette, but for the same reason that we pursue our own quest. Since how we live the second half is not just a question of personal life-style but of planetary survival, we will care for our home with the same integrity that we try to care for our bodies, our children, our soul/mate, and the seven generations.

Taking care of our planetary home is a challenging task of great technical complexity. But it is also a moral challenge that even a child can grasp. At a hearing held by the U.S. Department of Energy (DOE) in Oakland, California—one of twenty-three such events planned around the country in order to give the public an opportunity to participate in the decision about how to store, dispose of, and clean up the radioactive wastes from our nuclear reactors—a ten-year-old boy asked to speak. Although he could barely see over the top of the podium, he did not hesitate to speak his mind. "I am furious at you for dumping your waste," he said to the DOE officials. "In my house, we are taught to clean up one mess before we are allowed to make another."[10]

Whatever our quest or calling may be, cleaning up our home must be part of it. As Oren Lyons and the Iroquois put it, "We believe that every person born has a mission, and whatever that mission is, it should be fulfilled. Only the persons themselves can develop their gifts. It is our responsibility to share these gift with others. When each of us does so, then as a whole you have a functioning community and a livable planet."[11]

"To do what is given to you to do means that you cannot worry about doing *every*thing," agrees Joanna Macy, whom I interviewed with her husband Fran. "Shall I save the whales or help battered women? Shall I lobby for energy efficiency or work in the public schools? You have to understand that each problem is part of a larger whole. And you have to feel connected to other brothers and sisters who are doing what you cannot do."

"About twenty years ago I had a heart attack," recalls Fran, a former Peace Corps official who is now in his sixties. "Before that I had a compulsive drive to serve. I thought I should be a good executive, a good father, a good husband . . . so many 'shoulds.' But after the heart attack I was finished with all that. When I take a group of American environmental experts to the Soviet Union, as I am doing next week, to a conference on the aftermath of Chernobyl, I am not doing it because I think I should. I am doing it because that's what I *love* to do. It's who I *am*."

"That's terribly important," Joanna cut in. "It doesn't work to tell people what they *should* do, playing on their guilt or their fear. The fact is, it's boring as you get older to be self-concerned. It's like being in an elevator that's too crowded or wearing a girdle that's too tight. What we need to do is invite people to get out of those constraints. What could be more interesting, more expanding, than to care about the world we live in? It's the ultimate adventure: to let go of our defenses and fall in love with the world."[12]

Beyond Hope and Despair: Walking the Path of Integrity

Denis Hayes, the founder of Earth Day, is certainly one of the finest political organizers I have ever known. His dedicated and persevering leadership on environmental issues has directed his entire adult life. A soft-spoken, down-to-earth lawyer, Denis launched the first Earth Day in 1970, when he was barely in his twenties. This young man and his friends were sending out an SOS for Mother Earth that was heard, albeit faintly, around the world.

While he became a lawyer, married, had a daughter, bought a home, worked on a variety of causes (including the environment), and watched his hairline recede, twenty years passed. One day, when he tuned into a "golden oldies" radio station and heard a commercial for presold burial sites, he was struck by both his mortality and his power. Unlike twenty years before, he didn't have to waste energy thinking about "making it" in a career. "You reach a point where you don't have to suck up to anybody," Denis told me once when we talked privately. "After that, we no longer have to worry so much about jeopardizing our career. In law and medicine at least, you can prove yourself fairly quickly. Then you can do just what you care about." And what Denis cared about, he reaffirmed in his forties, was safeguarding his home—a decision that led to Earth Day 1990.

Only three months before the event, I happened to be with Denis in Moscow at a meeting with two dozen Soviet environmentalists who were trying to organize the Earth Day events in that troubled country. But as I watched Denis facing this group, he was so relaxed, patient, and calm that it was hard for me to grasp that this man was laying the groundwork for what would prove to be the largest global demonstration on behalf of the planet in history. In a gentle voice, but squarely facing the harsh realties, he explained to them what is happening to their country's and the planet's biosphere. Carefully avoiding telling them what they should do, he simply pointed out alternatives and encouraged them to seize the opportunities that seemed most effective. Their response was deep and clear. Although he was a lawyer from a capitalist country speaking English, by the time we walked out of that room, a national board for Earth Day had coalesced before his eyes.

But this same man who worked so hard and who inspired so many others in America and around the world is no stranger to despair. Even as he mobilizes his energies and organizes others, he knows that all his efforts may well not be enough. Even though the condition of the planet worsens, activism becomes more difficult. Even in the midst of a year of intense global organizing, Denis remained aware of his own despair. "The first time [Earth Day 1970], the economy was booming, and nobody had serious doubts that they would have a future. That made social activism easier. We felt we could take some chances and still get a seat on the boat. But now we've had some hard times, and there'll be

more. Everything's much tighter." Although he is proud of
the progress we have made, he is not optimistic. "Those of
us who set out to change the world are poised on the threshold of utter failure. Measured on virtually any scale, the
world is in worse shape today than it was twenty years ago.
How could we have fought so many hard battles only to find
ourselves now on the verge of losing the war?"

Even though I was inspired by Denis and the spirited
group of Soviet eco-activists, I shared Denis's despair. Bar-
raged by so many warnings of apocalypse, I entered the
Kremlin on the final day of the conference in a somber
mood. Yearning for a message of hope from Gorbachev, I
wondered if this visionary but embattled leader, who had
dared to challenge the ghost of Stalin, would also chase
away this specter of ecological suicide. As he began to
speak, his warmth and charisma sparked my hope. But instead of inspiration, we heard this leader confessing his
country's sins. He was well aware that, ever since the October Revolution, the position of the Communist party ideo-
logues had been that environmental destruction was a problem of capitalism—somebody *else's* problem. Because in the
USSR "the people" owned the means of production, not
greedy capitalists, it followed that "the people" would never
destroy the natural habitat in which they lived. For decades,
this ideological veil had hidden the truth about the ecological reality. But standing on the podium, Gorbachev stripped
this veil away.

"*We*'ve been thoughtless about the environment,"
Gorbachev said categorically. Not the capitalists, not the in-
dustrialists—no, he says, *we*. "Until a few years ago," he
continued, "we didn't think about the environment. We
thought only of the military threat. We couldn't see what
was happening to the environment because we were concerned about our military security. But for the last two
years, we've started to see the truth. We realize that the real
threat is not military. The real threat is what we're *all* doing

to our planet." And he concluded with a call to develop
global armies of "green helmet" forces, young men and
women who would not battle against each other, but safeguard the earth.

As the assemblage clapped enthusiastically, many of the
several hundred people gathered in the Great Hall of the
Kremlin rose to their feet. Scanning the extraordinary range
of men and women who were applauding, I saw Oren Lyons,
the Iroquois faithkeeper, and a small group of "indigenous
people" from around the world. To my right, seated between
Raisa Gorbachev and a Buddhist religious leader from Japan, was Tennessee Senator Al Gore, who many consider to
be one of the best-informed members of Congress on environmental matters. Behind Gore is the Grand Mufti of
Syria, one of dozens of religious leaders representing virtually every major religious tradition in the world, who had
earlier posed the question: Of what value is our faith in God,
if we destroy God's creation?

As I joined the throng squeezing out the narrow, carefully
guarded doorways, my anguish only deepened. Although the
Western world is filled with bright people who think they
have the answer (or at least part of it), the sobering truth is
that no economy has the right answer. Neither the ideas of
Karl Marx nor the ideas of Adam Smith will solve the planetary ecological crisis. Every nation is committing ecocide. "If
we define *sustainable* as 'meeting current needs without sac-
rificing the needs of future generations,'" the Worldwatch
Institute's Lester Brown had said, "then there is not a single
environmentally sustainable economy in the world today."
No nation—repeat, *no* nation—is living sustainably.

From the planet's point of view, communism is certainly
not the answer, but neither is capitalism. Both view the earth
as resources to be exploited for short-term profit. American
capitalism has done a much better job than Soviet communism at creating wealth, but both systems have had disastrous consequences on the water, soil, and air. Despite the

differences between private and public ownership, both systems consider a mountain as a resource to be mined for its wealth. Both systems consider a lake to be a repository for industrial waste. Both place a higher priority on this year's output than on next generation's ecology. For both Adam Smith and Karl Marx, the depletion of the forest cover was irrelevant. So was the depletion of the ozone and global warming. They both focused on who should own the means of production, not on who should take responsibility for the biosphere. "A Communist coal mine in Rumania," as Bill McKibben wrote in *The End of Nature,* is as deadly to the environment as "a capitalist utility in West Virginia."[13] And that is truly cause for despair.

In Erik Erikson's view of the stages of the life cycle, the final period of our quest will be a time of great inner struggle between hope and despair. According to Erikson, as our lives reach their closing years, we will look back on what we have done, and who we have been, and how we have loved. In each of us, hope and despair will compete for our attention, each trying to hold dominion over our consciousness. If we pursue our quest through this final "forest dark," we will learn a virtue that, in Erikson's view, comes into full play only in the second half, a virtue derived from the Latin word *integer,* meaning "whole": the virtue of *integrity.*

Although Erikson's definition, developed a quarter century ago, is psychologically compelling, in the nineties we must add an ecological dimension as well. For it is not only in the context of the *human* life cycle that we must demonstrate integrity but also in the context of the cycle of nature on which the flow of generations depends.

"What law are you living under? United States government law?" Oren Lyons asks each of us. "That's man's law. You break man's law, and you pay a fine or go to jail—maybe." But, according to Iroquois tradition, The law of nature is different. "Natural law prevails everywhere. It supersedes man's law. If you violate it, you get hit. There's no judge or jury, there's no lawyers or courts, you can't buy or dodge or beg your way out of it. If you violate this natural law, you're going to get hit and get hit hard."

As Oren sees it, we do not need a degree in environmental science to understand natural law. "All life on Mother Earth depends on the pure water, yet we spill every kind of dirt and filth and poison into it. That makes no common sense at all. Your legislature can pass a law saying it's okay, but it's not okay. Natural law doesn't care about your man's law. Natural law's going to hit you. You can't get out of the way. You don't fool around with natural law and get away with it. If you kill the water, you kill the life that depends on it, your own included. That's natural law."

Just as high-tech Anglo culture has come to symbolize dominion over the earth, traditional native American culture has become a symbol of protecting the earth. Just as we have destroyed the indigenous peoples who were one with the earth, so we now destroy their home. As Kevin Costner pointed out shortly before his film *Dances with Wolves* received seven Academy Awards, "we express concern about faraway injustices like apartheid in South Africa or the destruction of the Brazilian rain forest. But we still won't accept the fact that we've destroyed four hundred cultures systematically. . . . We pride ourselves on freedom, but we completely deprive others of theirs. We talk about how Cortez destroyed the Aztecs, but we don't acknowledge the extent of our own destruction. We pave it over."[14]

No doubt this is why we never invoke the words of President Franklin Pierce, who purchased the land from Chief Seattle and made it part of the United States of America. But again and again, we hear the words of Chief Seattle: "How can you buy and sell the sky—the warmth of the land?" he asked the man in the White House. "The idea is strange to us. Yet we do not own the freshness of the air or the sparkle of the water. How can you buy them from us? . . . We know that the white man does not understand our ways. One portion of the land is the same to him as the next, for he is a stranger who comes in the night and takes from the land whatever he needs. The earth is not his brother, but his enemy, and when he has conquered it, he moves on."

Little more than a century later, our generation can no longer "move on." We have reached the earth's frontiers. Expansion must be replaced with wisdom, conquest by integrity. We must begin walking the path of integrity. Specifically:

Integrity means ensuring that our children and grandchildren will not walk on an earth that grows hotter and hotter. Carbon is a vital, universal element of the biosphere, which has been present at relatively constant levels in the air, sea, and land. If humankind—by burning gas and oil and coal, or by burning rain forests—increases the level of carbon dioxide in the air, the biofilm will get hotter. If we human beings do not change our habits, and the temperature increases between three and nine degrees (Fahrenheit) in the next century as predicted, the earth will look more like hell and less like heaven.

Much of the mantle of green that covered the earth when we were born has been stripped away—stripped so fast that it will, at current rates of deforestation, disappear before we die. As our ancestors slaughtered buffalo, we slaughtered trees. We cut them down and did not plant them. And then we cut them down around the world, wherever we could find them.[15]

Integrity means ensuring that the life-giving rays of the sun will not make our children and grandchildren sick. About half a century ago, human beings invented one of many "miracle chemicals," CFC (chlorofluorocarbon). We did not know until 1975 that a CFC molecule poses a theoretical danger to the ozone, and we did not know until 1985 that these molecules had actually begun to thin the ozone layer over the Antarctic. Each invading CFC molecule will destroy one hundred thousand protective ozone molecules, a process that will occur over a century or more, long after we are gone and the next generations walk the earth. The ozone layer helps absorb the most harmful sun rays, preventing these cancer-causing rays from reaching us. The amount of ozone has already significantly decreased. Unless this trend is stopped, and stopped quickly, cancers may one day become as common as colds.[16]

Integrity means preserving resources for the generations to come. In little more than one generation (1940 to 1976) in one country (the United States), more minerals were used than in all of humanity in the tens of thousands of years before them. Our generation is using even more. The more we extract, the more we process; the more we process, the more we waste; and the more we waste, the more we pollute.[17]

Integrity means not burdening our children with an overwhelming burden of debt. Our children and grandchildren will inherit an enormous debt—almost $50,000 for each American family. Even as measured by our own paper currency, we are turning our offspring into debtors long before they are born. Because we will not live within our means, we are forcing them to carry the burden later.[18]

And integrity means not impregnating the earth with toxic and radioactive wastes that may poison our children and grandchildren long after we are gone. They may walk on an earth that contains radioactive wastes that will endanger them and their offspring for thousands of years. To toast our bread and boil our water, we have been persuaded that we must use methods that poison their future. The radioactive material is so toxic and so dangerous that no one wants it anywhere near them, so according to current plans, it will be buried deep in the body of the earth so that none of us has to see what we have done to it. This is clearly not the path of integrity.[19]

These are but a few examples of how we have lived the first half of our lives. You may not agree with these examples, or you may have many more. But whatever your view, it is, I believe, each of our responsibility to examine how we live, assess it in terms of the seventh generation, and change our way of life accordingly. By walking the path of integrity, we move beyond hope and despair. Our actions may save the planet, or they may not. We do not know. But we do know who we are and the path that we have chosen. It is our calling, not because we are "activists" or "environmentalists" but because we care about our own quest and the quests of those who follow.

Remember, it is by no means certain that the human life-span will continue to lengthen. In fact, if our abuse of the planet continues, it is likely that the human life-span will shrink, not grow. If humanity does not act as one body to preserve the living systems that sustain us, our children's lives may be shorter than ours. *Longer lives, and deeper quests, are not guaranteed. They must be earned by every generation.*

If we were to seize this destiny—if entering the second half were to become synonymous with renewal and questing rather than stagnation and crisis—a renaissance of creativity and activism would invigorate every corner of our society:

• A healthier generation in the second half of life, taking more responsibility for the care of our body/minds, would have a powerful impact on the young and would dramatically accelerate the shift toward healthier life-styles. Entire industries would be transformed. Others would be born. Medical expenditures would be reduced and, more important, realigned. An economic earthquake would shake not only the health care industry but the food, entertainment, advertising, and pharmaceutical industries, just to name a few.

• The status of older persons would change. Growing respect for elders would require a transformation in the role that "senior citizens" play in our culture. Their skills, resources, maturity, energy, money, and time are without a doubt among the most underused resources in America. If it were a genuine social movement led by them and supported by their children and grandchildren, it could be a desperately needed injection of human warmth and wisdom into schools, hospitals, day-care centers, businesses, nursing homes, and the like.

• Just as every well-publicized disintegration of a marriage sends out the toxic message that love is illusory and cannot grow, every revitalized marriage would send out a message of hope that love not only lasts but deepens. The impact of this turnabout would be felt directly in our homes, but its indirect impact throughout our society would be even greater.

• Job satisfaction would markedly increase and so would productivity. Men and women in midcareer would be encouraged, not discouraged, to reassess their job prospects and to receive new training—either in their current field or in a new, more compelling area of expertise. Our society would invest resources in the older worker just as we now invest in educating the young.

• Activism amongst those in the second half would skyrocket. More and more men and women would move beyond the care of their own household to a wider commitment to community and planet.

All this and more could occur during the closing years of this millennium and the beginning of the next. It would emerge, not because we decided to become activists but because we decided to become fully ourselves.

Multigenerational Activism: Bringing Our Heads Together as One

Vaclav Havel, who spent the first half of his life as a dissident playwright, entered the second half as leader of his country. Soon after its mercifully brief, largely nonviolent revolution, he became president of Czechoslovakia. But even while he was head of state, he found time to be interviewed by rock musician Lou Reed of the Velvet Underground, which had been one of Havel's favorite bands during the sixties. He told Reed that the "whole spirit of the sixties, the rebellion against the establishment," was an inspiration to him and his revolutionary colleagues and "affected significantly the spiritual life of my generation and of the younger people."

Having been imprisoned several times before leading a revolution that toppled a Communist regime, Havel is no starry-eyed, naive idealist. He recognizes why the cultural and political upheaval of the sixties was not enough.

> We differ from this twenty-year-old rebellion in that we made another step further. As small and inconspicuous a step as it might be, it's the knowledge that we can't just tear things down but we have to build in a new way. And many people took political responsibility. And, for example, Michael Kotap, probably the best-known rock musician in this country, is also one of the best-functioning deputies in our federal parliament now. He doesn't have much time for composing music. It is a sacrifice of a kind that he has brought to his society.

In urgent times, Havel argued, urgent change is required—not just politically, but personally. Kotap would rather write music than be a member of parliament. And Havel, presumably, would rather write plays than run a country. But in the second half of their lives, they have found themselves in extraordinary circumstances, requiring an extraordinary response.[20]

The scene of policemen or army soldiers (acting on behalf of conservative authority) beating and sometimes killing young demonstrators (gathering on behalf of change) has been replayed from Tokyo to Tiananmen Square, Chicago to Chile, Burma to Berlin, and Prague to Paris—indeed, in virtually every region of the world over the past thirty years. And it will be replayed many more times throughout the remainder of this century. That is because the young want change. They cause change. They symbolize change. They *are* change.

As Havel himself illustrates, however, a one-generation counterculture is not enough. Not only the young must be involved, but also those entering and in the second half who are able and willing to shape the forces of change through mature, responsible leadership. When change occurs and a new, more positive leadership steps forward, the new leaders are not those in their teens and twenties. They are most often those in midlife, those men and women in their thirties, forties, and fifties who are able to bring their experience, wisdom, and maturity to bear on the new circumstances. Without leaders in the second half who are capable of bridging the old and the new, youth rebellion alone rarely bears fruit. It is begun, but never completed. It challenges, but does not transform. It is necessary, but not sufficient.

What is missing is the energy of their elders, a quality of leadership that will be even more crucial in the future than it has been in the past. The necessary response is not a big demonstration (though that may help) or a raucous one-line slogan (though that may also be useful), but mature, sustained activism and a steady commitment over many years to change the very way we live.

Looking back at the years when he ran the Peace Corps program in several Third World countries, sixty-year-old Fran Macy is struck by the fact that the older men and women who became Peace Corps volunteers often dealt better than their younger counterparts with the physical hardships and psychological isolation. "They were more seasoned, more familiar with how change happens in life, less frustrated and impatient and easily discouraged," Fran recalls. "They were also more respected for their age in many of these less developed countries than they were back home, which also made them feel more empowered. Since they remembered a time in their lives that was more low-tech, they adapted more easily to a world without cars and motors and media. They were more comfortable with simplicity."

Not only do those in the second half have more maturity and perseverance; they also have more power. When New York businessman Allen Grossman became chairman of the board and CEO of a relatively large, privately owned distribution company, he was "the boss." He could go no higher. If he had so desired, he could have begun acquiring other companies. He could have strived to double his wealth and double it again. But instead, he found himself in his mid-forties drawn to the world of nonprofit organizations. "I knew I wanted to change my focus from monetary profit to social profit," he recalls. "I knew I had some important management skills. I wanted to use them—but how? I cared about so many international issues—global ecology, Third World development, democratic institution-building. But I didn't know where to turn."

And so began his journey out of the business world and into the complex world of managing public interest organizations involved with social change. In 1991 he completed the transition by becoming CEO of Outward Bound. It was a thrilling shift, but also disorienting. He had stepped "down"—but felt "up." Instead of being paid royally, he was unpaid; instead of being picked up at the airport, he rode subways or cabs; instead of having a staff of hundreds, he had one assistant; instead of managing a major corporation, he helped manage a few minuscule public interest groups; instead of being the boss, he advised executive directors. Despite the loss of status and respect in the world of the marketplace, Allen was excited again as he had not been for years. To his credit, he redefined the climb and began his quest.

"The cure for boredom is not diversion," wrote John Gardner in *The Recovery of Confidence,* "it is to find some work to do, something to care about."[21] Allen is not alone in following Gardner's visionary prescription. Scores of men and women are choosing to trade some of the rewards of climbing the old ladder for the benefits of pursuing more well-rounded goals. They are pursuing what Ralph Nader and Joan Anzalone call "good works," which enable us not just to make a living, but to make meaningful, sustainable lives.[22]

Peter Morton is not a kid; he's in his forties. Anna Sue Rafferty is not a young woman; she's sixty. Neither of them was an activist when young. It was only when they reached the second half that they recognized the earth was in danger and decided to take a stand. In Peter's case, he founded one of the trendiest restaurant chains, the Hard Rock Cafes. He decided that the restaurants should use only biodegradable takeout containers. Leftovers would be distributed to hunger projects. The cafes sell Save The Planet T-shirts and donate money to the National Resources Defense Council (whose board of trustees Peter recently joined). Because he was the middle-aged owner, it happened; if he had been a young waiter or busboy, it wouldn't have. Peter's stand was strengthened by having the enthusiastic support of his primarily younger staff, and the younger people became more active because they had the leadership of a socially responsible CEO.

Meanwhile, in Ponca City, Oklahoma, a low-income, multiethnic town, Anna Sue Rafferty and her neighbors were suffering from toxic waste resulting from decades of oil refining. Similar to the more famous case of Love Canal, residents of Ponca City discovered a toxic orange sludge seeping into their basements. Anna Sue organized the Ponca City Concerned Citizens, who sued Conoco (a subsidiary of faraway Du Pont), claiming it was responsible for undercutting the value of their homes and endangering their lives.

Her little group won a major settlement and, more important, served notice to the large chemical companies that even high-priced lawyers cannot defeat a determined grassroots organization.[23]

"I'm sixty years old now," Anna Sue told me after the battle had been won. "I know it's hard to believe that somebody'd take this up at my age. But when you live in a place for thirty-seven years, and you see people cramming this garbage down your throat every day, there comes a time when you've got to stand up and say stop!"

No one ever told her she was too old to become a citizens' activist. On the contrary, she was a natural leader for the cause. "I wasn't a stranger or outsider in our little town. People knew me. They knew that when I took something up, I usually had a reason. The worst of the mess was right close to the school. I'd put four children through there. I'd been president of the PTA. So when I said we gotta do something, they respected me for it." She is particularly proud of the way young people responded to her leadership. Once, when they were preparing for a closed-door meeting with the state governor, some of the hot-headed college-age kids who were part of her organization asked her to sit between them and the governor. "They figured they needed some kind of happy medium in there to keep things from getting outta hand," says Anna Sue.

But the power of the multigenerational movement did not result only from the young needing elders. It was also grounded in the elders needing the young. When young activists asked Anna Sue to give a crucial speech for the cause on the steps of the state capitol, she reluctantly agreed, but she told them somebody else would have to write the speech. After receiving the activists' version, she asked her youngest son, who was twenty, to type it for her. But he refused.

"Mom, this just isn't you," he told her. "This just isn't how you talk. It'd be a lot better speech if you wrote it yourself. I *know* you can do it." With his encouragement, she wrote it herself, he typed it—and it was front-page news in the next morning's paper. She had found her own voice, not hidden behind somebody else's.

There are many, many Peter Mortons and Anna Sue Raffertys already at work. As was evidenced by Earth Day 1990, when the generations work together, the synergy is phenomenal. When Denis Hayes looks back at what happened that day, he sees as one of the major differences between 1970 and 1990 that "the generation in midlife was out there with us. This time some of our most superb political operators were older men and women, often who had been inspired by their own kids who were now in college. We heard endless jokes about how parents could deal with the 'environmental policemen' in their homes. There is no question that the young were enormously effective change agents for their parents." (If Denis ever doubts the synergy of generations, he need look no further than the United States Congress, where he can visit several senators and representatives whose political careers started twenty years earlier on Earth Day, including one senator who then ran the mailroom.)

Fortunately, in the second half, many of us are not quietly drifting onto the golf course but are taking our skills, our money, our love, and our vote and are using it for service. This means not only helping repair our home—the air and water, the forest and soil—but also serving those who live within its walls: those whose lives, without assistance, will end before midlife; whose bodies are crippled and minds impaired; whose hopes have been crushed and self-esteem shattered; whose quests are in danger of being prematurely and unfairly foreclosed by poverty, confined by illiteracy, handicapped by illness, limited by immobility, and intimidated by authoritarian rule.

Some will advocate on behalf of the disenfranchised on grounds of economic justice. Others, in more fearful tones, will invoke political necessity. Still others will cite, as we did previously, ecological self-interest. And still others will argue for a new order on spiritual grounds.[24] But in the end, it will all come back to our quest. We can try to hoard the gift of the second half, like jewels in a safe-deposit box. We can flaunt it, like expensive designer clothes. We can boast about it, as if it were a promotion or award, or count it, as if it were a bank account. But if we do so, we are swimming against the very flow of the human cycle itself. The gift of the second half is fully received only when it is shared.

Don't wait for a leader. Become one. Stop complaining about being left with a choice between the "the lesser of two evils." Elders are meant to inspire us. So find someone, or become someone, worth following. If not us, then who?

Learn the facts. You can't repair your house if you don't know what's broken, or why. Before you swing your hammer or cut with your saw, develop some respect for the materials you are using. We are, after all, playing with Creation itself.

Don't run from your despair; follow it. Don't deny your own feelings of powerlessness in your rush to "make a difference." Those feelings are the key to your deepest power. Let them lead you first. Then you may lead others.

Enlarge your tribe. We need global elders now, not just tribal ones. Whatever your circle is, expand it. As the Iroquois say, "Every man is an uncle; every woman is an aunt." So get to know your nieces and nephews. They need you.

Pay your rent. We're all renters here, not owners. What you pay and how you pay it depends on your Calling. But unless each of us pays our share, our kids may well be homeless.

Remember your address. ZIP Code: E-A-R-T-H. That's home. That's where your quest begins and ends. Take care of it as if you were taking care of your own quest—because you are.

8

DISCOVERING HEAVEN ON EARTH
The Quest for the Sacred

Little by little, wean yourself.

This is the gist of what I have to say.

From an embryo, whose nourishment comes in blood,
move to an infant drinking milk,
to a child on solid food,
to a searcher after wisdom,
to a hunter of more invisible game.

RUMI, thirteenth-century poet

In the summer of 1985, I was thirty-five, a time of life that often seems connected to a spiritual coming of age.[1] I had just finished spending a week as part of a delegation hosting a visiting group of Soviets, who were closely monitored by what was undoubtedly a covert KGB member in their group. After a particularly tension-filled series of meetings, we held our final session at a hot springs where we finally relaxed and became playful. By the time our guests left, much of the hostility between the Soviets and Americans had washed away in the mineral-rich waters. Tired but satisfied, I went to a quiet spot upstream from the hot springs and sat on a rock in the sunshine.

I did not intend to meditate because, frankly, I had always found meditation elusive. Because Shelley and I have three children and demanding jobs, I reasoned that meditation was for solitary, self-involved spiritualists, not for working people like us who were raising families. Besides, particularly when our children were small, sleep seemed far more precious than nirvana. If God had offered me a choice between a good night's sleep and a glimpse of infinity, I admit I may well have chosen the former.

But this, too, was just another convenient excuse. In fact, my efforts to meditate were frustrating. Meditation is a mirror, reflecting the Self, and I did not like what I saw when I looked in it. The mirror revealed that I was divided. Part of me would sit and meditate, and part of me was busy doing hundreds of other things: planning my workday, feeling rushed, doubting that I was meditating "properly," and so on. Try as I might, I did not know how to be all in one place at one time. I could not truly sit still. I was not whole.

So when I sat down near that little stream to relax, I expected nothing more than a few minutes of peace. But something unusual happened. Enveloped by the sounds of the stream and the scents of the valley, a phrase emerged in my mind: "like a river, flowing into the sea." As I reflected on the phrase, I realized that I wanted to learn to live more like that stream—flowing, flowing, flowing effortlessly, flowing ultimately into the great sea. The river did not rage against boulders. It did not get impatient with quiet pools or tense in whitewater. It simply flowed.

Shortening the phrase to "like a river . . . into the sea," I said the first part as I inhaled, the second as I exhaled. I did not decide to do this; it was spontaneous. First out loud, then silently, saying the phrase guided me. It brought me into full presence. Now more centered, I felt my body grow light. Time altered. The sounds of the stream and the birds became a chorus of rapture. The environment felt like a cocoon, cradling me in warmth and light. I felt no boundary between the world and me.

Having never felt this way before, I was elated. As if to check on reality, I opened my eyes just to make sure everything was still "normal." Although my vision was clear and steady, what I saw was most certainly not normal. Even the stones were alive. Everything seemed to be made of energy, not matter. The world looked just as my body felt: one breathing, pulsating stream of life. For the first time in my life, I was one with the world. The river was moving me— carrying me home.

After surrendering to this timelessness, I felt the touch of fear. I wondered if this altered experience would end, and if so, when. As soon as that thought crossed my mind, this magical state began to loosen its hold on my consciousness. I looked at my watch. Only twenty minutes had passed. As I gazed at the trees and stream and rocks, the scene was beautiful but no longer luminous.

As I returned to the hot springs I could not understand why I had felt such joy and oneness. I felt like a little boy who, after losing his balance again and again, finally learned to ride his bike. I felt proud of myself. I had read about this mystical state and always felt that the people experiencing it were either making it up or that it was inaccessible to ordinary folks like me. But now, I had done it. Although I knew I was a beginner, I expected that the next time I climbed up on the seat and began to pedal, the ride would be as exhilarating as this one.

When I returned home, I began meditating regularly. I had tasted the fruit of heaven and was eager for another bite. But the next meditation, to my great disappointment, was not luminous. The next one was no better. Nor was the next one, or the one after that. Slowly, I realized that I had not *done* anything. It would be more accurate to say that a gift had been bestowed upon me. I had been given a fleeting experience of wholeness.

When I sat down to meditate by the river, I had not done so to "get away" from the world, or to "take a break" from my work, or to "recharge" my batteries. I had simply surrendered. But no sooner had I received this gift of bliss than I wanted it again. Now that I had tasted its sweetness once, I wanted to again. I had stumbled into the Garden of Eden, only to stumble quickly out again.

Spiritually speaking, I am obviously just a beginner, so I can share here only what a beginner knows. I do not even have a word to describe what happened to me that day (spirit? reverence? grace? God?). All I know is that, as I move more deeply into the second half of my life, I want to move toward that sacred place. I want to connect with the sacred more deeply. I want to embrace it and to be embraced by it. It matters to me now in a way that it never did before.

Even as I yearn for transcendence, I cling to the state of consciousness we call ordinary. Something prevents me from following my yearning and experiencing the *extra*-ordinary, as I did by the river that day. I think what prevents me, even now, from experiencing the sacred more fully is my spiritual passivity.

In the Beginning: Overcoming Spiritual Passivity

Childhood is a time of extraordinary curiosity, spiritually and otherwise. Questions abound. If we need authoritative confirmation of this fact, Robert Coles's *The Spiritual Life of Children* certainly provides it. But anyone who has been a parent or who has worked intimately with children knows this is so.

I remember playing in the bathtub with my youngest son, who was then four. We were laughing and playing with his bath toys when all of a sudden he stopped and turned toward me.

"I don't want you to die," he said, as if somehow saying it would make it so.

"You don't?" I replied, startled by the unexpected turn in our conversation.

"No, I'll keep you safe—here!" he said earnestly, and placed his forefinger on the side of his head. But then he paused, somehow dissatisfied with his solution to the problem of human mortality. "No, not there," he continued, putting his hand over his heart. "I'll keep you *here*."

When he resumed playing as if nothing had happened, I was left to marvel, as I have ever since, at the extraordinary power of the spiritual quest. Over the next few years, he would often ask about death, perplexed by its mystery and its meaning. He would also ask about God, rainbows (usually with pots of gold), babies, love, and whatever else puzzled him about life. Watching his spirit unfold, trying to grasp the mysteries of life that elude us all, has been one of the greatest joys of my life. But it has also touched my deepest wounds.

For me, childhood was not a time of spiritual curiosity, but of memorization. I attended a Presbyterian Sunday school in Indianapolis, Indiana, where I was told that Jesus was "*The* Way" and memorized long passages of the Bible by heart. I was told what words to say; told what the parables meant;

told about the Trinity; and so on. When, at the age of thirteen, I repeated back to the church elders what they had taught me, they confirmed me as a member of the church. Confirmation was for me, as it had been for Jung more than a half century earlier, spiritually *dis*confirming. The very way by which I was accepted proved to me that I did not belong.[2]

Since like all children I was spiritually hungry, I ingested what I was fed. So did my friends. My best friend went to a Methodist church because his parents did. He became a Methodist. My girlfriend was a member of a Disciples of Christ church where her father was a minister. She became a Disciple of Christ. Another girl in my class was Jewish. She went to synagogue. I naturally wanted to spend Sunday morning with my friends, but I soon learned that all Christians could not worship together. Our respective beliefs in God did not unite us, but separated us, which seemed strange to me. Each of my friends and I became members of our respective denominations without resistance. I had not earned my beliefs, for they had been given to me before I could even ask. I had not proved I was a good Christian, only a good parrot. And because I did not seek my *own* path to the sacred, I followed someone else's and got lost.

Like so many children, I became spiritually passive, by which I mean that I was trained to repeat other people's truths. Unlike the mystics, who counsel us not to adopt truths that we ourselves have not experienced, I was raised to think that the more closely I conformed to a preexisting religious tradition, the better a Christian I was. So by the time I reached adolescence, repeating other peoples' truths was all I knew how to do. I had never experienced God or Jesus. I had never seen a burning bush or any other kind of miracle. I would not recognize the Holy Ghost even if it came trick-or-treating on Halloween.

If you were fortunate enough to have your deepest spiritual seeking supported in childhood, I believe you are among a very few who were so blessed. Certainly in Western cultures, spiritual matters are usually explored with the young in the context of organized religions. And when the truth is organized, it usually loses its mystery and its magic. Thus we reach the second half either in a spiritual strait-jacket or secularly naked. Neither will suffice because both leave us spiritually passive. In the second half of our lives, our quest demands that we become active—not just politically or socially, but spiritually.

Dan Wakefield also grew up on the hearty but monotonous diet of corn-belt Christianity and, like me, had turned his back on it before he reached manhood. When I met him, he was a hard-drinking, hard-working, tough-minded, agnostic liberal, struggling to get dramas of genuine social value into prime-time television. An accomplished author and screenwriter, he was by most standards extremely successful. In our interview, he was eloquent, forthright, and dynamic as he regaled me with stories about his valiant, though not always successful, fights with network censors. Since he was making a living doing what he believed in, I considered him a hero of sorts. I had no idea that, only a few years later, his life would take a radically different turn.

One morning, just a month before his forty-eighth birthday, Dan Wakefield woke up screaming. But on this particular morning, he did not (as he was accustomed to doing) reach for a bottle of wine, or a bottle of pills. He reached for the Bible. Since leaving behind his childhood faith long ago, he had not thought much about God. But for the next several years, such thoughts become the focus of his daily life. As he reports in his book *Returning: A Spiritual Journey,* his quest took him through all the pain in his life and brought him, ultimately, back to the faith that he had rejected so many years before. Bible study became his ally in coming to grips with his shadow, which took the form of addiction.

> Bible study . . . was like holding up a mirror to my own life, a mirror in which I sometimes say things I was

trying to keep hidden, even from myself. The first scripture passage I was assigned to lead [in a Bible study
group] was from Luke, about the man who cleans his
house of demons, and seven worse ones come. . . . It
sounded unnervingly like an allegory about a man who
had stopped drinking and was enjoying much better
health, but took up smoking marijuana to "relax," all
the while feeling good and even self-righteous about
giving up the booze. It was my own story. I realized with
a shock, how I'd been deceiving myself, how much more
"housecleaning" I had to do.[3]

For Dan, seeking his path to the sacred meant reclaiming his
religious faith and returning to church. Since his spiritual
reawakening, he has spent several years teaching others how
to write their own "spiritual autobiography" as a way of
seeking their own personal path toward the sacred.[4]

Women too are reclaiming their spirituality. Sometimes
they return to their childhood faith, but more often today
their quest for the sacred leads them toward a different, less
patriarchal form of worship. The deep and widening
women's spirituality movement bears witness eloquently to
the creative yearning for true faith that often lies dormant
until well into adulthood. As Anthea Francine told us in the
opening chapter, these women are "questing for authenticity." To do so, they have no choice but to overcome their
spiritual passivity and let their soul seek its own answers.

When adults renew their search for the sacred in Western
cultures, it seems odd that we do not have a mainstream
tradition of spiritual quests in the second half. But in other
cultures, such grown-up spiritual seeking would be right on
schedule. In cultures such as India, for example, midlife was
traditionally considered to be the time in the life cycle to
renounce worldly involvements and turn toward the spiritual
realms. In the Hindu tradition, the idealized life cycle of a
hundred years was equally divided into four parts: student,

householder, hermit, and renunciant. "The first two represent engagement, the second two, detachment," comments Professor Arvind Sharma, a professor of comparative religion who was raised as a Hindu. "Very few live this scheme exactly, of course, but it is deeply embedded in Hindu consciousness. The problem in the West seems to be that you are only aware of the cycle up to the householder stage. That's why people don't know how to grow old gracefully. As a friend of mine said, 'In the West, they get stuck halfway through and don't know where to go.' If you discount an element of cultural chauvinism, there's certainly a grain of truth there."

Echoing Jung, Professor Sharma advises us to "accept the fact that *what one values before the second half will change.* Recognize that the spiritual dimension may well have a higher priority. If this happens, don't be perturbed. It is a natural, healthy, wholesome sequence with a long tradition."[5]

Whatever our age happens to be when we awaken from our spiritual passivity, it is our spiritual coming of age. We are no longer waiting lazily for the spirit to find us. Nor are we cynically armoring our souls against any experience of the sacred. We are opening our hearts and beginning to seek. And when our quest begins, we realize that it is, in fact, a vital part of our history.

After all, Jesus was not raised a Christian. Moses was not raised a Jew. Mohammed was not raised a Muslim. And Buddha was not raised a Buddhist. We do not need to be theologians to know that these men developed their faith as a result of personal midlife quests. None of the great teachers—neither Jesus nor Moses, Mohammed nor Buddha—took the ideas they were fed as children and repeated them like pious parrots for the rest of their lives. All four only came to their spiritual understanding later in their lives after years of seeking.

Genuine spirituality is not a finished product, something

that would be handed down to us from on high by an all-knowing God or guru. The great religious leaders did not look outward and upward to the current authorities; they looked downward and inward into their own souls. They faced doubt and anguish. They made mistakes. They lost their way, only to find it again. They were blind before they could see. Jesus, Moses, Buddha, Mohammed—*all* the holy prophets had to seek their own path toward the sacred. If we wish to follow any or all of them, then we cannot avoid *our* quest.

Remember: The word *quest* means "search." It is derived from the Latin word *quaerere*, "to seek," the same root from which the word *question* has grown. Jesus, Moses, Mohammed, and Buddha questioned. They were seekers. They undertook quests that today their followers memorize by heart. Through their quests they developed the belief systems to which so much of the world now adheres. Whether or not we personally believe in one of these belief systems, we should recognize the quest. *Without their spiritual quests, these faiths would not exist*—and the world as we know it would be a profoundly different place.

If we value their ideas, let us open ourselves to the possibility that we too must do spiritual learning in the second half as well. We must each seek the sacred as did the great spiritual leaders. To follow them does not mean to repeat their truths; it means to find ours. We must let go of our spiritual passivity and begin to discover the spirit within us. This, I believe, is what Christians mean when they say that Jesus is "The Way." They are pointing to the potential in *my* life, *your* life, and *every* human being's life of saving ourselves, of dying and being born anew, of discovering our place in the cosmic order of life. Like Jesus, we begin to search. We search for guidance—for an open door—for light. We are drawn to the paths that, throughout human history, have evoked the sacred. But which path do we take?

Where do we begin? How do we know in which direction to turn?

My brief and fleeting encounters with the spirit have been diverse—during the birth of our children, at that luminous moment when a fetus becomes a person, opens his eyes, and looks deeply into mine; in the wilderness, when a sudden glimpse of beauty leaves me breathless with wonder at creation; in meditation, on those rare occasions when stillness becomes a sacred silence; and in relationships, when the connection between my soul and another's is so clean and clear that we feel the holy current of love pass between us. Although I have learned much from these encounters, I cannot claim to have found the sacred, or even to have securely found the path that leads toward it. But I have found some signposts that have helped me and others find our way.

Let us follow these signposts in the same spirit that Bill Moyers explored the origin and meaning of the traditional hymn "Amazing Grace." Moyers discovered that this hymn means something different to everyone. This "something" is at the same time universal, yet unique to each person. "I once was lost but now am found" summarizes the quest; "was blind but now I see" embodies the search for the sacred. To me, the song is not about religion, not about heaven and hell. It is about grace. To live gracefully is the Holy Grail we all seek. No one owns grace. No one can codify or market it. It simply is. All Moyers could do, all any of us can do, is to sing its song.

Although this book is a product—bought, sold, distributed, and marketed like other goods—it is also my attempt to raise my untrained voice in song. As Ernest Becker says in the final line of *The Denial of Death:* "The most that any one of us can seem to do is to fashion something—an object or ourselves—and drop it into the confusion, make an offering of it, so to speak, to the life force." This is my offering, dropped into the collection plate, along with yours.

To Witness the Spirit:
Daily Life as Spiritual Practice

Whether the quest for the sacréd involves a dramatic experience of being "reborn" into an organized religious denomination, or a quiet, deliberate, and personal reaffirmation of faith, it is happening in the second half to many people of every faith. Since their childhoods, an estimated two-thirds of the postwar generation dropped out of mainstream religious organizations. More than a third of those who left, however, have recently returned to the fold. (Those with kids have returned to church in droves; childless couples have done so far less often.) "It turns out that the Forever Young generation did not escape the life cycle," summarized one reporter who was assigned to document the replenishing of the pews. As we "wed, aged, became fruitful and multiplied"—in other words, as we entered the second half—"we focused our attention on 'matters of the spirit.' "[6]

For two out of five in the postwar generations, their spiritual path has not led directly to the doors of a church or synagogue. Yet many of the remaining 60 percent who have no connection to organized religion are nevertheless deeply involved in a spiritual quest. Unlike those who pray "in Jesus' name," heed "the Will of Allah," count themselves among "the Chosen People," or adopt Buddhism or some other nonwestern religious tradition, nontraditional seekers want the authenticity of their spiritual journey to be respected, even if it lacks a simple, recognizable label. Indeed, despite the apparent chasm between those who do and do not profess a belief in God, we all face similar questions on our quest for the sacred.

Whether we look deeply into our own hearts or deeply into the heart of the major religious traditions, we find the same truth: The second half of life is a time for spiritual awakening. But now the spirit seems to reassert itself in our daily lives. In every chapter of this book, we have encountered it again and again. "This is the modern spiritual quest," writes Jungian analyst Murray Stein. "It is not going to a monastery and meditating all the time, not going to church more often. It is finding the spiritual dimension in our everyday lives."[7]

Although a few among us may become monks or mystics, priests or pilgrims, holy men or shamanesses, most of us will not. We hold jobs, nurture families, and live in the world. Our daily path is pedestrian, taking us through city streets and crowded freeways, fluorescent-lit offices and factory floors, funeral services and dirty diapers. As the artist Corita put it: "After ecstasy, the laundry." How can we stay attuned to the extraordinary while immersed in the ordinary?

Unfortunately, it is not easy to encounter the sacred in our daily lives. This is the perennial dilemma of the spirit, with which spiritual leaders throughout the ages have struggled. In the second half, the challenge to honor "things as they are" becomes greater, because the spiritual dimension is no longer in the wings but has moved to center stage. John Wellwood restates the dilemma well when he writes: "Although sacred vision may be vast and profound, it is also quite ordinary. It is a question of honoring the elemental qualities of things as they are—whether it be the solidity of the earth, the heat of passion, the fierceness of anger, or the pain of a broken heart."[8]

Lovers of Ray Lynch's uplifting albums *Deep Breakfast, The Sky of Mind,* and *No Blue Thing* may assume that this accomplished musician has always been able to find the sacred through music. But the truth is quite different. This native Texan was a successful classical guitarist and lutenist, dazzling audiences in New York with his virtuoso performances with the Renaissance Quartet. But one day, standing in his front yard, he realized that his comfortable life, including his music, no longer had meaning. He was tired of being paid for performing *other* people's music. "I felt like I was on the edge of an abyss looking down into a black hole,"

Lynch recalls, in words reminiscent of Dante as he got lost in the dark forest. "It was the most frightening moment of my life. I was looking at death and knew my life had come to a dead end."[9]

Fortunately, it turned out to be a new road, not a dead end. Lynch stopped performing professionally, apprenticed with a spiritual teacher (while working as a carpenter), and finally decided it was time to compose. The rest, as they say, is history. He soon became one of the most successful and respected performers in his genre. He has given all of us who are moved by his music a greater gift than his songs. He has let us listen to his personal quest for the sacred.

Learning to find the sacred in our daily lives involves wholeness—a breaking down of the barriers that we built within ourselves during the first half of life. It involves experiencing our connection with whatever before was separate from us. When I and Other become one, the spirit emerges in our daily lives at the most unexpected moments. Surgeon Richard Seltzer recalls precisely such a moment with a patient whose cancer surgery left her mouth misshapen due to a nerve that had been unavoidably severed during the operation. Lying in her hospital bed, she picked up a mirror and for the first time looked at her twisted mouth. Impassively, she asked Dr. Seltzer if her mouth would always be like this, and he replied that it was permanent. At which point the patient's husband, who had been standing quietly beside her bed, stepped forward and kissed her, twisting his mouth so that it fit hers.

"All at once I *know* who he is," Seltzer recalls. "I understand, and lower my gaze. One is not bold in an encounter with a god."[10]

This sensitive surgeon witnessed the sacred in a kiss between husband and wife. It can be found as well in a hug between parent and child; in the preparing of a meal; in the turning over soil for a garden; in caring for a pet; in the gentle union of a string quartet or a sailing crew; and in the birth of a child or the death of a parent. Just as it is present in the first breath and the last, so is it present in every breath in between—but only the gods are aware of it.

Spiritual growth takes root deeply only when it endures the return home. As we seek paths toward the sacred, they eventually lead us home—home not as in real estate, but as in wholeness. It is in the rhythms of daily life, as the authors of *Chop Wood, Carry Water* note, that we face the everyday spiritual challenges: "how to live more meaningfully with those we love, how to earn a living, how to find love and be loved, how to be a member of a family and community and planet, how to make play, health, art, sex and business a reflection . . . of our spiritual lives." These are the ways that we try "to bring heaven down to earth."[11] These paths, Heidegger observed long ago, "need by no means be high-flown" but can lead us back to "this patch of home ground."[12]

I experienced this distinction clearly a few years ago when I found myself dreaming about the need to expand our house. At first I thought the problem (too little space) was as obvious as the solution (make the house bigger). Since our small house lot made expanding horizontally difficult, most of the architectural images that began to flood my mind focused on building a partial second story that would include a third bedroom for our children and perhaps a small den or study with skylights illuminating the two rooms. These skylights, if properly designed, would allow new sources of light into virtually all the downstairs rooms. For several weeks, my mind's eye sketched and resketched how this upper level of the house would be constructed. I would wake up thinking about home design, building materials, Plexiglas, and solar angles. I could not understand why I was so obsessed and why I was thinking less and less about the actual rooms and more and more about the skylights.

I don't know how I would have unraveled this mystery if my son Ari, whose yearning for his own room had originally triggered our expansion plans, had not given me a copy of Alice Walker's essay "Oppressed Hair Puts a Ceiling on The Brain" from her collection of selected writings, *Living by the Word*. Because it was a transcript of a talk delivered to a mostly black and female audience at Spelman College, I was at first tempted to dismiss it as sorority pillow talk. Vowing not to speak "of war and peace, the economy, racism or sexism, or the triumphs and tribulations of black people or of women," she told her assembled audience: "I am going to talk about an issue even closer to home. I am going to talk to you about hair."[13]

For years Alice had endured a never-ending series of hairdressers, starting with her mother "doing missionary work on my hair. They dominated, suppressed, controlled." But Alice wanted to liberate her hair. She "wanted it to grow, to be itself . . . to be left alone by anyone, including me, who did not love it as it was." She was clearly as surprised by the outcome as I was: "The ceiling at the top of my brain lifted; once again my mind (and spirit) could get outside myself. I would not be stuck in restless stillness, but would continue to grow."

"This," she writes in the concluding paragraph, "was the gift of my growth during my fortieth year."

Here was a person of a different race and sex, with a background utterly different from my own, who was also trying to raise a ceiling. Her feminine metaphor was hair; my masculine metaphor was house. But we were both engaged in the same process of trying to let more of the light shine through. Ms. Walker's story enabled me to grasp that the problem was not the ceiling of my house, but the ceiling on my head. I wanted to connect to the spirit, and to the sky. For that, I did not need skylights at all. I simply needed to step outside (or simpler still, step inside).

In the Bible, the apostle Luke recorded Jesus' reply to the Pharisees when they asked if the Kingdom of God would come on earth. Jesus' answer was: "The Kingdom of God does not come in such a way as to be seen. No one will say, 'Look, here it is!' or 'There it is!'; because the Kingdom of God is among us."[14] This same message about witnessing the spirit in daily life was repeated in terms our generation was certain to grasp by two unlikely contemporary apostles, George Harrison and John Lennon:

> GEORGE HARRISON: Through Christianity, how I was taught it, they told me to believe in Jesus and in God and all that. They didn't show me any way of experiencing God or Jesus, so the whole point of it was to believe in something without actually seeing it—well, it's, you know, it's no good . . . if there's a God, we must see him; and that's the point in—of the whole thing. . . .
>
> JOHN LENNON: Yes, well, that thing about the "Kingdom of Heaven is within you," you know, that's all it means, to have a peep inside, you know—
>
> HARRISON: And to contact it—[15]

"Even using the word *sacred* may be a step in the wrong direction," says a specialist on comparative religion, Richard Heinberg, when I asked him to comment on this yearning to discover heaven during, not after, life. "What it comes down to are those moments of compassion and transcendence, and they make all the difference." Although these moments of grace are private and personal, Heinberg feels they are part of a major cultural shift. Every few generations there is a rebellion against prefabricated faith and followers set out to experience the sacred for themselves.

In the West there is more emphasis on dogma and hierarchy, according to Heinberg, while in Eastern religions, it's taken for granted that the follower needs to experience the sacred in daily life. "This is why there is a rising interest in

Oriental spiritual disciplines—we want to *witness* the spirit, not just worship it."[16]

True encounters with the spirit can change us. They do not just lead us home. They return us to the world. Whenever the spirit comes alive in the second half of life, a commitment to serve emerges. One can view this psychologically and call it "generativity," as Erik Erikson does, or "charity" (as do the Christians) or *seva* (as do the Buddhists). By whatever name, service is a path toward the sacred that imparts an understanding that self-absorbed seekers will never know.

During my interview with Murray Stein, he suddenly became passionate about my reading an obituary. It had recently caught his eye in *The New York Times* because it noted the death of William Larimar Mellon, Jr., heir to the banking and oil fortune. (Mellon's father had been the head of Gulf Oil; his great-uncle Andrew was an oil and aluminum tycoon.) Born into this empire, William decided to leave the East Coast and move out west. He bought a ranch, then another, becoming one of Arizona's most prosperous cattle ranchers. Using all his vast resources, he built the structure for the first half of his life. But when he entered the second half, it was no longer enough.

At the age of thirty-seven, he read an article in *Life* magazine about Albert Schweitzer, the famous doctor who had spent his adult life ministering to the sick in a small village in Africa. He wrote to Schweitzer, received a long handwritten letter in reply, and his life was changed. In midlife, he entered medical school and received his medical degree in 1954, at the age of forty-four. His wife, who had previously been a riding instructor, became a laboratory technician. They searched throughout Latin America for a place to build their hospital and finally selected Haiti, where they built a two-million-dollar hospital on the abandoned site of a United Fruit Company plantation. From then until his death in 1989, reported the *Times,* "the Mellons and their staff of Haitian doctors and nurses have treated tens of thousands of patients."[17]

"My speculation," Stein observed "is that Mr. Mellon experienced in midlife a loss of meaning. So he reorganized himself around a new identity. *Mr. Mellon had lived for himself; he now wished to live for others.*"

Having spent much if not all of our time looking after ourselves (and, if we are parents, after our children), many of us find ourselves wanting to help others. Working in an orphanage and volunteering in a project to safeguard an endangered species are certainly not the typical activities that come to mind when we talk about midlife crises. But it is precisely such acts of service to other human beings, other creatures, or the planet itself that spontaneously emerge in the quest for wholeness. It connects us to a world beyond ourselves. It places our own life in perspective. It enables us to have an impact, to make a difference. It allows us to learn what only service can teach.

There is no single, uniform way to serve, any more than there is a single way to pray. Each of us must focus our energies on different aspects of the circle. "Please show me the way to serve God," a rabbi once asked his teacher. But his teacher replied: "It is impossible to tell you what way you should take. For one way to serve God is through learning, another through prayer, another through fasting, and still another through eating. Everyone should carefully observe what way his heart draws him to, and then choose this way with all his strength." Martin Buber makes the same point when he recounts what Rabbi Zusya told his followers shortly before his death. "In the world to come I shall not be asked: 'Why were you not Moses?' " whispered the rabbi. "I shall be asked 'Why were you not Zusya?' "[18]

It is as if we were visiting a beautiful park for which no entry fee is required, but each of us who enters is asked to make some other kind of contribution to the park's well-being. Each visitor's response, of course, will be different. Someone might plant a tree. Someone else might pick up garbage. Another person might give a ride to elderly visitors who could otherwise not come. Someone else might paint a fence. There is no "right" way to contribute except, perhaps, with an open heart. Our challenge is not to try to live up to some externally imposed ideal of "social responsibility" or "global thinking," but to find within ourselves the genuine *enthusiasm* (literally, "to be filled with God") to make our own personal contribution to protecting the quest for those who follow.

Unless we want to be martyrs, we must also take care of ourselves. If we do not begin here, sooner or later we will not be able to take care of anything. If we are sick, depressed, or chronically poor, we are not well-equipped to take care of anybody or anything else. Altruism must be grounded in basic self-care, or it just won't work. *But a life that is focused entirely on "me" and "mine"—even "my" spiritual growth—will not work either.* On this point, the religions of mankind are in extraordinary unanimity. It is not only Christianity that advises us to "do unto others as you would have others do unto you." It is the universal ethical advice from every great religious tradition:

> Regard your neighbor's gain as your own gain,
> and your neighbor's loss as your own loss.
>
> TAOISM

> What is hateful to you, do not to your fellow man.
>
> JUDAISM

> Do not unto others what would cause you pain
> if done unto you.
>
> HINDUISM

> No one of you is a believer until he desires
> for his brother that which he desires for himself.
>
> ISLAM

> Hurt not others in ways that you yourself
> would find hurtful.
>
> BUDDHISM

It is in this spirit that we must serve the world. Our challenge is to keep that spirit alive, not just in our places of worship but in the places where we live and work and love. And fortunately, almost every night, we receive just the guidance we need.

The Sacred Storyteller: Dreaming as Spiritual Practice

We begin dreaming as soon as life begins. From childhood through adolescence and adulthood until the day we die, hundreds or thousands of dreams each year are delivered to the mailbox of our conscious minds. But what is unique about the second half is that we are more likely than ever before to open these letters and pay attention to what their author has to say. If we pay attention to the stories that this sacred storyteller shares with us, our quest will lead us deep into the country of the soul.

If God is a mystery, then our dreams are clues. Every major culture and religion throughout recorded history has been fascinated by the inner storyteller, whose tales do not come from Hollywood or Madison Avenue but from within. No matter how we desacralize our world—removing ourselves from nature, distancing ourselves from religion, abandoning ritual and ceremony, forgetting the holiness of holidays—it is almost impossible to remove the nocturnal storyteller. He or she is always with us, always ready to remind us of another reality. As Donald Marrs, the former Chicago ad man, concluded during one of his darkest hours: "dreams were my only spiritual reality."[19] Our dreams, particularly what Jung called our "big dreams,"[20] can inspire us far more than any minister's or rabbi's sermon and can guide us more clearly than any scripture. From high in the steeple of our selves, the church bells of our dreams call us. They are given to us, as the native American leader Chief Seattle put it, "in the solemn hours of the night by the Great Spirit."[21]

Robert Johnson had a dream when he was twenty-five that included an encounter with the Buddha and a snake. Despite extensive analysis of it, including help from Dr. Jung himself, the meaning of the dream eluded Johnson. Thirty-five years later, he had another "big dream" in which the snake appeared. This time he understood its meaning—not because a wise analyst explained it to him, but because he was less resistant and more open in the second half than he had been in the first.[22] Even those who began exploring their dreams at an earlier age often find that their power and vividness markedly increase at midlife. It is as if a veil has been removed, allowing us to see more clearly and feel more deeply what our inner storyteller is trying to show us.

Our dreams often point with the accuracy of a spiritual compass to the undiscovered regions of our Selves. We realize that living fully, which so many of us *say* we want to do, means following that compass.

Although I did not entirely ignore my dreams before midlife, I certainly did not attend to them either. Always impatient, I found them hard to remember and even harder to fathom. But then, in my thirties, my dreams began to hit me with such force that I could no longer ignore them. One of the first dreams that influenced my quest was triggered, I am certain, by my friendship with a remarkable artist who died a few years ago named Corita Kent. Her art, which made her famous, was for her a form of prayer. While a nun, she signed her art Sister Corita. But after leaving her order to devote herself to her art in the second half of her life, she signed it simply Corita. Her work adorned billboards and postcards, magazines and monuments. My favorite was a

drawing of purple flowers in a clear vase—like Corita, simple yet dignified. Even when she knew she was dying of
cancer, a halo of stillness surrounded her. She was truly a
holy woman.

Shortly after she died, I had the following dream:

> I am in the back seat of a car being driven by a man and
> a woman whose faces I cannot see. It has been raining
> heavily; the windshield wipers thrash madly. I am in a
> business suit with my suitcases on the seat beside me.
> As always, I am in a hurry, this time rushing to the
> airport. I peer nervously into the front seat and see the
> flashing red light of the gas gauge. It is on empty. Flat
> empty. Gripped by fear, I ask the couple in the front
> seat if there is a gas station nearby. "Yes," one of them
> replies, "just up the street."
>
> I look up the street, which runs along a river. My
> attention is totally focused on finding the gas station
> when suddenly, on the riverbank, I see a solitary little
> shop. No cars are parked around it, and no one is inside.
>
> I am so startled to see a shop along the riverbank that
> I ask the couple what it is. They tell me it is a flower
> shop run by a former nun. We are close to it now, wait-
> ing for a red light. I can see the shop more clearly now.
> Its name is clearly marked in front: DEEPLY CHARGED PUR-
> PLE. On the shelves in the little store are vases galore,
> each filled with purple, violet, and lavender bouquets.
>
> "Oh would I like to stop there!" I hear myself ex-
> claim. It is my voice, but I barely recognize it. But do I
> really want to stop? Aren't I in a hurry to find gas and
> get to the airport?

In this dream, I forgot my plans, my schedules, my itiner-
ary. I was on my way to the airport, armed with my ambitions and propelled by my high-flying energies. But then I
glimpsed a spirit so enthusiastic, so "filled with God," that it

penetrated my armor, navigated the labyrinth of my consciousness, and touched my soul. Through her art and her love, which is immortal, Corita wanted me to know the purple-splendored possibilities of being human. I never fully heard her message when she was alive. But I finally received it after she died, in my dreams.

The part of myself that had planned the first half of my life was no longer steering me in the right direction or at the right pace. If I had relied solely on that rational, planning part of myself, I would have been trapped. The realm I needed to enter required intuition, not mere intellect; faith, not just ideas; heart courage, not mere body strength. It required what understanding dreams requires: a willingness to go beyond my ordinary waking consciousness.

After that, I began paying attention to my dreams and writing them in a journal. I was encouraged to learn that I was not alone in having difficulty remembering or understanding the language that the sacred storyteller used. Even those who analyze dreams professionally, if they dare to step out from behind their degrees, admit that they often feel baffled. Robert Bosnak, a Boston-based Jungian analyst in his mid-forties, observed in *A Little Course in Dreams:* "My first reaction after listening to a dream is, 'I haven't the faintest idea what this is all about. It just proves that dreams are pure nonsense.' "[23] Paradoxically, this is precisely why our dreams are so vital. According to Bosnak: "Nobody likes to stumble, and dreams trip us up . . . trip up our daytime consciousness again and again in order to unhinge our fixed positions." This is at first precisely how they make us feel: unhinged. We lose our moorings. Or to use Jung's metaphor, we feel as if we have lost our footing and are suspended in midair.[24]

Lost, dislocated, abandoned, disoriented, overwhelmed, overcome—difficult as these feelings may be, without them we will never witness the sacred but will simply continue racing down the fast lane of our lives. Since our dreams are our "inner elders," wise voices that can be consulted as we make the pivotal decisions of our lives, it is crucial that we listen to them. Students of creativity and genius have long known that great mathematicians, scientists, artists, writers, and other inventive minds have made some of their most dramatic breakthroughs in their dreams. What is now becoming clear is that breakthroughs in the lives of ordinary men and women are often also seeded in our sleep.[25]

Perhaps no dream has spoken to me more clearly than the one that emerged in Moscow where I was organizing the Entertainment Summit, a politically highly charged project involving the film industries of the two superpowers. I had been able to negotiate an agreement between Moscow and Hollywood to allow the filmmakers from both superpowers to meet each other and, as a result, learn to make more accurate and thoughtful movies about each other. For months I was so caught up in my public role preparing for this second summit that I had no time for my inner life at all.

When I left for Moscow as head of a delegation of distinguished Hollywood producers, writers, and directors, I was exhausted. The pressure in Moscow was intense; the vodka flowed; sleep was elusive. When the day approached to negotiate our final agreement, I was still severely jet-lagged and lay awake at two in the morning (which is one in the afternoon back home). I was afraid I would not fall asleep and consequently would be lost in a haze of fatigue.

Finally, I fell asleep and dreamed.

> I am visiting a "woman healer." She has dark hair and dark eyes, like so many of the women in Russia. I am skeptical that she has anything to offer me, and I observe her with suspicion. I feel bored and doubt her power.
>
> The healer fixes her eyes upon me; I can tell that she sees everything I am feeling. She walks over to me and takes my right hand so that her fingertips rest on my

palm. Afraid, I pull back my hand. She steps away, yet I still feel the heat of her fingers on my hand. I look down and see her three finger joints in my hand. Terrified, I flick my hand, trying to throw off her fingertips as if they were poisonous spiders. The fingertips sail through the air but disappear before they hit the ground.

My indifference and arrogance vanish. My attention is riveted on her. I know in my soul that she knows me and is out to teach me, whether I am ready or not.

Later, all of us are lying on the floor. The woman healer walks over and touches the back of my neck (a place where I hold tension). Again I feel heat, but this time it is accompanied by deep relaxation. As I surrender to the feeling, my whole body begins to shake. I feel embarrassed, exposed. Finally, the shaking stops. Tears come to my eyes. I feel healed, relaxed, exorcised.

The next morning I awoke, feeling completely rested and at peace. The meetings went extremely well; the agreement was signed. Throughout the day I felt as if I were being protected and healed by this dark-haired angel who emerged from nowhere and whom I have never seen again.[26]

I felt as if my inner storyteller, who for the first half of my life had quietly told tales that I could ignore if I so wished, had grabbed me by the collar and would not let go. Now I *had* to pay attention. Like Abraham Lincoln, I had accepted the biblical fact that "*in the old days* God and his angels came to men in their sleep and made themselves known in dreams."[27] What I had not realized is that what happened in the Bible could happen to me.

Evidently, many others in the generation now entering the second half have had a similar awakening. A grassroots dreamwork movement emerged during the eighties and even founded its own newsletter, the *Dream Network Journal*.[28] Although certainly not a mass movement, the popularity of dreamwork signified the eclipse of an era in which the reigning conventional wisdom was that only someone *else* (usually requiring payment and speaking in jargon) could truly understand and interpret our dreams. Although few people participated in grassroots dreamwork groups, many people now share the movement's post-Freudian bias that the ultimate authority on a dream's meaning is the dreamer. As with any journey into uncharted territory, however, trained guides are often essential.[29]

To understand the potential value of your dreams, consider some of the following basic principles of dreamwork:

> The dream is a spiritual event.
> The dream can provide healing and wholeness.
> The dream releases energy or insight.
> The dream allows your waking ego to establish a relationship with your deepest self.
> In light of spiritual growth, the dream is more powerful when viewed as a question than as an answer.
> The dream is incomplete without dreamwork.[30]

Now substitute the word *quest* for *dream* in the above sentences, and you can see why these inner messages are such vital correspondence in the second half. They are our signposts on the journey, responding day by day with advice about the path we are choosing to follow.

In our dreams we are connected to a reality that embraces us all, a reality in which we are not separate selves, each with our own wallet or purse that records our identity, but part of a sacred whole that is often obscured by our day-to-day preoccupations. Our dreams strip away that veil. Bring ten people together sharing dreams, and you will find many stories of hurrying toward an intended destination only to be "sidetracked" (that is, divinely redirected) by a mysterious, sacred figure. Indeed, while researching this book I encountered several, including one in which the dreamer arrived at the airport and encountered a Trappist monk.[31]

I share my dreams here, not because they are special, but precisely because they are not. They illumine themes that, as we enter the second half of life at this point in history, dance around many bedsides, perhaps yours as well. These themes hit us with extraordinary power, I believe, when their message is particularly urgent. They are not ends, but means. They are challenging us to act.

Martin Luther King, Jr., did not have a dream, analyze its meaning, and then tell his therapist. He had a dream—and then he lived its meaning! During his famous speech at the March on Washington on August 28, 1963, he shared his dream with the world. In less than a page of printed text, King mentioned his dream not once, not twice, but nine times. "I have a dream," he said the final time, "that one day every valley shall be exalted, and every hill and mountain shall be made low . . . and the glory of the Lord shall be revealed."[32] Every time I hear King's voice speaking these words, I feel their riveting power. This was more than political oratory, more than a preacher's prose. It was the deepest vision from a man's soul translated into language so that every man and woman, black and white, could feel its power.

Not everyone can have a holy shrine, magnificent temple, towering mosque, or stained-glass church in which to worship in peace. But like Dr. King, each of us is endowed with an inner sanctuary that we enter every night. Each of us— free man or slave, pauper or millionaire, therapist or client —can dream.

The Power of Retreat: Meditation, Nature, and the Vision Quest

Although our quest for the sacred is rooted in daily living and nightly dreaming, many of us need a spiritual practice to keep us on our path. This practice may take many different forms. For some it may be precious moments with a baby;

for others, quiet labor in the garden; for still others, sitting with closed eyes engrossed in a symphony. But as different as our paths to the sacred may be in the second half, they usually have some common elements, including spiritual retreats.

In the ambitious, hurly-burly world where football metaphors prevail, *retreat* has an exclusively negative connotation. The term is used here, however, in keeping with its oriental meaning as one of many aspects of a fully lived life. Success, counsels the venerable *I Ching,* or "Book of Changes," requires carrying out the retreat correctly. "Retreat is not to be confused with flight," or with desperate and fearful running away. On the contrary, retreat can be a "sign of strength," a recognition that the time to advance has not yet arrived. "In this way we prepare, while retreating, for the countermovement"—for moving ahead when our energy is stronger and our vision clearer.

Historically, the most common retreats have been monasteries and other cloistered religious environments. For some seekers, such environments still seem appropriate for a modern solo quest. In many parts of the country, there are secluded spiritual hideaways where you can spend your days or weeks in quiet retreat surrounded by those who have chosen life in a religious order. Others who seek retreat take the opposite extreme, splurging on Club Med or some other oasis of pleasure and entertainment. Incredulous that anyone could find rejuvenation in a convent or monastery, these men and women retreat to the sun and surf, into a world of sensual pleasure and complete lack of responsibility. Still others find both convents and Club Med inappropriate for their retreats. Instead, they prescribe for themselves one of the myriad "human potential" seminars or workshops that are now available for individuals or couples. In every major city, in countless conference centers and hotel ballrooms, on almost any weekend of the year, groups gather for intense psychological encounters designed to promote growth, well-being, or happiness.

But hotel conferences, like convents and resorts, are man-made environments. For some who enter life's second half, peace-and-prayer retreat centers, fun-and-frolic resorts, or touch-and-talk workshops all miss the point. They prefer to retreat into nature. Yearning for solitude in the timelessness of creation itself, they do not want to exchange their own confining roof-and-wall reality for someone else's. To cope with their crisis, they need a retreat from the civilized construct altogether. Whether they venture out alone or with others, they seek renewal that only nature can provide.

But wherever and however we retreat, we need a way of communing with ourselves. For many, meditation seems to provide a useful context. What entered America as the flaky, weird preoccupation of hippies and rock stars has over the past quarter century become part of our culture. Doctors prescribe it. Talk-show hosts demonstrate it. TV moms, like Phylicia Rashad of *The Cosby Show,* practice it. (Meditation "is the most important thing," says the actress, now in her early forties. "Without that focus first, nothing works."[33])

Since many of us who came of age with (or soon after) the Beatles were impatient with religion that was abstract and unconnected to our experience, we knew what George Harrison meant when he sang passionately, "I really want to know you, Lord, really want to see you." He and his fellow minstrels would not settle for a definition of the sacred in some old book. They wanted to experience it—and quickly too. During the psychedelic craze of the sixties, the quest for instant enlightenment became downright ridiculous. We witnessed what Marilyn Ferguson, author of *The Aquarian Conspiracy,* recently referred to as the "candy cane" concept of consciousness: "People acted as though they would find enlightenment one day, perhaps on an LSD trip or a trek to Nepal, and the search would be over."[34] We did not want to wait a lifetime to become enlightened; we wanted nirvana now! This led to a spiritual hype that relied, in Aldous Huxley's phrase, on "too much nirvana and strawberry jam."[35]

Now in the second half, our quest for the sacred is maturing. Meditation has moved from the periphery toward the mainstream of Western culture. Along with the more traditional form of reflection known as prayer, meditation is now widely recognized as a method for relaxation and spiritual growth. Today its value is based, not on the opinions of rock stars or traveling gurus, but on scientific data that were simply unavailable to previous generations. In the mid-1970s, at precisely the time when the first members of the postwar generation were entering the second half of life, Dr. Herbert Benson, director of the Hypertension Section of Boston's Beth Israel Hospital, published *The Relaxation Response*. He and his colleagues proved that regular meditation lowers blood pressure. As long as their research subjects continued to meditate for two brief periods each day, their blood pressures remained measurably lower than before. When they stopped, it rose again.[36]

Equally important, Dr. Benson demonstrated that the relaxation response of meditation was not the property of any guru or religion. On the contrary, it was "simply a scientific validation of age-old wisdom" present in all the great religious traditions. The response was simple to learn—and free. All you had to do was:

1. Sit quietly and comfortably with your eyes closed.
2. Relax your muscles, moving from your feet up to your face.
3. Breathe through your nose, noting each breath with a word (spoken silently) that makes you feel good.
4. Continue for fifteen to twenty minutes, preferably twice a day.[37]

Since publication of *The Relaxation Response,* scores of doctors have demonstrated that regular meditation is useful not just in lowering blood pressure but in developing a healthy mental and physical way of living, particularly in the second half of life. Meditation, our physicians are telling us, is a vital tool for developing a trusting heart that lasts longer and makes life less stressful and allows life to become more deeply spiritual.[38] Those twenty minutes provide us with an invaluable experience of time and space when we are at peace. It is a journey that money can't buy—and Club Med can't provide. Like the inner storyteller of our dreams, meditation is a vital path toward the sacred.

Just as meditation is an inner path, nature seems to be an outer one. What the soul in all its mystery is within, the earth seems to be without. "Speak to the earth," reads the Bible (Job 12:8), "and it shall teach thee." So it is not surprising that, when author and philosopher Sam Keen runs seminars in which he asks people to draw their ideal future, images of nature almost always appear. He asks questions such as: "What is it that hasn't happened to you yet? What would have to happen to you in order for you to be able to die as a person who is fulfilled?" Keen is struck that more than 95 percent of the people draw *rural* environments, with oceans, farms, and trees. Even if they draw a city, says Keen, "they usually have an apartment: they will go into the city and they will come out. Or if they draw a city environment for themselves, they will also draw a rural environment."[39] In Abraham Maslow's phrase, we are "resacralizing" nature.[40]

Your way of finding the sacred in nature will no doubt differ from mine. To one person, a lotus flower may be an inspiration to ecstasy; for another person, such inspiration may come from the sound of wind in a sail. To define categorically and impersonally where the spirit can be found is not only arrogant, but *dis*piriting. For each of us, seeking the sacred landscape is a personal quest. (Thank God this is so;

otherwise, *the* universal holy place would be mobbed and would soon lose its sacredness anyway.)

Although sojourns in the wilderness can have many purposes, "vision quests" convey what seems to be the overriding motivation: the search for a new vision. There are other quests that involve individual or joint expeditions into difficult terrain (such as mountain climbing, transoceanic sailing, and extended wilderness treks) that accentuate the physical challenge. There are also various rituals, such as native American sweat lodge ceremonies and others involving chanting or breathing, that use both physical and psychological means for assisting transformation. But the vision quest experience is focused as much on the spiritual as on the physical and is part of a broader movement to realign ourselves with nature.

Diane Broderick—forty, separated, and the mother of three children—was drawn to the vision quest because she read that they were traditionally used for "shedding the old ways." She knew she was terrified by the idea of being all alone in the wilderness for three days and nights, without any support or companionship. But instead of running away from her fear, she decided to try to move through it. "I was ready for a challenging initiation," she recalls. "At midlife, I was learning to trust these intuitive impulses. I knew I had to do it. The only thing standing in the way was fear."

Her week in the wilderness turned out to be "powerful medicine" that forever changed her life.

> It was as if my socialized being dissolved. I became a creature again, a human creature, but very much a part of nature. I came to know myself in a new way, a deeper way. I felt welcomed by the earth, connected to mother earth and father sky. I felt that I was their child. Whatever my wounds from my biological parents, I realized that I had these other parents. In their world, I had an experience of inner strength and connectedness. I have

never forgotten that feeling. It was almost like being reborn.

The most powerful moment she remembers was in the middle of the first night under the stars, seated in the middle of the medicine wheel that she had constructed out of stones. She prayed, calling in the spirits of each person in her life and asking them to forgive her and heal her wounds. "As I pictured each person, I felt each wound I had ever had or had ever caused. I forgave myself. It was the most complete moment of self-love I had ever known. Until that moment, the word *mercy* had been just a word. That night, it entered my body."[41]

After returning home to her work and to her children, life was different. Her relationship to fear had changed. She felt far more self-reliant, far more clear. She felt less like a victim and more like the architect of her own life. Today she continues to feel deep gratitude to the woman who led the vision quest, Nancy Goddard. "Without her help," says Diane, "my intentions would not have been so clear. I would not have felt the presence of the sacred so vividly. Nancy is a wonderful model for trusting nature and relating to it."

"A lot of the people who do vision quests come right off the sidewalk," according to Goddard. "They want to have a relationship with the earth, but they don't know how to." She describes the first stage of the quest as one of severance, "leaving behind the world, cutting yourself from conveniences, comforts, possessions." It is a metaphor for what people are trying to do in their lives. Echoing Diane's experience, Nancy says that the quest "strips away acculturation and silences all the voices of people telling them who they are and what they should become. It prepares them to become who they want to be, and who they really are. It transforms people on every level: physical, emotional, psychological, spiritual. That's one of the beauties of the quest experience: it's all connected."

Nancy often finds that people do not even know they are in the midst of a major life transition until they are actually on the quest. Since, in our culture, "we don't honor our transitions," Nancy believes that "the process of change becomes blurred." We need to sharpen and clarify what is occurring. "Particularly at midlife," says Nancy, "people feel an urgency. They feel the need to grasp their lives. They still have the health and vitality to do this work. They want to make the most of it."[42] It is not coincidence that the vision quest involves journeying in nature, far from the man- and woman-made world where most of us spend our daily lives. Paths toward the sacred necessarily lead us to toward what was here before us and will remain after us—the *whole* of creation.

Seen from this perspective, spirituality is not a "higher" path. Whether we think of God the Father on his celestial throne, Moses climbing up to speak with God, the guru alone meditating on a mountaintop, or the steeple rising high above the church, we too quickly assume that the more "elevated" we are, the more "spiritual" we must be. According to this conventional wisdom, we push the archetypal "up" button for heaven and push "down" for hell. (Similarly, we call happy being "up," and sad "down.") This no doubt is why, without thinking, I first titled this chapter "Find Your Path to the Mountaintop." Based on the spiritual vocabulary of *"higher* motives" and *"consciousness-raising,"* and *"peak* experiences" that I had inherited, the classic image of a pilgrimage to the mountain was entirely predictable.[43]

But the challenge of the quest is not finding the mountaintop. It is learning to find our path to the sacred wherever we may be. All of nature is sacred, not just the sites that we humans so designate. As Frederic Lehrman writes in *The Sacred Landscape,* a sacred place "is one where the Earth's voices can be heard more clearly. Go to these places and listen. Once you've heard her, she can reach you any-where."[44]

The Circles of the Quest: Where All Roads Meet

Through every one of the preceding chapters, a spiritual thread is clearly visible in the fabric of the book. It was present in our vision of a quest rather than a crisis; in our view of the body's senses as a doorway to deeper meaning; and in our view of love as a path to the sacred. It was also present in our search for a calling, our exploration of what it means to age deeply, and our honoring of the elders and the cycle of generations. And finally, it was present in our view of the land, air, and water as the essence of Creation that has been placed in jeopardy by our way of life.

As I wrote about our quest for wholeness, I struggled to avoid fragmenting it but rather tried to portray its integrity. I focused so intently on the papers on my desk and on the flickering computer screen that for several years I never grasped the relevance of a diagram that hung on my wall. This diagram, which I had photocopied from a book about Oriental philosophy,[45] was so compelling that from time to time I would send a copy to friends at times when they were in a particularly difficult or challenging transition.

It looks like this:

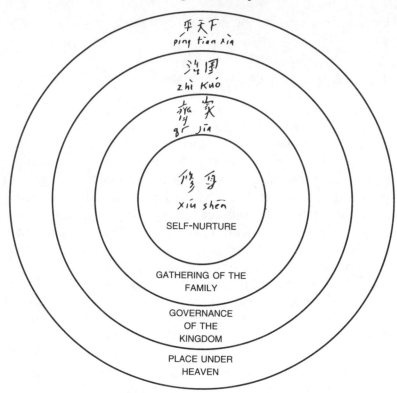

During the years while this ancient portrait of human wholeness patiently hung on my wall, this book evolved. Out of
hundreds of interviews and conversations and studies, the
book's structure slowly unfolded. Several times it would
shed its skin and take new form. After several years, when
the manuscript was finally near completion, the chapters finally settled into their current design.

   Then one day I happened to look up, and I witnessed
these concentric circles on my wall. For the first time, I realized that the chapters of the book began at the center of the
circle and moved outward. In the first two chapters, we focused on the emotional and physical dimensions of "self-
nurture" in the second half of life. In the next four, we ex-

plored the "gathering of the family," including issues of marriage, work, elderhood, and community. In the next chapter, we ventured into "governance of the kingdom" by directly facing the challenge of caring for our common global home. Finally, in this chapter, we focused directly on "peace under heaven" and the quest for the sacred in our lives.

To say that I had discovered the structure of this book would therefore be inaccurate. I had actually *re*discovered it. The design of this book on the contemporary quest for wholeness had been developed centuries ago by the elders of ancient China. Furthermore, they not only identified the different dimensions of our lifelong quest but made clear by their use of concentric circles that each was part of the others. If we do not sustain our own bodies and souls ("self-nurture"), we will not be able to serve the larger world. If our most intimate relationships ("gathering of the family") are not sound, all the larger social institutions (the "kingdom") will become ungovernable. The center of these circles—the personal, social, and political is the heart of true spirituality. Since all I had done was to rediscover ancient truths, it would have been much easier if I had just followed the diagram from the outset. Right from the start, I could have followed in the footsteps of the sages, I could have saved myself a lot of trouble and found my path much sooner. But it would not have been *my* path. If all we do is follow in someone else's footsteps, no matter how wise he or she may be, it is *their* quest. Learning to follow instructions is important, but it does not prepare us for the day when, lost in Dante's "forest dark," we find ourselves utterly alone. Nor does following instructions prepare us for the time of life when, as elders, we must give guidance to those who follow us. Copying someone else's map, in the end, leaves us empty-handed. Wherever their map leads us— whether it is a Wall Street brokerage or a Zen Buddhist monastery—is not our destination. And to make matters worse, their destination is probably obsolete. In our rapidly changing world, one generation cannot follow the maps of its predecessors.

Fortunately, the Founding Fathers were veterans of rapid social change. They wisely designed democracy based on this very notion of generational renewal. Shortly after the American Revolution, Thomas Jefferson wrote to his friend James Madison to remind him that the constitution must be revised at regular intervals. "What these periods should be," Jefferson wrote, *"nature* herself indicates." Based on the "tables of mortality" then available, Jefferson concluded that a new adult majority—"in other words, a new generation"—comes into place every nineteen years. In his view, as every new generation came into power, it should have the same inalienable right: "to choose for itself the form of government it believes most promotive of its own happiness."[46]

That our quest is connected to the wisdom of the Founding Fathers, as well as to that of native American elders and ancient Chinese sages, can be a great comfort to us. It confirms that, as we come into our own, we will not be alone. On the contrary, "we will be connected to all those men and women throughout time who have shared in this journey. Although those of us in the second half of life now find ourselves in new and dangerous terrain, there is a perennial wisdom on which every generation can rely."[47] In times of dramatic social change, every map requires revision. Not only our personal maps by which we intend to live the second half of our lives, but the political maps of our country and our planet, must be continually redrawn. Particularly as longevity increases, our capacity to grow throughout adulthood becomes absolutely critical—not only to our own personal happiness but to human survival.

As we come into our own, we are not only fulfilling our own personal potential. The wholeness we are discovering is not just *ours*. The love we find, the calling we discover, the sacredness that graces our lives—these do not belong to us.

The mystery of the adult metamorphosis is that we now experience ourselves interconnected with something larger. We sense sacred oneness with all of creation. We do not need religion to remind us; our souls can feel the magnetic field.

We are being called home. We do not know by whom, or to where, but that, after all, is our quest.

Notes

Preface

1. Toms, Michael, *An Open Life* (New York: 1990).
2. Adult development is one of the youngest in the overall field of human development. As recently as the late 1980s, major funding was allocated by the MacArthur Foundation for research in child development, adolescent development, and development of the elderly. Belatedly, they realized that there was a major gap in their funding—namely, the middle third of the life cycle. This remains the missing link in our understanding of the life cycle.

Chapter 1

1. Buzz Aldrin, *Return to Earth* (New York, 1973), p. 300. Aldrin is a favorite case study of midlife books, not only because of his prominence but because of the archetypal quality of his midlife experience. He went as far into space (into the archetypal "masculine") as man could possibly go, and then was forced to return to earth (and the archetypal "feminine"). His struggle to integrate the two continues. Further discussion of his story can be found in Peter Chew, *The Inner World of the Middle-Aged Man* (New York, 1976) and Otto Friedrich, *Going Crazy: An Inquiry into Madness in Our Time* (New York, 1977), pp. 229–33.
2. Timothy Leary, *Flashbacks* (Los Angeles, 1983).
3. Friedan's first statement was made in conversation with the author. The second statement is from an interview in *Modern Maturity,* April-May 1989.

4. Natalie Rogers, *Emerging Woman: A Decade of Midlife Transitions* (Point Reyes, Cal., 1980), chapter 3.
5. Daniel Levinson, *The Seasons of a Man's Life* (New York, 1978).
6. Jung cited in John Raphael Staude, *The Adult Development of C. G. Jung* (Boston, 1981), p. 92.
7. C. G. Jung, "The Transcendent Function," in H. Read, M. Fordham, G. Adler, and W. McGuire (eds.), R.F.C. Hull (trans.), *The Structure and Dynamics of the Psyche*, 2d ed., vol. 8 of the *Collected Works* Bollingen Series 20 (Princeton, NJ: Princeton University Press, p. 396; cited in Staude, Adult, p. 92.
8. Unpublished poem, copyright Peter C. Goldmark, Jr., April 1985. Used by permission of the author.
9. Personal conversation with the author, January 1991.
10. Unfortunately, labeling our experience a "midlife crisis" only serves to make a successful outcome more difficult. It implies that our life has careened out of control, like a train that has derailed. As doctors who specialize in treating heart attack victims have discovered, the worst response to a crisis is to panic. Unfortunately, that is precisely the response that the term *midlife crisis* inspires. It is a problem with no solution. It is like a fever: something to get over as quickly as possible. It is something to be ashamed of, to be finished and forgotten. We have no sense of its being part of any process of growth or change. Moreover, like many threadbare pop psychology labels, it has created a false split between those who suffered from the syndrome and those who did not. It has often been invoked in bedroom quarrels as an explanation for acting irresponsibly, when a frank and humble apology would have been more appropriate. And it has even been used, in at least one extreme example, as a courtroom defense—for murder! Having outworn its usefulness, this phrase should simply be gracefully retired, left behind in the graveyard of time-bound clichés.
11. Personal conversation with the author, February 1991.
12. Personal conversation with the author, January 1991.

13. Joseph Campbell with Bill Moyers, *The Power of Myth* (New York, 1988), pp. 146–47.
14. As I worked on this book:

- The Texas Rangers' forty-three-year-old Nolan Ryan became the oldest man in the history of baseball to ever pitch a no-hitter. "It's a great symbol," said President George Bush, whose son owns the team. Nolan appears in television commercials, drawling: "I feel ready to go another nine innings." And who can doubt it?
- Mark Spitz, winner of seven gold medals at the 1972 Olympics, is training in his forties toward the goal of winning in Barcelona in 1992.
- Former world champion gymnast Kurt Thomas is planning an unheard-of comeback in his midthirties.
- Carlton Fisk, who trains his forty-two-year-old body as hard as any of his teammates, is still slamming the ball over the fence for the White Sox.
- Boxer George Foreman, who retired long ago, is putting in grueling ten-mile training sessions as he prepares to fight his thirty-one-year-old opponent. "I represent a whole class of people who thought they were too old," Foreman said. "I'm proving something. . . . You can dream at any age."
- Martina Navratilova continues to beat opponents half her age at Wimbledon and around the world.

The darker side of these extraordinary performers, however, is that, when their careers end, midlife will hit these athletes with even greater force.
15. "Slow Start, Fast Pace for New US Attorney Baird," *Los Angeles Times*, (July 19, 1990), p. B1.
16. This is why treatises on adult development are often so frustratingly vague. For example, Jeffrey S. Turner et al. *Lifespan Development* (New York: 1983), describes the second half in terms of polarized stereotypes:

- Some researchers indicate that the second half is a time of conflict and upheaval; *but* other research shows it is a time of quiet achievement and deeper harmony.

- Some studies show that the "empty nest" is a crisis when parents become restless and dissatisfied; *but* others argue that children leaving home leads to "new levels of marital satisfaction and fulfillment."
- Midlife for many couples involves feelings of regret about their marriage, leading to boredom or divorce; *but* for other couples "increases in communication abilities, intimacy, companionship and mutuality are reported."
- In the second half many individuals stably maintain the work life that characterized their early adult years; *but* others engage in a "full-scale reorientation" and find radically different lines of work.

On the one hand, there are those whose lives come apart in a midlife crisis; on the other hand, there are those whose lives are locked in stultifying stability. In fact, we are as varied as the young or the old. Some of us have never married, some are married, and others divorced; some are childless, some have a full house, and others have empty nests; some are ill and ailing, others more fit than ever; some are in rewarding careers, others seeking change; some wealthy, others just getting by. Some are mothers just starting careers; others are career women just starting mothering. Some are trying to beat the fertility deadline and finally get pregnant; others have many pregnancies behind them and are dealing with college tuition. Some are overachievers just beginning to "balance out"; others are laid-back late bloomers belatedly trying to make some money.

17. Murray Stein, *In Midlife* (Dallas: Spring Publications, 1983).
18. William Nolen, *Crisis Time* (New York, 1984).
19. Jane Fonda quoted in "Jane Raw" *Los Angeles Magazine* (October 1989).
20. Stein, *In Midlife;* John Bradshaw, *Homecoming* (New York, 1990); Maureen Murdock, *The Heroine's Journey* (Boston and London, 1990); Robert Bly, *Iron John* (New York, 1990); Connie Zweig and Jeremiah Abrams, *Meeting the Shadow* (Los Angeles, 1991).
21. Ralph Metzner, *Opening to the Light* (Los Angeles, 1986).

22. Jan Struther cited in Stanley Brandes, *Forty* (Knoxville, Tenn., 1986), p. 100.
23. Cited in Donald Marrs, *Executives in Passage* (available from Barrington Sky Publishing, P.O. Box 49428 Los Angeles, Cal. 90049).
24. M. Scott Peck, *The Different Drum* (New York, 1987).
25. Raymond A. Moody, Jr., *Life after Life* (New York, 1975). In a later chapter, we explore the parallels between near-death experience and midlife in more detail.
26. *Selected Letters of C. G. Jung 1909–1961,* ed. Gerhard Adler and Aniela Jaffe, (Princeton/Bollingen, 1984), p. 97. In a handwritten note to an anonymous "Dr. N.," dated 10 June 1950, Jung wrote: "You get nowhere with theories. Try to be simple and always take the next step. You needn't see it advance, but you can look back at it afterwards. There is no 'how' of life, one just does it as you write a letter, for instance. It seems, however, to be terribly difficult for you not to be complicated and to do what is simple and close at hand. You barricade yourself from the world with exaggerated saviour fantasies. So climb down from the mountain of your humility and follow your nose. That is your way and the straightest. With kind regards, Yours sincerely, C. G. Jung."

Chapter 2

1. I wish to express my indebtedness to Morris Berman, whose book *Coming to Our Senses* inspired the title of this chapter.
2. Personal interview with the author, January 15, 1991.
3. Lillian Rubin, *Women of a Certain Age* (New York, 1979), p. 59.
4. Mary Kay Blakely, *Wake Me When It's Over* (New York, 1989), p. 15.
5. Diane Ackerman, *A Natural History of the Senses* (New York, 1990), p. xviii.
6. "Age Busters," Erik Fair, *Citisport* [West Los Angeles] (September 1989), p. 26.
7. Roger Gould, *Transformations* (New York, 1978), p. 307.
8. Comfort excerpted from "Aging: Real and Imaginary," in

Ronald Gross et al., *The New Old: Struggling for Decent Aging* (New York, 1978), p. 79.

9. Ackerman, *Natural History*, p. xix.

10. M. Friedman and R. H. Rosenham, *Type A Behavior and Your Heart* (Greenwich, Conn., 1975), cited in *Treating the Burnout Syndrome: Resource Guide* (available from HealthComm, Inc., 3215 56th St. N.W., Gig Harbor, Washington 98335).

11. American Heart Association proceedings reported in *Los Angeles Times* (January 17, 1989), p. 3.

12. Anne Morrow Lindbergh, *Gift from the Sea* (New York, 1955), pp. 88 and 96–7.

13. "No Rush to Corporate Wellness," *Fortune* (September 25, 1989).

14. "The Search for the Fountain of Youth," *Newsweek* (March 5, 1990), p. 47.

15. Dr. Gershon Lesser, *Growing Younger* (Los Angeles, 1987), pp. 27ff. As Dr. Dean Ornish points out, another way of lowering calories is not eating less, but eating differently, particularly less fat, sugar, alcohol and animal protein. Thus "eating less" does not mean going hungry; it does mean changing what we eat.

16. "A New Menu to Heal the Heart," *Newsweek* (July 30, 1990), p. 57.

17. In addition to the three S's—strengthening, stretching, and stillness—we should really add a fourth: sweating. Its cleansing and rejuvenating powers are too often ignored as we get older. Some women's fitness experts actually call sweat a "home-brew estrogen" because it tunes up the endocrine system and naturally simulates positive hormonal changes. Sweating is an old-fashioned prescription that more of us should follow. See, for example, Jane Fonda's *Women Coming of Age* (New York, 1984), p. 137.

18. *Medicine and Science in Sports and Exercise* 21 (April 1989), p. 2.

19. Stephen N. Blair, director of fitness study at the Institute for Aerobic Research in Dallas, Texas, as reported in "To Live Longer, Take a Walk," *Newsweek* (November 13, 1989), p. 77.

Chapter 3

1. Stuart Walzer, *Los Angeles Times* (December 8, 1989), p. E1.
2. Harville Hendrix, *Getting the Love You Want* (New York, 1988).
3. M. Scott Peck, *The Road Less Traveled* (New York, 1978).
4. In order to protect the privacy of others—and sometimes my own—I have slightly fictionalized some of the stories in this chapter. Nevertheless, the deeper human drama in these stories remains firmly grounded in the truth.
5. John Wellwood, *Journey of the Heart* (New York, 1990), p. 141.
6. C. G. Jung, "Marriage as a Psychological Relationship," in *The Basic Writings of C. G. Jung,* ed. Violet Staub de Laszlo (New York, 1959).
7. For a profile of couples who make such painful transitions but stay together, see Floyd and Harriet Thatcher, *Long Term Marriage: A Search for the Ingredients of a Lifelong Partnership* (Waco, Texas, 1974), chapter 10. Read any of the books mentioned in the footnotes to this chapter as well.
8. Erich Fromm, *The Art of Loving* (New York, 1956), chapter 1.
9. Michael Liebowitz's *The Chemistry of Love,* cited in Hendrix, *Getting the Love,* pp. 40–41.
10. The Jungian analyst is Adolph Guggenbuhl-Craig, writing in John Wellwood, *Challenge of the Heart* (Boston, 1985), pp. 157–63.
11. Phillip and Lorna Sarrell, *Sexual Turning Points* (New York, 1984), pp. 109–10, 159.
12. A strong misogynist streak in our culture permits men to denigrate the "bitch" or the "old lady," as if somehow the woman they freely chose to marry had been transformed by some bizarre marital alchemy from alluring maiden to old hag. The acid tongue of Al Bundy, the character on the controversial TV series *Married With Children,* epitomizes such barely controlled hatred. (He actually stoops to characterizing his wife as a monster that emerged from a swamp and trapped him.) Meanwhile, for women, outspoken advocates of husband-hating have recently stepped forward, with both literature and nonfiction offering counsel to distraught wives and bitter divorcees who pity themselves for having married conniving,

lying, cheating, good-for-nothing scoundrels. Nora Ephron's thirty-eight-year-old heroine Rachel in *Heartburn,* for example, portrays herself as being conned by her ex-husband's "big brown eyes and his sweetheart roses" (as if he had the acting powers of Sir Laurence Olivier and she, a veteran journalist, had the innocent gullibility of a dewy-eyed sixteen-year-old).

13. For several examples of couples caught in each other's shadow, see Wellwood, *Journey,* pp. 123–24. Robert Bly calls these early marriages a "union of two slices," because so much of each spouse is parked away in their shadows. See his *Little Book on the Human Shadow* (New York, 1988).

14. Robert Johnson, *We: Understanding the Psychology of Romantic Love* (New York, 1983), pp. 29–30.

15. Hendrix, *Getting the Love,* p. 27.

16. By "untold story," I do not mean that our marriages should be in the newspapers. I mean that they are part of what Jean Houston, in *Search for the Beloved* (Los Angeles, 1987), calls the "Larger Story" of our time, a concept to which we will return in the final chapter.

17. I tell their story in *A Choice of Heroes* (Boston, 1983).

18. For deepening my understanding of what it means to be free and faithful, I am indebted to Robert Stein's essay "Coupling/Uncoupling," in *Spring* (Dallas, Texas, 1981).

19. Judith Viorst, *Necessary Losses* (New York, 1986), p. 309.

20. M. Esther Harding, *Women's Mysteries* (New York, 1971); Jean Shinoda Bolen, *Goddesses in Every Woman* (San Francisco, 1984).

21. I explore the men's movement and its reaffirmation of "deep masculinity" more thoroughly in the afterword to the new edition of my previous book, *A Choice of Heroes: The Changing Faces of American Masculinity,* to be published by Houghton Mifflin in the spring of 1992. For an overview of the men's movement itself, see Aaron Kipnis, *Knights without Armor: A Practical Guide for Men in Quest of Masculine Soul* (Los Angeles, 1991). It includes references to most of the current men's literature.

22. Johnson, *We,* p. 53.

23. Saul H. Rosenthal provides an excellent summary of the data in *Sex over Forty* (Los Angeles, 1987).

24. Patrick Dougherty, "Men and Shame," audiocassette (available from P.O. Box 40387, Saint Paul, Minn. 55104).
25. Diane Medved, quoted in "Marrieds' New Creed: Make It Work," *USA Today* (March 12, 1990), p. 1.
26. Ralph Earle, quoted in "Therapists Begin Taking a Dim View of Divorce," *Los Angeles Times* (November 28, 1989).
27. Despite piles of statistics, the meaning of the numbers are hotly debated. Some simple mathematics support the conclusion that in midlife marriages there is an epidemic of pain. The current odds that a marriage will end in divorce are roughly one out of two. (Among the generation now in midlife, the odds of divorce are even higher.) Now add to those who divorce the many, many more who are caught in "cold war" marriages. Finally, let us add to the fiery divorces and the icy marriages, the catastrophic failure of *re*marriages. (The odds do not improve the second or third time around: 60 percent of remarriages also end in divorce.) Clearly marriage in America is in a stage of red alert, right?

    Wrong, say other researchers, who argue that the married couple in America is in a state of loyal bliss. According to a 1989 Gallup poll, four out of five married Americans say they would marry the same person if they could do it all over again; three out of four say their spouse is their "best friend"; and two out of three say they are "very happy" in their marriage. Even more startling, nine out of ten among the more than six hundred currently married men and women in the poll say that they've never had an affair during their marriage. Another poll corroborates this finding, with 95 percent of husbands and wives claiming they have been sexually faithful *during the previous year* (*Psychology Today* [March 1990]).
28. Pollack is quoted in "Compassion and Comfort in Middle Age," *The New York Times* (February 6, 1990), p. C1.
29. If a marriage is bad (particularly if it is horrible and the adversaries famous), the press is interested. Indeed, the husband or wife can write a book or screenplay about it, as Nora Ephron did in *Heartburn,* and feel quite comfortable. We also learn of every couple who, like the one portrayed by Michael Douglas and Kathleen Turner in Danny DeVito's film *War of the Roses,* would rather kill each other than face their shadow.

When this happens in real life, the media once again smell a sensational story.

The positive stories of enrichment, meaning, and joy, however, are not so easy to tell. They are hard to tell publicly because the deepest reaches of marital intimacy involve the spirit. They are private and, in a way, sacred. We do not know how to talk about spiritual matters in public without sounding foolish. So if your marriage is wonderful and you encounter marital ecstasy, do not expect any news coverage or calls from agents asking for screen rights. Marital collapse sells; marital breakthroughs do not. Indeed, the very act of opening private joys to public scrutiny is dangerous. As Garrison Keillor put it in *We Are Still Married:* "Telling the world the truth about your true love is a doomed enterprise, amusing for the world but disastrous for you."

Chapter 4

1. Donald Marrs, *Executive in Passage* (Los Angeles, 1990), p. 51.
2. Personal interview with the author, January 1990.
3. Maureen Murdock, *The Heroine's Journey* (Boston, 1990).
4. Ram Dass cited in Stanislav Grof and Christina Grof, *Spiritual Emergency* (Los Angeles, 1989).
5. "Farewell, Fast Track," *Business Week* (December 10, 1990). Data cited include research of Ross A. Webber, professor of management at the University of Pennsylvania's Wharton School.
6. Johnson's comments from "Farewell, Fast Track." The *Times* report was reprinted in *The International Herald Tribune* (March 3–4, 1990).
7. Cheryl Smith cited in ibid.
8. Daniel Goleman, "The Strange Agony of Success," *The New York Times* (August 24, 1986).
9. One of the most provocative midlife transformations is the Apollo/Hermes relationship. Apollo was rich and successful, with a huge herd of cattle. Hard up for cash, Hermes steals some cattle from his older brother's herd. Hermes knows they are Apollo's most prized possession, but figuring his brother might not even notice the loss, Hermes steals them anyway.

"The older brother god, Apollo, is surprised and angry," summarizes Stein in *In Midlife*, and "the search for the thief and for the lost treasure begins. This is the first act of the drama that unfolds at midlife: 'What do you mean I've lost it? I'll get it back!' "

Always full of surprises, Hermes instead brings Apollo his invention, the lyre, which resembles what today we would call a harp. Apollo falls in love with music, and it becomes for him, as Stein puts it, "his greatest and most singular attribute as a god." When Hermes finally offers to return the cattle, Apollo no longer wants them. He has found a deeper meaning to his life than counting his cattle. He has become enraptured by music.

10. Joseph Campbell, *The Hero with a Thousand Faces* (New York, 1972).

11. "The following myth is made possible by a grant from Bill Moyers: on the road with the Odysseus of the small screen." Bill Moyers cited in David Zurawik, *Esquire* (October 1989), p. 145.

12. Alex Comfort, *Say Yes to Old Age* (New York, 1990). For a thoughtful look at the retirement blues as well as the no-retirement blues, see Eda LeShan, *It's Better to Be Over the Hill Than Under It: Thoughts on Life over 60* (New York, 1990). Depression following work, says LeShan, is usually not due to missing work, but to the feeling "I have never really lived." See also Ruth Harriet Jacobs, *Re-engagement in Later life: Re-employment and Re-marriage* (Stamford, Conn., 1979).

13. Donald LeBier cited in Ronni Dandroff, "Is Your Job Driving You Crazy?", *Psychology Today* (July/August 1989). To follow up on LeBier's comments, read his *Modern Madness: The Emotional Fallout of Success* (Addison-Wesley, 1986).

14. Jim Hubbard, "Shooting Back" *Life* (November 1990).

15. "Last of the Big Spenders: New-Style Consumer Will Scaledown, Save More," *Barron's* (March 11, 1991), p. 10.

16. Marie Gallagher, "Home Lust," in *Beyond the Boom: New Voices in American Life, Culture, and Politics,* ed. Terry Teachout (New York, 1990).

17. Steven Foster and Meredith Little, *The Trail Ahead* (Big Pine, Calif.: Rites of Passage Press, 1988).

18. Personal interview with the author, 1989. She was also interviewed by *Newsweek* (February 13, 1989), p. 73.

19. Duane Elgin, *Voluntary Simplicity: Toward a Way of Life That Is Outwardly Simple, Inwardly Rich* (New York, 1986) p. 31: "Voluntary simplicity involves both inner and outer condition. It means singleness of purpose, sincerity and honesty within, as well as avoidance of exterior clutter, of many possessions irrelevant to the chief purpose of life. It means an ordering and guiding of our energy and desire, a partial restraint in some directions in order to secure greater abundance of life in other directions. It involves a deliberate organization of life for a purpose."

20. Michael Ventura, "The Solutions to All Our Problems (Guaranteed)," reprinted in *The Utne Reader* (July/August 1990). Of the thirty-four solutions to life's problems, "make mistakes" was the first one Ventura listed.

21. Personal conversation with the author; also reported in *Time* (January 8, 1990), p. 72.

22. In a personal conversation with the author, Pilder discussed seeing signs that corporate culture is at last beginning to realize the need to reconnect work to deeper values and motivations. "The corporations may become part of that school for forty-year-olds that Jung talks about," said Pilder. "A major bank in New York City is putting together a strategic workforce plan. They're not clear what to do with many segments of their workforce, particularly their older workers. If you look at the plateaued employee, the challenge is to enable them to go deeper in relationship to what they are doing."

23. Richard N. Bolles, "The Decade of Decisions," *Modern Maturity* (February–March 1990), p. 36.

24. Marsha Sinetar, *Do What You Love, The Money Will Follow* (New York, 1987), p. 120.

25. Spike Lee quoted in *Newsweek* (October 2, 1989), p. 37.

26. This is the moment Marsha Sinetar calls "learning to let go." See her *Living Happily Ever After: Creating Trust, Luck and Joy* (New York, 1990).

27. Personal interview with the author, January 1991.
28. Dr. Jeannette Gerzon. Copyright 1991. All rights reserved.

Chapter 5

1. Nancy Collin, "The Real MacLaine," *Vanity Fair* (February 1991).
2. John G. Penn quoted in "Early Face-Lifts: Stopping Appearance Slides Before They Even Start," *Longevity* (October 1990), pp. 38–41.
3. A detailed, overenthusiastic report on human growth hormone is "The Hormone That Makes Your Body Twenty Years Younger," *Longevity* (October 1990).
4. Joseph Knoll quoted in Carol Kahn, "An Anti-Aging Aphrodisiac" *Longevity* (December 1990).
5. Interview with the author, December 10, 1990.
6. For a journalistic account of some specific anti-aging remedies, see Alastair Dow, *The Deprenyl Story* (Toronto, 1990), chapter 12, "The Fountain of Youth." For a broader and more impartial discussion of these and related issues, see Kenneth R. Pelletier, *Longevity: Fulfilling Our Biological Potential* (New York, 1981), particularly chapter 4, "Regeneration and Rejuvenation."
7. Eda LeShan, *The Wonderful Crisis of Middle Age* (New York, 1973).
8. Janie Matthews, "Early Face-Lifts" *Longevity* (October 1990).
9. Myron Brenton, ed., *Aging Slowly* (Emmaus, Pa., 1983).
10. Phyllis Diller, *The Joys of Aging and How to Avoid Them* (New York, 1981).
11. Bill Cosby, *Time Flies* (New York, 1987).
12. Dave Barry, *Dave Barry Turns 40* (New York, 1990), pp. 20, 174–75.
13. The reason the age of forty takes on special meaning in our culture is explored by Stanley Brandes, *Forty: The Age and the Symbol* (Knoxville, Tenn., 1985).
14. Landon Y. Jones, *Great Expectations: Americans and the Baby Boom Generation* (New York, 1980), p. 253.
15. "Peddling Youth Over the Counter," *Newsweek* (March 5, 1990), p. 50.

16. George F. Will, "Slamming the Doors" *Newsweek* (March 25, 1991).

17. Steven Levine, *Who Dies?* (New York, 1982), p. 154.

18. "20 Ways to Wipe Away 10 Years," *Men's Health* (June 1990), p. 62.

19. *Los Angeles Times* (September 3, 1989).

20. John Bradshaw, "Addiction: Our Families, Ourselves," *Lear's* (April 1990), p. 55.

21. Frances Lear cited in "The Coming of Age: The Over-40 Model Is Coming Into Vogue as Fashion Caters to Graying Boomers," *Los Angeles Times* (March 30, 1990), p. E6.

22. Ken Dychtwald, *Age Wave* (Los Angeles, 1989).

23. Stanley Ellin, "The Blessington Method," in Dorothy Sennett, *Full Measure: Modern Short Stories on Aging* (available from Graywolf Press, P.O. Box 75006, Saint Paul, Minn. 55175, 1988).

24. Kenneth Ring, *Heading Toward Omega: In Search of the Meaning of the Near-Death Experience* (New York, 1984).

25. Ernest Becker, *The Denial of Death* (New York, 1974).

26. Elisabeth Kübler-Ross, *On Death and Dying* (New York, 1969); Joanna Macy, *Despair and Personal Power in the Nuclear Age* (Philadelphia, 1983).

27. Levinson, *Seasons,* pp. 214f; and Elliott Jacques, "Death and the Midlife Crisis," In *Death: Interpretations,* ed. Hendrink M. Ruitenbeek (New York, 1969), pp. 140–65, originally published in *International Journal of Psychoanalysis* 46:502–14.

28. Hermann Hesse cited in A. L. Vischer, *On Growing Old* (Boston, 1967), p. 195.

29. Lewis Thomas cited in Levine, *Who Dies?,* p. 1.

30. Susan Sontag, *Illness as Metaphor* (New York, 1977).

31. Marvin Barrett, *Spare Days* (New York, 1988), pp. 90–91. The remainder of his comments were in an interview with the author, October 1990.

32. Joseph Campbell and Bill Moyers, *The Power of Myth* (New York, 1988).

33. Quoted in Paula Brown Doress et al., *Ourselves, Growing Older* (New York, 1987).

34. Jean Houston, "Developmental Emergence in Later Life," 1991 Mystery School.

35. Maggie Scarf, *Unfinished Business* (New York, 1980) p. 412.

36. Becker, *Denial of Death,* p. 265.

37. Dr. Ornish's remarks are from a personal interview with the author, January 15, 1990. Also Ornish, *Dr. Dean Ornish's Program for Reversing Heart Disease* (New York, 1990), pp. 221–22 and 215. In countless books, writers from vastly different backgrounds who have entered the second half of their lives are rediscovering the ancient truths about forgiveness. For example, scientist-turned-philosopher Gary Zukav writes that the "authentically empowered person is one who forgives." See Gary Zukav, *The Seat of the Soul* (New York, 1989), p. 227. Another physician, Dr. Redford Williams, feels forgiveness is so vital that he makes it the final and ultimate step in his twelve-step method for developing a "trusting heart." See Redford Williams *The Trusting Heart* (New York, 1989), p. 195. We will explore the spiritual dimension of this more fully in Chapter 8.

38. "Paul Newman's Dream," *Life* (September 1988).

39. This theme is explored well from a feminist perspective by Naomi Wolf, *The Beauty Myth* (New York, 1991).

40. Robert Grudin, *Time and the Art of Living* (New York, 1982), p. 186.

Chapter 6

1. This disguised obituary was cited in Robert Fulton, "The Many Faces of Grief," *Death Studies* 11 (1987), pp. 243–56, reprinted in *Aging: Seventh Edition,* (available from Dushkin Publishing Group, Sluice Dock, Guilford, Conn. 06437).

2. Robert Bellah, *Habits of the Heart* (New York, 1986).

3. Steven Wall and Harvey Arden, *Wisdomkeepers* (Beyond Words Press, 1990).

4. These and subsequent comments by Steve Wall are from a personal interview, January 1990.

5. *New Options* 70 (September 24, 1990) (available from P.O. Box 19324, Washington, D.C. 20036).

6. Just as a meteorologist's vocabulary must go beyond cold and hot, so ours must look beyond childhood and adulthood. For

the purpose of building community, at least five terms are needed instead of two.

Childhood, first of all, must be considered at least two distinct phases: *childhood* itself, during which the young are in the care of their parents or guardians and more or less under their control; and *youth*, when young people become increasingly able to express their own values and develop their own life-styles. If nothing else, the sixties established that childhood does not extend from birth to adulthood. The stage of "youth" became a vital, living part of our life cycle vocabulary because, without it, it was impossible to describe what was occurring around us. On October 21, 1967, journalists simply could not write that half a million children were marching across the Potomac and descending on the Pentagon to protest the war in Vietnam. Similarly, it is impossible to watch several thousand college students arrive on a college campus for freshman orientation and consider them children. They are not children; they are "young people" or "youths."

Similarly, we cannot speak simplistically of "adulthood" as if this were still the nineteenth century. This catch-all word applies to everyone from a self-involved college student barely out of his teens, completely dependent on parental support; to a fifty-year-old parent, executive, and city council member who carries on his or her shoulders responsibilities for a family, a business, and a metropolitan area; to an eighty-year-old great-grandparent who seeks only to pass on some wisdom to others and to die with dignity and respect. It is a useful term to distinguish those who are physically grown from those who are not, and those who have the legal rights and social privileges of being over twenty-one years of age from those who are younger. But otherwise the term, by itself, has been stripped of all meaning. Indeed, as an adjective describing films, for example, "adult" is now synonymous, not with "mature," but with "pornographic."

Adulthood is still a useful term to describe those who, having left youth behind, are eligible to serve in the military; to consume alcohol; to marry without parental permission; to drive motor vehicles; to work and receive payment as adults; to have a social security number and pay taxes; to fall under the jurisdiction of the law as a "major," rather than a "minor"; and other related rights and responsibilities. But as a stage of life, it describes accurately only the twenties and early thirties of the contemporary Western life cycle. (Indeed, for many of those in this early phase of adulthood who continue their education and training beyond college, their life-styles resemble youth more closely than those of older adults.)

By the mid-thirties or early forties, *midlife* begins. Physically, this period is different because the body has begun to show discernible signs of aging. Socially, it is different from the early stage of adulthood because for the vast majority in midlife family responsibilities become of paramount importance. Economically, it is a different stage because careers are better established and earning power is greater or, in most cases, reaching a clearer plateau. Unlike entering adulthood, which confers a whole new set of rights and obligations, midlife carries with it no automatic external change in status. Yet the middle decades of adulthood are so different from the first decades that they clearly require a status of their own.

7. "What Do We Call . . . Them?" *Newsweek* (April 23, 1990), p. 74.
8. Wrote Simone de Beauvoir in *The Coming of Age* (New York, 1972). Unlike the entrance to adulthood, which is "nearly always accompanied by initiation rites," entry into elderhood is ignored. "The time at which old age begins is ill-defined; it varies according to the era and the place, and nowhere do we find any initiation ceremonies that confirm the fresh status."
9. "Depression Leads to Elderly Suicide," *Brain Mind Bulletin* (April 1989).
10. Ornish, *Reversing Heart Disease,* p. 87.
11. These and other studies cited in Ornish, *Reversing Heart Disease,* pp. 86ff.
12. Margaret Mead, *Blackberry Winter* (New York, 1972).
13. Mead quoted in Ronald Gross et al., *op. cit.,* p. 270. Ronald Beatrice Gross, Sylvia Siedman, eds. *The New Old, Struggling for Decent Aging* (Garden City, N.Y., 1978).
14. Dychtwald, *Age Wave,* p. 107.
15. Gail Sheehy, *Pathfinders* (New York, 1968).

16. Wendell Berry, *What Are People For?* (San Francisco, 1990), p. 13.

17. Mihaly Csikszentmihalyi, "Bring on the Hairy Mentor," *The New York Times Book Review* (February 11, 1990), p. 15.

18. Howard Gardner, *To Open Minds* (New York, 1989), p. 46.

19. Erik Erikson, *Identity, Youth, and Crisis* (New York, 1968). The term *independence* is implicit in Erikson's work, but is stressed more directly by John Bradshaw, in *Homecoming: Reclaiming and Championing the Inner Child* (New York, 1990). Bradshaw draws on Erikson and argues that dependency needs correspond to childhood; counterdependency needs to adolescence and early adulthood; independence needs to the years twenty-six to thirty-nine; and interdependence needs to the second half (pp. 39–52).

20. Erik H. Erikson, Joan Erikson, and Helen Kirnick, *Vital Involvement in Old Age* (New York, 1986) especially "Potential Role of Elders," p. 333.

21. Robert Coles, *The Spiritual Life of Children* (Boston, 1990), p. 334.

22. Jane Jacobs, *The Life and Death of Great American Cities* (New York, 1961), pp. 38ff.

23. Paul S. Hewitt and Neil Howe, "Generational Equity and the Future of Generational Politics," *Generations: Journal of the American Society on Aging* (Spring 1988), pp. 10–13.

24. Personal interview with the author, March 7, 1991. For further information, see Neil Howe and William Strauss, *Generations* (New York, 1991).

25. Robert Samuelson, "Pampering the Elderly" *Newsweek* (October 29, 1990), p. 61.

26. Mark S. Tucker, testimony before the Joint Economic Committee of the U.S. Congress, Subcommittee on Economic Resources, Competitiveness, and Security Economics, July 1986.

27. Zimmerman is president of the Ojai Foundation and founder of the Human Development Program at Crossroads School, which now has a rite of passage as part of the human development program that is required for graduation. The foundation is currently developing rites of passages for midlife and elderhood as well.

28. Cited in Wall and Arden, *Wisdomkeepers.*

Chapter 7

1. Lester Brown, speech delivered in Moscow at the Global Forum, January 1990. Elaborated in Lester Brown et al. *State of the World 1990* (Worldwatch Institute, Washington, D.C.). Other responsible experts think we have even less time than Lester Brown does. James MacNeill is director of the Sustainable Development Program, Institute for Research on Public Policy, Ottawa, Canada, and the former secretary general of the World Commission on the Environment and Development (Brundtland Commission). As he told interviewer Stephen D. Lerner of the Commonweal Sustainable Futures Project, "Lester Brown at the Worldwatch Institute and a few others have come out with a figure of forty years, but it is not clear to me what they mean by that. I hesitate to say we have forty years, because to say that is to imply that we don't have to start for forty years. In fact, if we are to complete the transition to sustainable development (that we must accomplish in the next twenty to thirty years), we have to start now."

2. Personal interview with the author, February 11, 1991.

3. Mark Gerzon, *A Childhood for Every Child: The Politics of Parenthood* (New York, 1973).

4. "Atwater Regrets Campaign Tactics," UPI report, *The International Herald Tribune* (January 15, 1991).

5. Personal interview with the author, February 14, 1991.

6. *Campaign & Elections* (December-January 1991), p. 19.

7. E. J. Dionne, *Why Americans Hate Politics* (New York, 1991), and P. J. O'Rourke, *Parliament of Whores* (New York, 1991).

8. Document circulated prior to the 1992 elections by Daniel Cantor and Joel Roberts (May 1990). "You can support an organization that represents the whole you," they write passionately, "not just a fraction of you."

9. Joanna Macy, *World As Lover, World As Self* (Berkeley, Cal., 1991).

10. *Los Angeles Times* (January 9, 1991), p. 3.

11. To learn more about the views of Oren Lyons and other native American elders, read the book he recommended: *Wisdomkeepers,* a book profiling a number of living native Amer-

ican elders who speak about how to live on this planet. Oren referred me to the publisher, a small-scale enterprise called Beyond Words located in a town thirty miles outside Portland, Oregon. When I told the secretary who answered that I wanted to get a copy of *Wisdomkeepers* and learn about how the book came into being, she told me I should speak to the publisher, Richard Kohn, and she put him on the phone. When I asked him about the story behind the book, he began his reply with a question: "Do you know the movie 'Field of Dreams'?" And there unfolded another person's quest into the second half.

12. Personal interview with the author, January 1991.
13. Bill McKibben, *The End of Nature* (New York, 1990), p. 38.
14. *US* magazine (March 7, 1991), p. 28.
15. Many excellent sources on deforestation are available, including *State of the World 1990* (Washington, D.C.: The Worldwatch Institute).
16. Denis Hayes, Natural Resources Defense Council's Marshall Lecture, American Museum of Natural History, November 8, 1989.
17. Sources cited in John E. Young, "Discarding the Throwaway Society" Worldwatch Paper 101 (January 1991).
18. This applies equally to the nations of the South. The poor nations of the South actually transfer to us billions of dollars a year. While after much debate we give out crumbs of aid, the lenders take in $50 billion from the poor in the form of debt repayments and purchase of critical imports. It is a case of Robin Hood in reverse: taking from the poor and giving to the rich. We *think* we are assisting the debtor nations when, in fact, they are enriching the lenders. *World Debt Tables 1990–91, External Debt of Developing Countries,* vol. 1: *Analysis and Summary Tables* (World Bank, Washington, D.C., 1990). Discussed in Sandra Postel and Christopher Flavin, "Reshaping the Global Economy," chapter 10 of *State of the World 1991.*
19. Both facts and feelings about this timeless tragedy are well presented in Macy, *World As Lover, World as Self.*
20. *Musician Magazine* (October 1990), reprinted in *The Utne Reader* (January-February 1991).

21. John Gardner, *The Recovery of Confidence,* cited in John F. Reynolds and Eleanor Reynolds, *Beyond Success* (New York, 1988), p. 58.

22. Joan Anzalone, ed., *Good Works: A Guide to Careers in Social Change* (New York, 1985), p. 23. Another guide to such careers is Reynolds and Reynolds, *Beyond Success,* in which they directly contrast "making a life versus making a living." See also Thomas Pile and William Proctor, *Is It Success or Is It Addiction?* (New York, 1988). The authors actually use such phrases as *cult* and *faith* to describe the fervor with which fast-trackers pursue success. It is interesting to note that these books heralded the end of the decade of greed and the beginning of the nineties.

23. The Morton and Rafferty cases are cited in *Los Angeles Times* (April 21, 1990), p. A28. Other information was obtained from personal interviews with Rafferty and the publicity department of Hard Rock Cafes.

24. In *Iron John* (Boston, 1988), the young protagonist is told: "You know a great deal about gold now, but nothing about poverty," In effect, says Bly, he is being told: "You know a lot about going up, and nothing about going down." Explains Bly: "To fall from being a king's son to being a cook is the step the story asks for." And this may be what history asks of the rich countries of the North as well.

Chapter 8

1. This phrase "spiritual coming of age" comes from Gary Zukav, *The Seat of the Soul* (New York, 1990), p. 248. Jung pointed out the importance of the mid-thirties, as we have seen, but it also appears in the writings of various spiritual seekers from the twelfth-century poet Rumi to recent Indian spiritual figures like Gopi Krishna to twentieth-century mystics like Ram Dass (Richard Alpert).

2. Jung eloquently described his own confirmation, which was administered by his own father, in his autobiography, *Memories, Dreams and Reflections:* "I ate the bread; it tasted flat, as I had expected. The wine . . . was thin and rather sour, plainly, not the best. Then came the final prayer, and the peo-

ple went out, neither depressed nor illumined with joy, but with faces that said, 'So that's that.' . . . Only gradually, in the course of the following days, did it dawn on me that nothing had happened. I had reached the pinnacle of religious initiation, had expected something—I knew not what—to happen, and nothing at all had happened. I knew that God could do stupendous things to me, things of fire and unearthly light; but this ceremony contained no trace of God—not for me, at any rate" (pp. 54–55).

3. Dan Wakefield, *Returning: A Spiritual Journey* (New York, 1984), p. 21.
4. Dan Wakefield, *The Story of Your Life: Writing a Spiritual Autobiography* (New York, 1990).
5. Interview with the author, January 8, 1990. Sharma is professor of comparative religion at the Faculty of Religious Studies, McGill University, Montreal.
6. "A Time to Seek," *Time* (December 17, 1990).
7. Personal interview with the author.
8. Wellwood, *Journey of the Heart,* p. 140.
9. Ray Lynch quoted in Jeff Wagenheim, "Deeper Breakfast," *New Age Journal* (September-October 1989), p. 76.
10. Richard Seltzer, *Mortal Lessons: Notes on the Art of Surgery* (New York, 1976).
11. Rick Fields et al., *Chop Wood, Carry Water* (Los Angeles, 1984), p. xv.
12. Heidegger cited in Len Hixon, *Coming Home: The Experience of Enlightenment in Sacred Traditions* (Los Angeles, 1989), p. 5.
13. Alice Walker, *Living by the Word* (New York, 1990).
14. Luke 17:20–21. I am grateful to M. Scott Peck for suggesting the use of the Aramaic translation "the kingdom of God is *among* us," which stresses the importance of community.
15. "There's no big scene there, or some old fellow," Lennon added, as they spoke on British television with David Frost, September 29, 1967. I first cited this dialogue in my book *The Whole World Is Watching* (New York, 1969).
16. Personal interview with the author, December 26, 1990.
17. *The New York Times* (August 5, 1989).
18. Martin Buber, *The Way of Man* (London, 1963).

19. Marrs, *Executive in Passage,* p. 88.

20. Carl Jung, *Memories, Dreams and Reflections* (New York, 1965). According to Jung, his "big dreams" often foreshadowed his future with uncanny precision. Jung asked: "Who brought the above and below together, and laid the foundation for everything that was to fill the second half of my life?"

21. T. C. McLuhan, *Touch the Earth,* (New York, 1971).

22. For a more detailed account of these two dreams, see Robert Johnson, *Ecstasy: Understanding the Psychology of Joy* (New York, 1987).

23. Robert Bosnak, *A Little Course in Dreams* (Boston, 1988).

24. Jung, *Memories, Dreams and Reflections,* p. 170.

25. Gayle Delaney, "Personal and Professional Problem-Solving in Dreams," in Stanley Krippner, *Dreamtime and Dreamwork* (Los Angeles, 1990).

26. Looking back, I see that some of the central lessons of my quest were locked away in this one dream. The wisdom of the dream is still beyond me. I can reread it, year after year, and learn something new. If probed deeply enough, everything I have learned since then, and everything that you have read so far in this book, is embedded in that one fleeting dream. In that dream I confront my arrogance that this superpowerful woman (a symbol of the eternal feminine) has nothing to teach me. I experience a spiritual force that is strong enough, when awakened, to heal my wounds. By surrendering to her power (the miraculous power of Life) I discover a peaceful, enduring strength. The woman healer, this nondenominational Virgin Mary, opens me to a deeper level of trust in the feminine and in my soul, and blessed my search for the sacred.

27. Abraham Lincoln quoted in William J. Wolf, *The Religion of Lincoln* (New York, 1963); cited in John Sanford, *Dreams and Healing* (Ramsey, N.J., 1978). Said Lincoln: "It seems strange how much there is in the Bible about dreams. There are, I think, some sixteen chapters in the Old Testament and four or five in the New in which dreams are mentioned."

28. The dreamwork groups ranged in size (from less than half a dozen to as many as twenty) and in composition (artists, women, new mothers, recovering alcoholics). They shared a belief that reclaiming their dreams would empower them. The

movement has continued to grow to the point that dream workshops are now offered in cities around the country; the Lucidity Institute has been founded by Stanford University dream researcher Stephen LaBerge, author of *Lucid Dreaming,* (Los Angeles, 1985), who has turned to direct mail appeals to recruit members. In addition to the academic researchers and psychotherapists who naturally populate this movement, there are many with explicitly social and political goals. One community organizer, who uses dreamwork to bridge racial, sexual, and ethnic barriers, wrote that "dream work has the potential to be deeply 'radical,' not only in the original sense of *radix,* getting to the 'root' of things, but also in the political and social sense of dramatic transformation of collective fears, opinions, attitudes and behaviors." See Jeremy Taylor, *Dream Work* (Ramsey, N.J., 1983), p. 17.

29. Although, as the dreamwork movement stresses, we are the authorities on our own dreams, it is worth remembering that we also need help. As we seek the sacred, we need elders and allies too. Learning the language of our dreams is like learning any language: We must hear it spoken by others in order to speak it ourselves. Without them, I doubt I would have ventured into it so far. The first guides were some older friends of mine—Dick, a family therapist, and Laura, a specialist in psychodrama—to whom I casually mentioned the fact that they had appeared in one of my dreams. They responded by offering me a gift. They volunteered to give me a session in which they would do for me what they sometimes do for their clients: to walk me through my own dream.

My other important dream guide has been a Jungian therapist with whom I have worked intermittently for several years. I would enter his office with a dream that seemed opaque and mysterious. Again and again, I would leave his office with my eyes—and heart—opened by the clear and compelling message that the dream had in my life.

30. Louis M. Savary, "Dreams for Personal and Spiritual Growth," in Stanley Krippner, *Dreamtime and Dreamwork* (Los Angeles, 1990).

31. Bradshaw, *Homecoming,* p. 277.

32. *The Words of Martin Luther King, Jr.*, selected by Coretta Scott King (New York, 1983).

33. Phylicia Rashad quoted in *USA Today* (August 18, 1987), p. 4D.

34. Personal interview with the author, December 28, 1990.

35. Aldous Huxley quoted in Jay Stevens, *Storming Heaven*, (New York, 1988), p. 64.

36. Herbert Benson, *The Relaxation Response* (New York, 1975), p. 102.

37. Benson, *Relaxation*, pp. 114–15.

38. Redford Williams, *The Trusting Heart* (New York, 1989), p. 186.

39. Interview with Sam Keen in *On Beyond War* 53 (October 1989).

40. Abraham Maslow, *The Farther Reaches of Human Nature* (New York, 1976), p. 48.

41. Personal interviews with the author. A similar story is told by Natalie Rogers. The daughter of the renowned psychologist Carl Rogers grew up in a cultural milieu apparently dedicated to psychological thinking and personal self-expression. She married and raised a family. But when she found herself in midlife terribly unsatisfied, with her marriage unraveling and her future clouded, she turned to nature for her healing. She went on a "vision quest," a journey into the wilderness that she credits with providing crucial insight that helped her find out who she was separate from the roles of daughter and sister, mother and wife. Natalie Rogers, *Emerging Woman: A Decade of Midlife Transitions* (available from Personal Press, Box 789 Point Reyes Station, Calif. 94956).

42. Personal interview with the author, December 1989.

43. Metzner, *Opening to the Light*, p. 120.

44. The sacred is not limited to the heights, but is also present in the depths. In his essay entitled "Peaks and Vales," James Hillman explores the sacredness of the low-lying regions, the valleys of our consciousness. *Vale* in the usual religious language of our culture is a depressed emotional place—the vale of tears; Jesus walked this lonesome valley; the valley of the shadow of death. The very first definition of *valley* in the Oxford English Dictionary is a "long depression or hollow." The

meaning of *vale* and *valley* include entire subcategories refer-ring to *such sad things as the decline of years and old age,* the world regarded as a place of troubles, sorrow, and weeping, and the world regarded as the scene of the mortal, the earthly, the lowly.

"There is also a feminine association with vales," Hillman continues. And no wonder. While men (who have tried so hard to guard the higher elevations for themselves) went off as mystics, gurus, saints, and prophets to the mountaintop, women stayed home and raised children, tended garden and hearth, and gathered firewood to heat the water that they carried up from the stream.

45. I copied this diagram so many years ago that I have no memory of its source. If anyone can place it, please inform me so that I can cite the proper references in future editions.

46. Thomas Jefferson, *The Complete Jefferson,* ed. Saul Padover (Salem, N.H.: Ayer Co. Pub., 1943), pp. 124–25, 291–93.

47. Aldous Huxley, *The Perennial Wisdom* (New York, 1974).

I am grateful to Shepherd Bliss for introducing me to the concept of the "midlife quest," and to Murray Stein for his evocative dis-cussion of crossing the "threshold" into the second half.